THE CYCLIST'S TRAINING BIBLE

THE CYCLIST'S TRAINING BIBLE

A Complete Training Guide for the Competitive Road Cyclist

BY JOE FRIEL

Photos by Beth Schneider

VeloPress • Boulder, Colorado • USA

The Cyclist's Training Bible
Copyright © 1996 by Joe Friel

Before embarking on any strenuous exercise program, including the training described in this book, everyone, particularly anyone with a known heart or blood-pressure problem, should be examined by a physician.

ISBN: 1-884737-21-8

First edition
Printed in the U.S.A.

VeloPress
1830 N 55th Street
Boulder, Colorado 80301-2700

303/440-0601
303/444-6788 fax
e-mail: velonews@aol.com

To purchase additional copies of this book or other Velo products,
Call 800/234-8356
International 303/440-0601

Cover photo: Robert Oliver

To Dirk:
my friend, my training partner,
my mentor, my pupil,
my son.

COΠTEΠTS

FOREWORD

Dr. Tudor O. Bompa is considered the "father of periodization" and is currently a professor at York University in Toronto, Canada. He consults with national Olympic organizations and sports federations throughout the world on the development of training programs for elite athletes.

In 1963, while on the faculty of the Romanian Institute of Sport, I was asked to coach one of the country's young and promising javelin throwers. As I looked at the "traditional" training programs at the time, I came to realize that something was missing in the way athletes were trained. Everyone followed the "ancient" program of preparatory, non-specific training during the winter, followed by the competitive phase during the summer and a transition during the fall. Later on, the Russians even called this "periodization." One of the missing links, the change I introduced, refined the sequence and type of strength and endurance training performed for each training period so that athletes ultimately would reach higher levels of strength and endurance. Later, I called this the "periodization of strength" and the "periodization of endurance."

From the 1960s on, Romanian coaches, as well as other Eastern European training specialists, adopted my principles of periodization and dominated world and Olympic competition for many years in many sports. Today, these systems, along with periodization of training for young athletes, are used by most top athletes in Europe and are gaining popularity in the United States as well.

In *The Cyclist's Training Bible*, Joe Friel has carefully provided the competitive road cyclist with all of the tools necessary to design and employ a periodization program following the principles I have laid down. He didn't come to this level of expertise by accident. I have spent time with Joe and know him as a very knowledgeable and masterful coach and teacher who is an authority on periodization. Unlike many other training specialists, Joe has spent many years trying different types of periodization and training schedules to determine what works best for cyclists and other endurance athletes. If he were in Eastern Europe, he would be called a "master coach."

The Cyclist's Training Bible is perhaps the most comprehensive and scientific book ever written on training for road cycling, and yet it is also practical and easy to follow. It will soon become the bible on training for cycling coaches and athletes alike. This book will have you systematically training just as world-class cyclists do. If you scrupulously follow the guidelines presented here, I'm confident your racing performance will dramatically improve.

Prof. Tudor O. Bompa, Ph.D.
July 1996

ACKNOWLEDGMENTS

I am indebted to Greg Haase and Ross Brownson for questioning my ideas and methods when I was first starting to train adult athletes. Their reasoned approach encouraged me to discover the "whys" of training through science and formed the basis for much of my thinking for the last 16 years.

I gratefully acknowledge Gale Bernhardt for reading and critiquing each chapter, Jennifer Koslo for keeping my coaching business running while I worked on this book, Todd Telander for converting my rough sketches into understandable illustrations, Dr. Loren Cordain for guidance on the Paleolithic diet and for reviewing that section, Oliver Starr for his input on supplements and ergogenic aids, Ulrich and Beate Schoberer for loaning an SRM Powermeter, Bob Dunihue for a historical perspective and for providing several old cycling magazines, The Fort Collins Club for the use of their equipment for illustrations, Charles Pelkey for his expert editing, and Mark Saunders for keeping me focused on the project while pulling together the many pieces of the project.

I am forever indebted to the many athletes I have coached since 1971 for teaching me so much about training for sport.

Finally, I want to thank my wife, Joyce, for her unselfish encouragement while I spent many long hours writing, reading and sitting at a computer. I would never have made it without her patience and support.

PROLOGUE

Training for cycling is much like sculpting in marble. A sculptor painstakingly chips away small pieces of the stone to reveal the masterpiece hidden inside. It's a long and tedious process, with the artist's mind's eye always on the end product. Careful planning is necessary before picking up the hammer and chisel the first time. If the artist loses sight of the plan and begins to enjoy swinging the hammer more than creating a work of art, the stone may be ruined. The artist must then start again with a fresh stone.

For an athlete, the human body is a remarkable medium. It can be sculpted and molded to create a wide array of fitness outcomes — from speed, to strength, to endurance. Each athlete is a sculpture in progress, using training to shape a work of art called fitness.

The purpose of this book is to help you create a plan and the skills to carry it through so that the final product of your training is no less a masterpiece than a marble statue. *The Cyclist's Training Bible* will teach you to see the sculpture within and to develop a plan to make it a reality. It will also provide the practical skills needed to use the chisel carefully and wisely so that you can gently remove small chips — not just pointlessly hammer away.

Why another book on cycling? Aren't there plenty, already?

Most books for cycling cover a wide variety of topics and are aimed at riders ranging from those who occasionally use a bike for general fitness to century riders to novice racers. *The Cyclist's Training Bible* is strictly meant for those who race, especially cyclists who have been at it a few years and are ready to move up to the next level or performance. My goal is to help you make that next step.

I have always been fascinated by how athletes improve and have sought to understand and conceptualize the process for others. As a teenager, my high school football and track coach, Leonard Scotten, was the first to introduce the notion of creating fitness to me. He taught me the value of hard work and started me thinking of one day becoming a coach myself. Now, some 34 years, later he still remains my coaching model.

In the early 1980s, I owned a bike shop and running store, and people kept coming to me for training advice. I soon found myself coaching runners, cyclists and triathletes, and discovered I enjoyed that much more than retail. In 1986, I decided to coach more athletes and sold the business. About the same time, I began writing training columns and stories for magazines and newsletters. Eventually, I became a regular contributor to publications such as *VeloNews*, *Inside Triathlon*, *Triathlete*, *Racing West*, *Masters Sports*, *Performance Conditioning for Cycling* and others.

The monthly pressure to provide a variety of science-based training articles for athletes in different sports helped keep me current on the scientific literature. Every day, the readers of these columns ask me training questions via e-mail, fax and telephone. This book grew from those questions, many of which were asked repeatedly. The answers to these questions come from 20 years of reading sport science literature coupled with the experiences I have had competing in a variety of sports and coaching hundreds of athletes over 25 years.

In the same way, this book is an interplay of science and experience. I've tried to present the scientific information in a way most cyclists can relate to. Much of what is included is an educated guess based on related research and tempered by experience. It's quite possible that by the time this book is in print, science will resolve some of the issues addressed here in contradiction to my suggestions. In fact, while I was writing the book, there were changes. For example, I recommended for several years that the athletes I train take beta carotene and other antioxidants to bolster their immune systems. In early 1996, studies revealed that beta carotene has little or no health benefits. I took it out of the manuscript.

There is nothing in *The Cyclist's Training Bible* that specifically relates to racing tactics, aerodynamics, equipment, bike setup, cornering, or professional profiles. This book is meant strictly for the self-coached rider who wants to know more about how to train and ultimately race better.

Coaching yourself is more difficult than it sounds, especially if you have high aspirations. Most athletes would be better off with a professional coach. Another person's point of view is frequently better than our own as it is more objective. Still, some simply prefer the challenge of self-coaching. Others simply don't trust a coach to do their planning. Still others must settle for self-coaching due to financial constraints. Whatever the reason, I have tried to make this book current and relevant to the needs of amateur cyclists.

I offer this book with the hope that it will make you a better racer and that one day you will return the favor by teaching me something you learned along the course.

Joe Friel
Fort Collins, Colorado
August 1996

ÌΠTRⱣODUCTÌΘΠ

How should I schedule hard workouts? How is it best to train during the weeks of my most important races? How many miles do I need before starting speed work? Is it OK to ride the same day I lift? How long should my recovery rides be? What can I do to climb better?

These are a few of the questions I hear from cyclists nearly every day. The athletes who ask these questions are intelligent and curious people — much like you, I'll bet. They have been riding and racing for three or more years, seeing substantial improvements in fitness merely from putting in the miles and going to races. In the first two years, the competition was fun and they finished well in races. But now they've upgraded and things are different. They can no longer expect to improve by just riding a lot, and begin to train harder only to find out they have more questions than answers.

The purpose of this book is to provide options for solving training questions in order to help you achieve racing success. The answers aren't always as simple and straightforward as you might like them to be. While the science of training has come a long way in the last 30 years, training is still very much an art.

The answer to most training queries I receive almost always starts with: "It depends." It depends on what you've been doing prior to this time. It depends on how much time you have to train. It depends on what your strengths and weaknesses are. It depends on when your most important races happen.

I'm not trying to be evasive, but I want to make sure you understand that there usually is more than one way to solve a training problem. If you asked 10 coaches to answer the questions that started this Introduction, you'd get 10 different answers. All could be right, as there's "more than one way to skin a cat" or train a cyclist. My aim in this book is to assist you in answering your own questions. To that end, *The Cyclist's Training Bible* builds on ideas and concepts presented in each chapter. Following the chapter-by-chapter progression will help you understand the "whys" of my training suggestions.

In Part I, the self-trained cyclist's need for commitment and a common-sense training philosophy are detailed. Chapter 1 describes what it takes for success in cycling, other than physical talent. Chapter 2 proposes a way of thinking about training that more than likely runs counter to your tendencies. I hope the 10 Commandments of Training cause you to occasionally stop reading and reflect on how to train intelligently.

Part II lays the scientific foundation for the remainder of the book by describing generally accepted concepts that guide the training process in Chapter 3. Chapter 4 takes the most critical aspect of training, intensity management, and teaches you how to do it with four methods. The sections of this chapter dealing with lactate analysis and power measurement are somewhat ahead of their time as the equipment for these techniques is not readily available and still in the early stages of development. I expect that by the year 2000, these devices will be less expensive and perhaps nearly as common as the heart-rate monitor is today.

Part III addresses the idea of training with a purpose and offers a framework for accomplishing that purpose. Chapter 5 shows you how to test your strengths and weaknesses, while Chapter 6 tells you what the results mean in terms of racing.

The heart of *The Cyclist's Training Bible* is Part IV. Here, I take you through the same process I use in designing a year-long training plan for an athlete. Chapter 7 provides an overview to the planning process. Chapter 8 describes the step-by-step procedures of planning in a workbook format. By the end of this chapter, you will have determined where you're going in the race season and how you will get there. Chapter 9 puts the cap on the process by showing you how to schedule workouts for the season and, more specifically, on a week-to-week and daily basis. It also suggests workouts. If you're doing a stage race during the season, be sure to read Chapter 10 before completing your annual training plan. Chapter 11 offers examples of other cyclist's annual training plans with discussions of the thinking behind their design. You may find in Chapters 8 and 9 that skipping forward to this chapter for examples helps in designing your plan.

Several other aspects of training that effect the annual plan are discussed in Part V. The importance of strength training for cycling and how to follow a periodized plan is explained along with illustrations of exercises in Chapter 12. Chapter 13 shows how stretching can benefit cycling performance. Training concerns specific to women, masters and juniors are detailed in Chapter 14. If you are in one of these special groups, it may help you to read this chapter before beginning the planning process in Chapter 8. The importance of keeping a training journal is the topic of Chapter 15. A sample journal is provided that complements the weekly scheduling described in Chapter 9. A different way of thinking about eating overlies the discussion of diet in Chapter 16. Also included are supplements and ergogenic aids. Chapter 17 provides guidance for how to deal with training problems common to cyclists — overtraining, burnout, illness and injury. Chapter 18 discusses the most important, but most neglected, aspect of training — recovery.

Finally, the last chapter attempts to answer common training questions posed by cyclists, including those listed at the start of this introduction. All of them are real questions asked by real cyclists regarding their real problems.

Before beginning, I want to offer this note of caution: This book is meant for cyclists who have been training and racing for some time. If you are new to the sport or considering starting to train, you should first have a medical examination. This is particularly important for those over age 35 who have been inactive. Much of what is suggested here is strenuous and designed for those with highly established levels of fitness and riding experience.

While I believe this book will help most cyclists improve, I do not pretend that it will make everyone a champion. It takes something more than just inspiration and guidance for that. No training program is perfect for everyone. Consider my suggestions critically and take from this book what will benefit you now. I hope you will use it as a training reference for years to come.

As you can see, *The Cyclist's Training Bible* is quite methodical. I hope that you don't feel as some do, that analyzing the process of training detracts from the fun of riding and racing. I don't believe it does. Being on a bike is most enjoyable when every starting line is a challenge and every finish line is jubilantly crossed with arms held high. Let's start.

Part I

THE SELF-TRAINED CYCLIST

TRAINING A HALF-CENTURY AGO

Hints on Bicycle Racing
BY NORMAN HILL
As it appeared in Review of Cycling *Magazine, 1943*

In training or conditioning for bike racing, one must remember that for best results it must be considered as a full-time job, and the entire mode of living must be directed toward one objective, namely, the best possible health which is the basis of all athletic ability.

Another important fact to remember is that adoption of a correct training program will not produce overnight results but must be followed religiously for a period of time. In fact, athletic champions are seldom, if ever, developed with less than several years of constant training and experience.

The correct conditioning program can and will improve anyone's ability but cannot, of course, guarantee that everyone will become a champion, as there are hereditary factors plus an element of luck to be considered. A correct training program can be likened to proper care of a car, the proper care insuring maximum efficiency, performance and endurance.

Chapter 1

Commitment

We're on a mission from God.

— Elwood, The Blues Brothers

Talk is cheap. It's easy to have big dreams and set high goals before the racing starts. But the true test of a commitment to better racing results is not in the talking, but in the doing. It doesn't start with the first race of the season — it's all the things you do today to get stronger, faster and more enduring. Real commitment means 365 days a year and 24 hours a day.

Talk to the best riders you know. Ask them about commitment. Once you probe past all of the "aw, shucks" stuff, you'll discover how big a role cycling plays in their lives. The better they are, the more you'll hear about life revolving around the sport. The most common remark will be that each day is arranged around training. It's a rare champion who fits in workouts randomly.

Racing to your potential cannot be an on-again, off-again endeavor. It's a full-time commitment — a passion. Excellence requires living, breathing, eating and sleeping cycling every day. Literally.

The greater the commitment, the more life pivots around the basic three factors of training — eating, sleeping and working out. Eating fuels the body for training and speeds recovery by replacing depleted energy and nutrient stores. Sleeping and working out have a synergistic effect on fitness: Each can cause the release of growth hormone from the pituitary gland. Growth hormone speeds recovery, rebuilds muscles, and breaks down body fat. By training twice daily and taking a nap, the dedicated rider gets four hits of growth hormone daily resulting in higher levels of fitness sooner.

In the final analysis, greater fitness is what we're all after. It's the product of three ingredients: stress, rest and fuel. Figure 1.1, Suggested Daily Routines, illustrates how training, sleeping and eating can be built into your day. (See page 6)

This kind of commitment may not be for you. In fact, there comes a point at which each of us has to check our "want to" against our "have to." Jobs, families and other responsibilities can't be forsaken for sport. Even the pros must consider other aspects of life. Those elements that contribute to making you a great cyclist may detract from your being a great employee, a great mother, father or spouse. Realistically, there have to be limits to passion, otherwise we'd soon alienate everyone who wasn't equally zealous and be reduced to slobbering zombies.

CHANGING

What can you do to improve your fitness and race performances? The first thing is to make small changes in your life. Balance can be hard to achieve, but remolding daily activities by 10 percent in the direction of better cycling doesn't take much and can bring noticeable improvement. How about committing to hitting the sack 30 minutes earlier each night so that you're more rested? Another small, daily change that could bring better results is healthier eating. Could you cut out 10 percent of the junk food every day replacing it with wholesome foods? What you put in your mouth is the stuff the body uses to completely rebuild and replace each muscle cell every six months. Do you want muscles made from potato chips, Twinkies and pop; or from fruits, vegetables and lean meat? What can you change?

The Cyclist's Training Bible can help you make some small changes that will bring big results. But what are the most important changes needed for success? What makes a champion a champion?

THREE ATTRIBUTES OF CHAMPIONS

Successful athletes and coaches ask two questions in their quest for peak athletic performance:

What does science say?

How do champions train?

Much of this book is based on answers to the first question, but the second is no less important. Often the top athletes are ahead of science when it comes to knowing what works and what doesn't. Exercise scientists become interested in some aspect of training because it seems to work for some athletes. Their studies are designed to determine why it's beneficial.

If we eliminate their individual abilities and boil the remainder down to the most basic elements, what is left are the attributes that bring success to the champions. I believe there are three such attributes: mission, support system and direction.

MISSION

When you think of champions such as Merckx, Hinault or LeMond, what comes to mind? More than likely, it is winning the Tour de France. Why do you think of that? Probably because these athletes had a passion for winning the Tour that was evident for all to see. Their motivation to succeed was exceptional. They were willing to make any sacrifice, to ride any number of miles, to do any workouts deemed beneficial to achieving the goal. Approaching the peaks of their careers, riding was their lives. Everything else was just details.

The dispassionate race faces on this group of elite women riders awaiting their start belies their emotional commitment to the sport.

What you can learn from these champions is that motivation and dedication are paramount to achieving your dreams: The greater the dreams, the bigger the mission. Neither this book nor anyone else can help you choose dreams and become more dedicated. Only you can do that. I can tell you, however, that without passion, without a mission, you'll always be just another rider in the peloton.

SUPPORT SYSTEM

The greatest rider with the biggest dreams will never become a champion without a support system — others who also believe in the mission and are committed to it. Surrounding champions are family, friends, teammates, directors, coaches, soigneurs and mechanics, all of whom are there to help the champion attain his or her dream. The rider becomes immersed in the we-can-do-it attitude. The mission is no longer singular — it becomes a group effort. Once this is achieved, success is 90 percent assured.

Do you have a support system? Do those around you even know what your goals, let alone your dreams, are? Is there a mentor or close friend with whom to share your challenges and vision? Again, this book can't help you develop a support system. Only you can do that. Support systems start with you offering to help others, perhaps teammates, attain their highest goals. Support is contagious. Give yours to someone else.

DIRECTION

Champions don't train aimlessly. They also don't blindly follow another rider's training plan. They understand that the difference between winning and losing is often as slight as a cat's whisker. They know their training can't be haphazard or left to chance. Merely having a detailed plan provides confidence. It's the final, and smallest, piece in the quest for the dream. Without a plan, the champion never makes it to the victory stand.

This is where *The Cyclist's Training Bible* can help you. While this book offers the reader individualized, results-oriented and scientific methods, following its program won't guarantee your success. But if you already have a mission and the support system is in place, you're practically there. This just may be the final and decisive element.

Figure 1.1
Suggested Daily Routines

	Two Workouts Daily		One Workout Daily	
	Work day	No-work day	Work day	No-work day
6:00 am	Awake	Awake	Awake	Awake
:30	Workout 1	Eat	Workout	Eat
7:00	|	Stretch	|	Stretch
:30	|	Personal	|	Personal
8:00	Eat	|	Eat	|
:30	Shower	Workout 1	Shower	Workout
9:00	Work	|	Work	|
:30	|	|	|	|
10:00	|	|	|	|
:30	|	Eat	|	|
11:00	|	Shower	|	|
:30	Eat	Nap	|	Eat
12:00 pm	Nap	Stretch	Eat	Shower
:30	Work	Personal	Nap	Nap
1:00	|	Eat	Work	Personal
:30	|	Personal	|	|
2:00	|	|	|	|
:30	|	Workout 2	|	|
3:00	Eat	|	|	|
:30	|	|	Eat	Eat
4:00	|	|	|	Personal
:30	|	Eat	|	|
5:00	End work	Shower	End work	|
:30	Workout 2	Nap	Personal	|
6:00	|	Stretch	|	|
:30	Eat	Personal	Eat	Eat
7:00	Shower	|	Personal	Personal
:30	Personal	Eat	|	|
8:00	|	Personal	|	|
:30	Eat	|	|	|
9:00	To bed	To bed	To bed	To bed

Chapter 2

SMART TRAINING

Ya gotta do what ya gotta do.

— ROCKY BALBOA

Why is it that some start their cycling career with little sign of physical talent and years later reach the pinnacle of the sport as elite amateurs or pros? Why are there others who excel at an early age, fizzle, and eventually drop out of the sport before realizing their full potential?

Those who persevere probably had talent all along, but it wasn't immediately evident. More than likely, the young athlete had a parent, coach or mentor concerned about the long term. They were probably someone who wanted to see their protégé in full bloom, so brought the athlete along slowly and deliberately.

The successful athlete's workouts may not have been the most scientific, but a sensible training philosophy was established early in his or her career. In contrast, the young cyclist who failed to make it as a senior may have been driven too hard by a parent or coach whose intentions were well meaning, but whose techniques left something to be desired.

A philosophy that works for young riders also works well for older and more experienced athletes who want to improve their results.

PHILOSOPHY

The philosophy of training proposed in *The Cyclist's Training Bible* may seem unusual. I have found, however, that if it is followed, serious athletes improve. Here is my training philosophy.

An athlete should do the least amount of the most specific training that brings continual improvement.

The idea of limiting training is a scary thought for some. Many cyclists have become so used to overtraining that it seems a normal state. These racers are no less addicted than drug users. As is the case with a drug addict, the chronically overtrained athlete is not getting any better but still can't convince himself or herself to change.

Read the philosophy statement again. Notice that it doesn't say "train with the least amount of miles." Another way of stating it might be "use your training time wisely." For those of us with full-time jobs, spouses, children, a home to maintain and other responsibilities, using training time wisely is more than a philosophy — it's a necessity.

To help you better understand this philosophy I'd like to explain it using the "10 Commandments of Training." By incorporating each of these guidelines into your thinking and training, you'll be following this philosophy and getting a better return on your time invested. Your results will also improve regardless of your age or experience.

THE 10 COMMANDMENTS OF TRAINING

COMMANDMENT 1 — TRAIN MODERATELY

Your body has limits when it comes to endurance, speed and strength. Don't try too often to find them. Instead, train within those limits most of the time. Finish most workouts feeling like you could have done more. It may mean stopping a session earlier than planned. That's OK. Do not always try to finish exhausted.

The biggest mistake of most athletes is making their easy days too hard, so when it comes time for a hard training day, they're unable to go hard enough. This leads to mediocre fitness and performance. The higher your fitness level, the greater the difference between the intensities of hard and easy days.

Many cyclists also think that pushing hard all the time will make them tough. They believe that willpower and strength of character can overcome nature and speed up their body's cellular changes. Don't try it — more hard training is seldom the answer. An organism adapts best when stresses are slightly increased. That's why you've often heard the admonition to increase training volume by no more than 10 percent from week to week. Even this may be high for some.

By progressing carefully, especially with intensity, you'll gradually get stronger and there will be time and energy for other pursuits in life. An athlete who enjoys training will get far more benefits from it than one who is always on the edge of over-training. When in doubt — leave it out.

Udo Bölts seeks his limits in the 1993 Tour de France prologue. Intense effort demands the balance of training and rest to bring consistent improvement.

COMMANDMENT 2 — TRAIN CONSISTENTLY

The human body thrives on routine. Develop a training pattern that stays mostly the same from week to week — regular activity brings positive change. This does not mean do the same workout every day, week after week. Variety also promotes growth. Later in this book you'll see that there are actually slight changes being made throughout the training year. Some of the changes are seemingly minor. You may not even be aware of them, as when an extra hour is added to the training week during the base-building period.

Breaks in consistency usually result from not following the Moderation Commandment. Overdoing a workout or week of training is likely to cause excessive fatigue, illness, burnout or injury. Fitness is not stagnant — you're either getting better or getting worse all the time. Frequently missing workouts mean a loss of fitness. This doesn't mean, however, you should work out when ill. There are times when breaks are necessary.

COMMANDMENT 3 — GET ADEQUATE REST

It's during rest that the body adapts to the stresses of training and grows stronger. Without rest there's no improvement. As the stress of training increases, the need for rest also accumulates. Most cyclists pay lip service to this Commandment; they understand it intellectually, but not emotionally. It is the most widely violated guideline. You will not improve without adequate rest.

Most athletes need seven to 10 hours of sleep daily. Professionals, with few other demands on their time than training, usually include naps to get their daily dose. The rest of us need to get to bed early every night. The younger you are, the more rest you need. Junior riders should be sleeping nine to 10 hours daily.

Refer back to Figure 1.1, Suggested Daily Training Routines, to determine a daily schedule that will ensure you get adequate rest every day. Until you establish a schedule, you're not really training — you're playing on a bike.

COMMANDMENT 4 — TRAIN WITH A PLAN

This is fundamental to improvement in almost any endeavor of life, yet few self-trained athletes do it. Sometimes I find riders who use a sound plan from a magazine, but as soon as a new issue comes out, they abandon the old plan and take up a new one. Most people will improve if they follow a plan — any plan. It can be of poor design, yet still work. Just don't change it.

COMMANDMENT 5 — TRAIN WITH GROUPS INFREQUENTLY

There's a real advantage to working out with others — sometimes. Pack riding develops handling skills, provides experience with race dynamics, and makes the time go faster. But all too often, the group will cause you to ride fast when you would be best served by a slow, easy recovery ride. At other times, you'll need to go longer or shorter than what the group decides to ride. Group workouts too often degenerate into unstructured races at the most inopportune times.

For the winter base-building period, find a group that rides at a comfortable pace. During the spring intensity-building period, ride with a group that will challenge you to ride fast, just as when racing. Smart and structured group rides are hard to find. You may need to create your own. Stay away from big packs that take over the road and are unsafe. You want to get faster, not get killed.

Use groups when they can help you. Otherwise, avoid them.

Team Banesto and admirers training near Boulder, Colorado for the 1995 world championships. Group rides should always have a purpose.

COMMANDMENT 6 — PLAN TO PEAK

Your season plan should bring you to your peak for the most important events. I call these "A" races. The "B" races are important, too, but you won't taper and peak for these, just rest for three to four days before. "C" races are tune-ups to get you ready for the A's and B's. A smart rider will use these low-priority races for experience, or to practice pacing, or as a time trial to gauge fitness. If all races are equal, don't expect much.

This book will show you how to peak for "A" races two or more times in a season. Each peak may last for up to six weeks. You will still race between peaks, but the emphasis will be on re-establishing endurance, strength and speed to prepare for the next peak.

COMMANDMENT 7 — IMPROVE WEAKNESSES

What do riders with great endurance, but not much speed, do the most of? You guessed it — endurance work. What do good climbers like to do? Why of course — they

like to train in the hills. Most cyclists spend too much time working on what they're already good at. What's your weakest area? Ask your training partners if you don't know. I'll bet they do. Then spend more time on that area. *The Cyclist's Training Bible* will help identify your weaknesses and teach you how to improve them.

COMMANDMENT 8 — TRUST YOUR TRAINING

Few of us trust our training when it comes time to race. There's a great fear as the big race approaches that we haven't done enough, so we train right up to race day. I've seen people the day before an important race go out for a long ride because they think it will help. It takes 10 to 21 days of reduced work load for the human body to be fully ready to race, depending on how long and hard the training has been. Cut back before the big races, and you'll do better. Trust me.

Zenon Jaskula in the hills near Colorado Springs. Riding alone is often the best training alternative.

COMMANDMENT 9 — LISTEN TO YOUR BODY

A few years ago, after the fall of the Berlin Wall, I attended a talk by the former head of the East German Sports Institute. After conceding that East German athletes had indeed used illegal drugs, which he felt was a minor aspect of their remarkable success, he went on to explain what he saw as the real reason for their great number of Olympic medals. He described how elite athletes lived regulated lives in dormitories. Every morning on awakening, each athlete met with a group of experts — an event coach, a physiologist, a doctor or nurse, and a sports psychologist, for example. The group checked the athlete's readiness to train that day and made adjustments as necessary to the schedule. In effect, they were listening to what the athlete's body was saying. The athlete trained only to the level they could tolerate that day. Nothing more.

It would be nice if each of us could afford such attention. We can't, so we must learn to listen to our bodies for ourselves. If you listen to what the body is saying, you'll train smarter and get faster. Cyclists who train smart always beat athletes who train hard. *The Cyclist's Training Bible* will teach you how to hear what your body is saying every day.

Tony Rominger's focused determination is evident in the 1995 Tour de France. Complete commitment to goals usually requires a lifestyle change.

COMMANDMENT 10 — COMMIT TO GOALS

Talk is cheap. If you want to race farther, faster and stronger this season you need to train differently and may even need to make changes in your lifestyle. What could be holding you back? Is it too little sleep? Maybe you need to go to bed earlier. Or perhaps you eat too much carbohydrate and not enough protein. You may benefit from putting more time in the weight room in the winter to build greater force. Maybe your training partners are holding you back.

After you set your goals in a later chapter, take a look at them and determine how they relate to your lifestyle and training. Determine that if change is needed, you can do it. Only you can control how well you race. It's time to put up.

Part II

FROM LAB
TO ROAD

Training Tips at Random
BY FRED KUGLER
As it appeared in Bicycling Magazine, April 1946

A stunt that we have often used in road training was to walk rapidly for about a half a mile but carrying the bicycle with your arm cocked so the bicycle's cross bar is just off your shoulder. This tends to throw your shoulders back and stretches your chest and lungs, developing your grip, wrists and arms. Change arms in carrying at will, but at no time during your set distance for this exercise let the bike touch the ground or your shoulder. If in a group, it can be made interesting by seeing who can carry their bicycle the farthest, or race to a given point under the above rules. Do this at the beginning or end of a ride, or just before or after a rest stop.

If interest is dull during a training ride, try this. The man in front stick in ten hard kicks (counting on one foot only), then swing out and drop back to last place and the next fellow stick in his ten hard kicks, drop back, etc. You will soon find the going quite tough, that is if each rider really puts in ten good hard kicks.

Chapter 3

THE SCIENCE OF TRAINING

People who think they know everything
are very irritating to those of us who do.

— UNKNOWN

It wasn't until the 1960s that the study of exercise as a science became widespread, and not until the 1970s before it began to significantly change the way serious cyclists trained. In the 1980s, exercise science made a quantum leap. We learned more about the human athlete in those 10 years than in the previous 80.

The earliest scientists learned more from studying the methods of top athletes than they did from independent study in their ivory towers. That is still the case today; as the people in white lab coats seek to find out why some athletes succeed and others do not.

Even in the early days, riders learned through trial and error that they couldn't develop both maximal endurance and top speed simultaneously. Coaches and athletes found that by first establishing an aerobic endurance base and later by adding faster riding, they could come into top form at the right time. This method of training was often imposed on them by the weather. Winter made long easy rides a necessity, while summer favored faster riding.

Since those leather shoe and wool jersey days, we've learned a lot from the best athletes, coaches and scientists. It's been a long and winding road. The entire range of training elements, including nutrition, recovery, strength, mental skills, fitness measurement and workouts, has been explored and greatly refined. Still, many athletes continue to train as if it were 1912. They go out the door day after day with no plan, deciding as the ride develops what they will do. Some are successful despite their backward ways. Could they do better? Probably. Will you improve if you adopt a more scientific way of training as described in this book? I believe you will.

I hope to help you reach toward your potential by taking advantage of the most recent training knowledge available. This knowledge has been gleaned from research studies, from the training methods of top cyclists and coaches and from athletes and coaches in other sports such as swimming, running, rowing and triathlon. Some of it is proven beyond doubt, but much is still theory. You need to determine how everything applies to you and your training. Even well-established and proven practices may not be applicable to you. Some things may not work for you although they do for others.

Before getting scientific, I want to explain a few basics about training for cycling. These may be so elementary that they seem evident, but I'll describe them just in case.

No one starts out at the top. Many of those who get there make it because they are more patient than others. Training has a cumulative effect from year to year. If done correctly, a cyclist should see improvement over time. Don't expect miracles overnight.

Physical and psychological breaks from training are normal and necessary. No one can improve at an uninterrupted pace forever. If you don't build in down time, your body will force you to. It doesn't matter how mentally strong you are: You need rest and recovery. And racing does not qualify as a break from training.

If you're new to cycling, the most important thing you can do is ride consistently and steadily for a year. Don't be concerned about all of the detail stuff this book will describe until you've put at least one season under your belt. Then you can begin to plug in the finer elements of training.

PERIODIZATION

In the late 1940s, Soviet sports scientists discovered that athletic performance was improved by varying the training stresses throughout the year rather than maintaining a constant training focus. This led to the development of annual training plans.

The Training Bible

The East Germans and Romanians further developed ths concept by establishing goals for the various periods and the system of "periodization" was born. One Romanian scientist in particular, Tudor Bompa, Ph.D., so refined the concept that he is known as the "father of periodization." His seminal work, *Theory and Methodology of Training* (Kendall/Hunt Publishing, 1983), introduced Western athletes to this training system.

While athletes and coaches have "Westernized" periodization, they have done so largely without the help of science. Scientific literature offers no direction as to a long-term training approach for endurance athletes.

The basic premise of all periodization programs is that training should progress from the general to the specific. For example, early in the season, the serious cyclist uses much of the available training time to develop general strength with weights, while also cross-training and doing some riding. Later in the season, more time is spent on the bike in conditions that simulate bicycle racing. While there is no scientific evidence to support such a pattern of training, logic seems to support it. In fact, most of the world's top athletes adhere to it.

Figure 3.1

General to specific training emphasis throughout the training year.

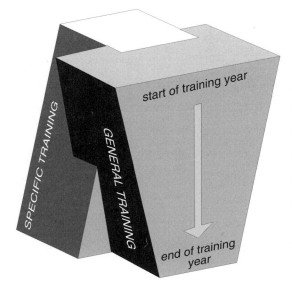

Of course, periodization means more than simply training more specifically. It also involves arranging the workouts in such a way that elements of fitness achieved in an earlier phase of training are maintained while new ones are addressed and improved. This modular method of training means making small changes in workouts during four- to eight-week periods. The body will gradually become more fit with such a pattern of change.

TRAINING STRESS

In order to bring positive physical changes, stress is necessary. That's where the workouts fit in. Workout stress can be changed by manipulating three elements of training: frequency, duration and intensity.

FREQUENCY

How often you work out is the most basic element. Beginners typically ride three to five times each week. That's appropriate for their level of need. An Olympic-hopeful might work out 12 to 15 times in a week — also appropriate.

Studies have found that training three to five times a week brings the greatest gain for the time invested, and that additional workouts have diminishing returns. If trying to realize your racing potential, however, those small gains are worth it since the competition will be quite close in ability.

Early in the training year, frequency increases, so as to add beneficial stress. Just prior to and during the race season, it decreases to allow more time for recovery.

DURATION

Workout length varies dramatically from day to day. Some workouts are long to build greater endurance, while others are short to allow more emphasis on higher intensities or to provide active recovery.

Typically, the longest workouts are about the same duration as the longest race the athlete will compete in. Early in the season, the higher-intensity workouts are done on lower-duration days, but as the racing season approaches, harder workouts incorporate both long duration and high intensity. This prepares the body for the stresses of racing.

INTENSITY

Frequency and duration are easy to measure. Workout intensity is somewhat tougher, but is the most important to get right.

High intensity is powerful medicine. Too much and you wind up overtrained and on the sidelines watching. Too little in training and you're off the back in races. Chapter 4 explains how to accurately determine your individual intensity zones, and Chapter 8 outlines how to use them wisely in training. Pay close attention to everything you read here on the intensity of training. If you get this part wrong, it doesn't matter what else you may be doing right.

General fitness development is encouraged during the early preparatory period of the annual periodization plan.

WORKLOAD

The combination of the three stress agents — frequency, duration and intensity — results in workload. A rider who works out frequently with long durations and high intensity is training with a high workload. Infrequent, short duration workouts at a low intensity produce a low workload. By manipulating the three elements, workloads can be designed to fit every athlete's needs.

PRINCIPLES OF TRAINING

The principles on which periodization are based are individualization, progression, overload and specificity. Bear with me here as these may sound somewhat scientific and theoretical. Understanding the principles will make you a better cyclist — one capable of smart self-coaching.

INDIVIDUALIZATION

The capacity of an athlete to handle a given workload is unique. Each athlete can be considered an ecosystem influenced by three categories of factors — sociocultural, biological and psychological. Each has the potential to impede or promote improvement.

Sociocultural factors such as lagging career progression, economic pressure and poor interpersonal relationships often undercut how much time and energy, both mental and physical, is available for training. Examples of biological factors are allergies, use of drugs and inadequate nutrition. These factors may restrict the individual's physical ability to train successfully. Psychological factors are perhaps the most overlooked, yet the most likely to compromise the benefits of training. Some examples are fear of failure, low self-esteem and the unreasonable expectations of others.

In addition, some athletes are "fast responders" while others are "slow responders." This means that if you and a teammate do exactly the same training in precisely the same way, you probably won't reach a common level of fitness by a given race. Being a slow or fast responder is probably genetic — you may have inherited a body that changes at a given rate. Generally, four to eight weeks of a given type of training are necessary to show significant results. While you can't change how quickly your body responds, you can learn to design your training program around your unique characteristics.

The bottom line is that you cannot simply do what others are doing and expect to get the same benefits — or any benefits at all. What is an easy day for one rider

may be race effort for another. Chapters 5 and 6 will address the issue of individual-
izing training to fit your unique set of abilities.

PROGRESSION

Have you ever done a workout so hard that you were sore for days afterwards
and didn't have the energy to even ride easily? We've all done that. Such a workout
violated the progression principle. The body didn't get stronger, it lost fitness. The
workout caused you to waste two very precious resources: time and energy.

The workload must be gradually increased, with intermittent periods of rest and
recovery, as the athlete focuses fitness for the most important races of the season. The
stresses must be greater than the body is accustomed to handling. The workloads,
especially the intensity component, are increased in small increments, usually of five
to 15 percent. This allows the cyclist to avoid overtraining and injury, yet provides
enough stress to allow adaptation to occur. Workload increases are largely individual
matters, especially as regards intensity.

Chapters 5 and 6 will guide you through the maze of building race fitness progressively.

Miguel Indurain and
Alvaro Mejia, two athletes
with exceptional, but
different abilities and
body types, climb the
Col du Galibier in the
1993 Tour de France.
Each rider comes to the
sport with a unique set of
capabilities that must be
individually developed.

OVERLOAD

The object of training is to cause the body to positively change in order to better manage the physiological stresses of racing. In order to stress the body, it must be presented with a load that challenges its current state of fitness. Such a load will cause fatigue, followed by recovery and eventually a greater level of fitness known as "overcompensation."

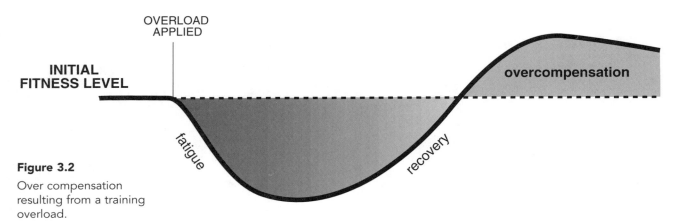

Figure 3.2

Over compensation resulting from a training overload.

Top-level performance is the result of years of well-planned overload resulting in adaptation. This optimum training repeatedly places measured stresses on the athlete. If the workloads are of the right magnitude, slightly more than the body can handle, adaptation occurs and fitness steadily improves.

It's important to note that overload happens during workouts, but adaptation occurs during rest. If you repeatedly short-change your rest, the body will not continue to improve. You'll actually lose fitness. This is called "overtraining." The biggest mistake I see self-coached athletes make is disregarding their need for rest. Smart athletes know when to abandon a workout early. They know when to do less instead of more. In short, they understand and listen to their bodies. You must learn to do the same. In Chapter 15, I'll teach you some techniques to help you refine this skill.

If the load of training is decreased for extended periods, the body adapts to lower levels of fitness. We call this "being out of shape." But once a rider has reached optimal fitness, it can be maintained with infrequent, but regular and judiciously spaced stress allowing for increased recovery between hard workouts.

SPECIFICITY

According to this principle, the stresses applied in training must be similar to the stresses expected in racing. Sometimes the workload must include long, steady

distance. At others, brief bouts of high intensity are required to bring the needed changes. Riding slow all the time is just as wrong as always going hard.

In Chapter 6, I'll teach you how to isolate the various stresses required in road races and show you how to blend them into a comprehensive program.

PEAKING

The purpose of periodization is to reach peak form just as the most important races roll around. Since these races are seldom on back-to-back weekends and may be separated by several weeks, it's usually necessary to peak more than once. I've found that the athletes I train race best when they peak two times each season. I believe you'll find that this works for you, also. Chapter 8 will help you design a twin-peaks season using the same procedure I use with my clients. (See page 24 for Figure 3.3.)

Chris Horner and Nate Reiss contest the finishing sprint climaxing a long breakaway in the 1996 Tour DuPont. High-level performance is the result of years of well-planned overload combined with adequate recovery.

Figure 3.3

A twin peaks season.

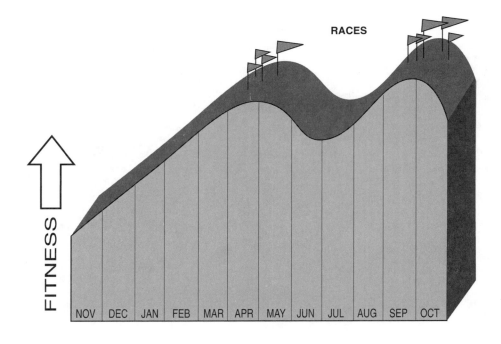

RACES

FITNESS

NOV | DEC | JAN | FEB | MAR | APR | MAY | JUN | JUL | AUG | SEP | OCT

REFERENCES

Bompa, T. Physiological intensity values employed to plan endurance training, *New Studies in Athletics*, vol. 3(4), pp. 37-52, 1988.

Bompa, T. *Theory and Methodology of Training*, Kendall/Hunt, 1983.

Brynteson, P. and W.E. Sinning. The effects of training frequencies on the retention of cardiovascular fitness, *Medicine and Science in Sports*, vol. 5, pp. 29-33, 1973.

Costill, D.L., et al. Effects of reduced training on muscular power in swimmers, *Physician and Sports Medicine*, vol. 17(2), pp. 94-101, 1985.

Costill, D.L., et al. Adaptations to swimming training: Influence of training volume, *Medicine and Science in Sports and Exercise*, vol. 23, pp. 371-377, 1991.

Daniels, J. Training distance runners — A primer, *Sports Science Exchange*, vol. 1(11), pp. 1-4, 1989.

Fitts, R.H., et al. Effect of swim-exercise training on human muscle fiber function, *Journal of Applied Physiology*, vol. 66, pp. 465-475, 1989.

Matveyev, L. *Fundamentals of Sports Training*, Progress Publishing, 1981.

Wenger, H.A. and G.J. Bell. The interactions of intensity, frequency and duration of exercise training in altering cardiorespiratory fitness, *Sports Medicine*, vol. 3(5), pp. 346-356, 1986.

Chapter 4

Intensity

Either this man is dead or my watch has stopped.

— Groucho Marx

In training both elite and recreational athletes, I've noticed a curious difference. Elite riders generally treat high-intensity training as if it's a powerful drug. They use it carefully and in measured doses at pre-selected times. Recreational cyclists, on the other hand, almost always devour high intensity as though it's candy.

Why the difference? Perhaps elite riders are more patient, or maybe they've learned the hard way that too much, too soon, means doom.

I sometimes ask a train-too-hard athlete I'm trying to break of this bad habit: If you owned an expensive horse capable of winning the Kentucky Derby, would you run it hard every day? The answer is always "no." They would allow time for recovery and bring the horse along slowly so as to avoid injury and overtraining. Then my next question is, "Why do you train yourself hard every day?" Few have an answer.

Of the three elements of training — frequency, duration and intensity — the most important to get right is intensity. Oddly enough, this is the part cyclists all too often get wrong. Most train too intensely when they should be going easy. Then when it's time to go fast they are a little too tired to push near their limits. As a result, all of their training becomes moderate. They race the same way: Stay with the pack until it's time to put the hammer down. Then they're off the back wondering why.

Developing peak fitness is like making a cake. First you whip up the batter and bake it. This is the most time-intensive part of the process. Developing the aerobic base is like this. Then, after the cake is baked, the icing is put on. This part doesn't take as long, but it's what really makes the cake appealing and tasty. The icing is much like high-intensity training. Without the large aerobic base that comes from easy riding, the intensity of training won't be as great or last as long. There's nothing to build the intensity on to — similar to having no cake and simply putting the icing on the plate.

Another training comparison that has stood the test of time is that of a pyramid. The broader the base of the pyramid (easy, aerobic training), the higher the peak will be (fast racing speed).

The bottom line is that high-intensity training needs to be undertaken with thought and planning in order to peak at the right times of the year. Too much, too soon and you won't be able to maintain the fitness. Too little, too late and you're off the back.

Learn to apply the intensity concepts in this chapter and you'll avoid overtraining and undertraining, and your racing fitness will be high when the time is right. Read carefully.

MEASURING INTENSITY

What's going on inside a cyclist's body during a race or workout? How does a rider know to go faster or back off during a time trial? Is a workout too hard or too easy? How is it possible to finish with enough left for a sprint?

The answers to these and other questions come down to keeping close tabs on your use of energy. By measuring intensity and comparing the information with what you have learned about your body in training and racing, you can make decisions as new situations such as breakaways, head winds and hills occur. Today's technology allows an athlete to measure intensity quickly and accurately.

The oldest, and still one of the best gross indicators of intensity, is perceived effort. An experienced cyclist is able to judge his or her intensity quite accurately by taking a subjective survey of the entire body at work. This is a skill honed by years of riding, making mistakes and relearning as fitness changes.

Perceived exertion is quantifiable using the Borg Rating of Perceived Exertion Scale (see Table 4.1) and is frequently used by scientists to determine at what level an athlete is working. Some athletes are so good at using a Rating of Perceived Exertion (RPE), that in a laboratory, graduated-effort test they can pinpoint their lactate threshold precisely just from feel.

Table 4.1

Borg Rating
of Perceived
Exertion Scale

Purpose	Rating	Exertion
Recovery	6	
Recovery	7	Very, very light
Recovery	8	
Recovery	9	Very light
Aerobic development	10	
Aerobic development	11	Fairly light
Aerobic development	12	
Tempo development	13	Somewhat hard
Tempo development	14	
Subthreshold development	15	Hard
Subthreshold development	16	
Superthreshold development	17	Very hard
Aerobic capacity development	18	
Aerobic capacity development	19	Very, very hard
Aerobic capacity development	20	

SYSTEMS

The body is made up of several interconnected systems, such as the immune system and nervous system. No matter what method of measurement used, you're taking a peek into the body through a small systems window, but since the systems are linked, you can draw conclusions about the entire body once you have experience and knowledge. I'll help you with the knowledge part in this chapter; you'll need to acquire the experience by using what you learn here.

The systems we can presently use to peek into the body while out on the road, and the measurable indicator of each are:

- Energy production system — lactate
- Muscular system — power
- Cardiovascular system — heart rate

ENERGY PRODUCTION SYSTEM

The metabolic system provides fuel to muscles in the form of carbohydrate, fat and protein. Within the muscle, these fuels are converted to a usable energy form called adenosine triphosphate (ATP). This process happens either aerobically or anaerobically.

Aerobic energy production occurs while you are riding easily. It relies primarily on fat and to a lesser extent on carbohydrate for fuel and uses oxygen in the process of converting these fuels to ATP. The slower you go, the greater the reliance on fat and the more carbohydrate is spared. As the pace of your ride increases, there is a gradual shifting away from fat and toward carbohydrate as the fuel of choice. At high efforts, around 15-17 RPE, oxygen delivery no longer keeps up with the demand, and you begin producing ATP anaerobically, meaning "without oxygen."

Anaerobic exercise relies heavily on carbohydrate for fuel. As carbohydrate is converted to ATP, a by-product called lactic acid is released into the muscle. This causes the familiar burning and heavy-legged sensations you've experienced while riding hard. As lactic acid seeps through the muscle cell walls into the blood stream, it gives off a hydrogen molecule and becomes lactate. Lactate accumulates in the blood, making it possible to measure its level in blood samples. The unit of measurement used in labs is millimoles per liter and is expressed as "mmol/L."

Since carbohydrate is in use during both these types of energy production, to a lesser extent in aerobic and more so anaerobically, lactic acid is always being produced. Even while you are reading this book, your muscles are producing measurable amounts of lactic acid.

By measuring lactate, an athlete, or more than likely his or her coach, could determine quite precisely several key aspects of fitness, such as:

• **Lactate threshold.** The level of exertion at which metabolism shifts from aerobic to anaerobic marked by lactate being produced so rapidly that the body can't keep up with its removal. I often explain lactate threshold using an analogy. If I slowly pour water into a paper cup that has a hole in the bottom the water will run out as fast as I pour it in. This is what happens to lactate in the blood at low levels of exertion. If I pour faster, there comes a point when the water begins to accumulate. This is similar to the lactate threshold point that is achieved at higher levels of exertion. Lactate threshold is an important concept that will be used throughout this book.

Table 4.2

Lactate Zones

RPE	Purpose	Lactate (mmol/L)
<10	Recovery	<2
10-12	Aerobic	2-3
13-17	Threshold	3-5
18-19	Aerobic Capacity	5-12
20+	Anaerobic Capacity	12-20

- **Training zones.** Training and racing intensities may be determined based on lactate levels (see Table 4.2).
- **Physiological improvement.** The faster a rider can go or the more power that can be generated without accumulating high levels of lactate, the better his or her racing fitness.
- **Economy of pedaling.** The smoother one pedals, the less effort he or she uses, and therefore, the less lactate that accumulates in the rider's muscles.
- **Equipment selection.** Optimal crank arm lengths, saddle heights and handle bar adjustments create a greater pedaling economy, which then produces low levels of lactate in the rider's muscle.
- **Recovery interval.** Reduced levels of lactate indicate that a cyclist is ready for the next work interval in a workout.

The key piece in achieving all of these benefits is the ability to accurately measure lactate in a "field" setting, rather than a lab — in other words, inexpensively.

Until recently, the only way to measure lactate was in a lab using an analyzer such as the YSI 2300, the accepted standard in the United States. Its size, expense and the need for electricity, however, make it impractical for field use.

Recently, a relatively inexpensive portable lactate analyzer was introduced to the U.S. cycling market (the AccuSport portable lactate analyzer), but as of this writing there are many problems to be worked out.

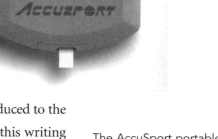

The AccuSport portable lactate analyzer.

MUSCULAR SYSTEM

The product of the neuromuscular system is power — the capacity to apply force to the pedals quickly. On the bike, this translates into gear size and cadence. It is a pretty simple formula: The higher the gear you can drive at a high cadence, the more powerful you are and the faster you can ride.

There are two ways of producing power — slowly pushing big gears, or rapidly turning small gears. "Mashers" rely more on the force side of the equation using high gears and low cadences. "Spinners" are best with low gears, but high cadences. Power results from either combination. A talented cyclist is able to use a bigger gear in a situation where it is demanded, such as time trialing, but can also spin comfortably in criteriums.

Just as low lactate production at high RPE is a good indicator of a metabolic fitness, high power outputs at all levels of exertion indicate a fit neuromuscular system.

Time spent in the weight room and training on hills using big gears develops force. Regularly pedaling at a high cadence improves speed. Working on both cre-

Table 4.3

Power of selected male cyclists

	Weight (in lbs)	Max Watts	Avg Watts	Avg as % of Max	Watts per lb
SS	155	740	519	70%	4.8
CM	170	987	707	72%	5.8
SC	145	955	762	80%	6.6

ates a powerful rider with a wide range of capabilities.

Power on the bike is usually measured in watts. As the cyclist's power rises, so does his or her wattage output.

Recently I tested all of the athletes I coach. Each sprinted 0.2 miles on a flat course using CompuTrainer to measure power. (This test is described in the next chapter.) Table 4.3 summarizes the results of three selected males.

SS wanted to upgrade to category 2, but his low power output was holding him back, as was his average power and watts per pound. Watts per pound can be a good indicator of climbing potential. At 4.8, SS will be off the back on hills. Strength training and hill work coupled with pedaling drills will help him develop more power.

CM is new to cycling, but has good potential based on his tests. A maximum power of 987 watts is excellent, but we need to work on his ability to maintain his power output. His average power fades too quickly. He needs to focus on anaerobic endurance training.

SC is a master. In his fourth year of competitive racing he has tremendous potential. As the smallest man in the group, he produced the second highest maximum power reading, his average power was the highest, and his power per pound was also highest. Given the right nurturing of racing skills, SC will become one of the best riders in his district.

For an endurance cyclist, another good indicator of current fitness is the amount of power he or she can generate at lactate threshold. As fitness improves, this should increase.

Table 4.4

Power Training Zones

RPE	Purpose	Watts as % of LT
<10	Recovery	<40%
10-12	Aerobic	40-79%
13-14	Tempo	80-87%
15-16	Subthreshold	88-99%
17	Superthreshold	100-104%
18-19	Aerobic Capacity	105-149%
20+	Anaerobic Capacity	150%+

Table 4.4 suggests training zones based on power. Since power is somewhat easier to measure and monitor during a workout than lactate, there are more narrowly defined zones in the power table.

There is no doubt that power is closely related to performance in cycling. A cyclist who increases his or her power is capable of riding faster, or riding at the same

Table 4.5
Power-Time-Weight Comparisons

Watts	120 lb Time	150 lb Time	180 lb Time
150	1:18:21	1:20:28	1:21:56
160	1:17:32	1:18:22	1:20:29
170	1:16:07	1:17:24	1:18:22
180	1:13:31	1:14:16	1:16:09
190	1:12:24	1:13:32	1:14:18
200	1:11:37	1:12:27	1:13:33
210	1:09:41	1:10:21	1:11:40
220	1:08:41	1:09:44	1:10:23
230	1:08:07	1:08:07	1:09:45
240	1:06:24	1:06:58	1:08:11
250	1:05:30	1:06:25	1:07:00
260	1:04:59	1:05:32	1:06:27
270	1:03:27	1:03:58	1:05:04
280	1:02:38	1:03:29	1:04:00
290	1:02:10	1:02:46	1:03:31
300	1:00:50	1:01:21	1:02:21
310	1:00:07	1:00:54	1:01:23
320	0:59:56	1:00:42	1:01:11
330	0:58:39	0:59:34	1:00:02
340	0:58:19	0:58:46	0:59:41
350	0:57:40	0:58:23	0:58:47
360	0:57:08	0:57:33	0:58:15
370	0:56:24	0:57:14	0:57:40
380	0:56:03	0:56:27	0:57:18
390	0:55:21	0:55:56	0:56:21
400	0:55:01	0:55:24	0:56:03

Power output is directly related to speed as illustrated here. This table compares average power in watts to 40km-time-trial times on a flat course for three hypothetical riders of different combined bike and body weights. It assumes a similar drag for all three riders.

The Training Bible

The RacerMate CompuTrainer makes indoor training with power possible.

speed with less energy expended. The accompanying Power-Time-Weight Comparisons illustrate this point for a 40-kilometer time trial. Note that as power rises, time falls for any given rider's body weight.

Accurately measuring power is an excellent way for not only determining a rider's strengths and weaknesses, but also for determining exertion levels at which to train.

There are presently two pieces of equipment available to measure power — the RacerMate Compu-Trainer (800/522-3610) and the SRM Powermeter system (Germany: 011-49-2463-3156).

CompuTrainer is an indoor cycling device that resembles a magnetic trainer. The similarity stops there. The CompuTrainer connects to a TV-Nintendo system through a handlebar control unit that allows the user to select and design courses, and race against a programmable "competitor." Hills, wind and drafting make workouts realistic, and in some instances better than training on the road. The CompuTrainer measures and displays power, heart rate, time and distance.

The SRM (Schoberer Rad Messtechnik, or Schoberer Bicycle Measuring Technique) is a replacement crank for the bicycle that measures power and displays the

The SRM Powermeter displays on a handlebar control unit and records for later downloading to a computer power, heart rate, cadence, speed, time, distance, average heart rate, average power, average cadence and average speed. Such devices are the wave of the future and will change the way cyclists train.

result on a handlebar unit similar to a bike computer. The information is stored in the handlebar unit for later computer downloading and analysis.

While both of these systems are quite effective at measuring power, the catch is cost.

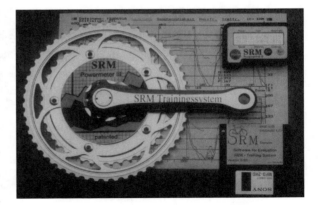

The CompuTrainer sells for about $1,500, while the SRM starts at $2,100. Not cheap. These may be the sort of tools your club could purchase for member use.

CARDIOVASCULAR SYSTEM

In the early 1980s, the introduction of the portable heart rate monitor brought about a profound change in athletes' approaches to training. It is now a commonly used training device, second only to the handlebar computer in popularity.

When heart rate monitors first hit the market, until about 1990, they were "gee whiz" toys — fun to play with, but didn't mean much. Now that nearly everyone has one, athletes are becoming more astute in their use. At criteriums, road races and time trials around the country you can find most cyclists using them to control and monitor exertion.

Trent Klasna adjusting his heart-rate monitor at the 1996 Tour DuPont. Heart-rate monitors have changed training in the last 10 years.

A heart rate monitor is much like the tachometer in an automobile. Neither one tells how fast you're going, but rather how hard the engine is working. Just as a car can rev up the engine without moving and redline the tachometer, heart rate can zoom while running in place.

Knowing how hard the heart is working is important information that allows you to make decisions as a workout progresses. Sometimes motivation, or lack of it, gets in the way of rating your perceived exertion during high-quality training sessions. Here are some typical questions that can be answered with a heart rate monitor.

• **Is the workout hard enough?** Quality workouts, such as intervals and tempo rides, require that you reach certain levels of stress to cause adaptation. A heart rate monitor tells you if you're working hard enough.

• **Is the workout too hard?** Even though during hill repeats you may feel as if you're working as hard as possible, a heart rate that won't rise to the prescribed zone says that this one is too hard — it's time to stop and get more recovery. Without the monitor you may talk yourself into continuing the workout and risk overtraining.

• **Is recovery complete?** Judging when it's time to do another hard workout

The Training Bible

is made easier with a heart rate monitor. A high resting heart rate, or one that stays abnormally elevated during low intensity, warns you to rest more.

• **Am I more fit?** In Chapter 9, I'll show you how to use a heart rate monitor to determine how your fitness is progressing. This is especially valuable early in the season before starting to race.

For a cyclist, knowing lactate threshold (LT) heart rate is as important as knowing frame size. But forget about trying to find maximum heart rate. Not only does this require great motivation — as in gun to the head — but it's not as good an indicator as LT.

Heart rate training zones are best if based on LT, since the percentage of maximum at which one becomes anaerobic (lactate accumulates) is highly variable. For example, one cyclist may have a LT that is 85 percent of his maximum heart rate, while another goes anaerobic at 90 percent of max. If both riders train at 90 percent of max, one is deeply anaerobic and the other is at the threshold. They are not experiencing the same workout or getting the same benefits. If, however, both train at 100 percent of LT or any other percentage of LT, they experience the exact same exertion level and reap the same benefits.

Finding LT requires scientific precision, but don't let that scare you away. It's actually a simple procedure. I'll describe how to do it in the next chapter.

One "easy" way of finding your lactate threshold heart rate is to time trial while wearing a monitor. The distance of the individual time trial (ITT) could be 5k, 10k, 8 miles, 10 miles, or 40k. The test can be done at an established race or as a workout you do alone. The average heart rate from this test will serve as a predictor of your LT. Since you will undoubtedly have higher motivation in a race than when doing this test alone, the results should be interpreted differently. Table 4.6 provides guidelines for determining LT heart rate from an ITT.

Table 4.6

Predicting Lactate-Threshold Pulse Rate from an Individual Time Trial Average Heart Rate

Distance of ITT	As Race	As Workout
5k	110% of LT	104% of LT
10k	107% of LT	102% of LT
8-10 miles	105% of LT	101% of LT
40k	100% of LT	97% of LT

Example: A 10-mile individual time trial is done as a race when the athlete is rested and highly motivated. The average HR is 176. Divide 176 by 1.05 = 167 for LT. See bold number 167 in table 4.8 for HR training zones. Table 4.6 may also be used to determine HR to be used in an ITT. Example: A 40k ITT should be ridden at 100% of LT.

Once you've found your LT, you can determine your heart rate training zones by using Table 4.7 or Table 4.8.

Zone	RPE	Purpose	% of LTHR
1	<10	Recovery	65-81%
2	10-12	Aerobic	82-88%
3	13-14	Tempo	89-93%
4	15-16	Subthreshold	94-100%
5a	17	Superthreshold	100-102%
5b	18-19	Aerobic Capacity	103-105%
5c	20+	Anaerobic Capacity	106%+

Table 4.7
Heart Rate Training Zones based on Lactate Threshold Heart Rate (LTHR)

Since we'll be referring to it frequently, I've numbered each zone for heart rate. Zones 1 through 4 are all aerobic zones and the 5 zones are all anaerobic.

Heart rate varies with sport. If you're cross training in the winter by running, your lactate threshold heart rate will be different from cycling, as will all of your training zones. Because of this, you should either determine heart rate zones for each sport you cross train in, or go only by RPE for other sports.

RACE-FIT SYSTEMS

Coming into top racing form means optimizing the performance of each of the three systems. A cyclist with a great muscular system but poor energy production and cardiovascular systems won't last long on the roads. It takes all three systems working together.

These systems must go through many changes during the training year for you to race effectively and attain your goals. Here's a partial list of changes that occur as a result of training:

Energy Production system

• Greater utilization of fat and sparing of glycogen.
• Enhanced conversion of lactate to fuel.

The Training Bible

Table 4.8

Heart Rate Training Zones
Find your **LT heart rate**
in the "5a Zone" column
(bold number). Read
across from left to right
for training zones.

| 1 Zone | 2 Zone | 3 Zone | 4 Zone | 5a Zone | 5b Zone | 5c Zone |
| | | | Sub- | Super- | Aerobic | Anaerobic |
Recovery	Aerobic	Tempo	Threshold	Threshold	Capacity	Capacity
90-108	109-122	123-128	129-136	**137**-140	141-145	146-150
91-109	110-123	124-129	130-137	**138**-141	142-146	147-151
91-109	110-124	125-130	131-138	**139**-142	143-147	148-152
92-110	111-125	126-130	131-139	**140**-143	144-147	148-153
92-111	112-125	126-131	132-140	**141**-144	145-148	149-154
93-112	113-126	127-132	133-141	**142**-145	146-149	150-155
94-112	113-127	128-133	134-142	**143**-145	146-150	151-156
94-113	114-128	129-134	135-143	**144**-147	148-151	152-157
95-114	115-129	130-135	136-144	**145**-148	149-152	153-158
95-115	116-130	131-136	137-145	**146**-149	150-154	155-159
97-116	117-131	132-137	138-146	**147**-150	151-155	156-161
97-117	118-132	133-138	139-147	**148**-151	152-156	157-162
98-118	119-133	134-139	140-148	**149**-152	153-157	158-163
98-119	120-134	135-140	141-149	**150**-153	154-158	159-164
99-120	121-134	135-141	142-150	**151**-154	155-159	160-165
100-121	122-135	136-142	143-151	**152**-155	156-160	161-166
100-122	123-136	137-142	143-152	**153**-156	157-161	162-167
101-123	124-137	138-143	144-153	**154**-157	158-162	163-168
101-124	125-138	139-144	145-154	**155**-158	159-163	164-169
102-125	126-138	139-145	146-155	**156**-159	160-164	165-170
103-126	127-140	141-146	147-156	**157**-160	161-165	166-171
104-127	128-141	142-147	148-157	**158**-161	162-167	168-173
104-128	129-142	143-148	149-158	**159**-162	163-168	169-174
105-129	130-143	144-148	149-159	**160**-163	164-169	170-175
106-129	130-143	144-150	151-160	**161**-164	165-170	171-176
106-130	131-144	145-151	152-161	**162**-165	166-171	172-177
107-131	132-145	146-152	153-162	**163**-166	167-172	173-178
107-132	133-146	147-153	154-163	**164**-167	168-173	174-179
108-133	134-147	148-154	155-164	**165**-168	169-174	175-180
109-134	135-148	149-154	155-165	**166**-169	170-175	176-181
109-135	136-149	150-155	156-166	**167**-170	171-176	177-182
110-136	137-150	151-156	157-167	**168**-171	172-177	178-183
111-137	138-151	152-157	158-168	**169**-172	173-178	179-185
112-138	139-151	152-158	159-169	**170**-173	174-179	180-186
112-139	140-152	153-160	161-170	**171**-174	175-180	181-187
113-140	141-153	154-160	161-171	**172**-175	176-181	182-188
113-141	142-154	155-161	162-172	**173**-176	177-182	183-189
114-142	143-155	156-162	163-173	**174**-177	178-183	184-190
115-143	144-156	157-163	164-174	**175**-178	179-184	185-191
115-144	145-157	158-164	165-175	**176**-179	180-185	186-192
116-145	146-158	159-165	166-176	**177**-180	181-186	187-193
116-146	147-159	160-166	167-177	**178**-181	182-187	188-194
117-147	148-160	161-166	167-178	**179**-182	183-188	189-195
118-148	149-160	161-167	168-179	**180**-183	184-190	191-197
119-149	150-161	162-168	169-180	**181**-184	185-191	192-198
119-150	151-162	163-170	171-181	**182**-185	186-192	193-199
120-151	152-163	164-171	172-182	**183**-186	187-193	194-200
121-152	153-164	165-172	173-183	**184**-187	188-194	195-201
121-153	154-165	166-172	173-184	**185**-188	191-195	196-202
122-154	155-166	167-173	174-185	**186**-189	190-196	197-203
122-155	156-167	168-174	175-186	**187**-190	191-197	198-204
123-156	157-168	169-175	176-187	**188**-191	192-198	199-205
124-157	158-169	170-176	177-188	**189**-192	193-199	200-206
124-158	159-170	171-177	178-189	**190**-193	194-200	201-207
125-159	160-170	171-178	179-190	**191**-194	195-201	202-208
125-160	161-171	172-178	179-191	**192**-195	196-202	203-209
126-161	162-172	173-179	180-192	**193**-196	197-203	204-210
127-162	163-173	174-180	181-193	**194**-197	198-204	205-211
127-163	164-174	175-181	182-194	**195**-198	199-205	206-212

- Increased stores of glycogen and creatine phosphate.
- Improved ability to extract oxygen from blood.

Muscular system

- Increased force generation within a muscle fiber.
- Enhanced recruitment of muscle fibers.
- More economical movement patterns.
- Enhanced endurance qualities.

Cardiovascular system

- More blood pumped per heart beat.
- Greater capillarization of muscle fibers.
- Increased blood volume.
- Enhanced oxygen transportation to the muscles.

MULTISYSTEM TRAINING

The serious cyclist intent on reaching his or her potential as a racer will use several methods to monitor training depending on the intended benefits and demands of the workout. All endurance athletes should become adept at using the RPE scale to listen to what the body is saying about exertion. This is essential no matter how many technical devices may be at the rider's disposal.

Observing heart rate is not only effective, it's also affordable with basic monitors starting at about $100. The cardiovascular system is a good indicator of exertions longer than about 60 seconds. For short, especially high-intensity repetitions, as in sprint training, heart rate monitoring is not very effective since heart rate lags behind intensity in the first few seconds of a high effort, and the monitor lags even more. In such cases, using power is highly recommended.

Roberto Gaggioli time trialing without a heart-rate monitor or SRM in the 1996 Tour DuPont. No matter how many high-tech devices an athlete has, the ability to subjectively rate exertion is still a critical skill.

Once lactate measurement has been refined, it will become an effective way for the athlete to pinpoint lactate threshold, determine short-term recovery and measure fitness changes.

In referring to training zones throughout this book, I specify the system being monitored. I will frequently use heart rate since it is the most commonly available measuring tool at the present time.

REFERENCES

Baker, A. Training intensity. *Performance Conditioning for Cycling, vol. 2* (1), p. 3, 1995.

Friel, J. *CompuTrainer Workout Manual,* RacerMate, 1994.

Janssen, P.G.J.M. *Training, Lactate, Pulse Rate,* Polar Electro Oy, 1989.

Kindermann, W., et al. The significance of the aerobic-anaerobic transition for the determination of work load intensities during endurance training, *European Journal of Applied Physiology, vol. 42,* pp. 25-34, 1979.

Skinner, J.S., et al. The transition from aerobic to anaerobic metabolism, *Research Quarterly for Exercise and Sport, vol. 51,* pp. 234-248, 1980.

Weltman, A. *The Blood Lactate Response to Exercise,* Human Kinetics, 1995.

Part III

Training

with a

Purpose

TRAINING A HALF-CENTURY AGO

The Racing Cycle
BY WILLIE HONEMAN
As it appeared in Bicycling *magazine, October 1945*

The Novice, with rare exceptions, will find himself lacking in one or more of the following: 1—ABILITY TO REPEAT, in other words ride five or six times at one race meeting, 2—ABILITY TO CARRY A SPRINT, 3—ABILITY TO RIDE AROUND THE MAN IN FRONT, 4—NO ENDURANCE, 5—CONCERNED ABOUT NERVOUSNESS, 6—DISCOURAGED UPON FAIL-URE TO PLACE.

An important point to keep in mind is, that nothing can be accomplished by a rider in Racing, if he does not try to improve on his Weak Points in Training. To ride around the Track or Road accepting pace (known as sitting in) at a slow speed and with no purpose, will accomplish nothing toward the rider's preparation for a coming event.

Chapter 5

TESTING

I yam what I yam and that's alls that I yam.

— POPEYE THE SAILORMAN

What is your potential as a cyclist? Do you have what it takes to consistently get good results? What must you work on to improve? What are you best at?

These are some of the questions to ask yourself every year. For the novice cyclist, these are difficult to answer since there is so much self-discovering to do. Even for an experienced rider, the answers are not always easy to come by. The problem is that athletes often "can't see the forest for the trees." Subjective self-evaluation is always difficult. They often need someone else to do the evaluation and tell them the direction to take. That someone else is often a coach. But since the purpose of this book is to make you your own coach, I'm going to show you how to determine what you need to emphasize in training and race preparation.

You may not like what you discover about yourself. In the winter of 1995-96, a master rider asked me to coach him. He described how when it came to climbs he was unable to hang on with the peloton and was off the back early in most races. Although unhappy with the situation, he wasn't completely dejected. He had given it a lot of thought and decided that the problem was a lack of power. So over the course of the winter he took a plyometrics class with a trainer who worked with professional power athletes such as football players.

My new charge had attended workouts four times a week that winter and had been so committed to improving that he actually stress-fractured both feet. What he wanted to know was how could I help him improve his power.

The first thing I had him do was test power on his CompuTrainer. What we discovered was that he had tremendous power, despite inactivity due to the stress fractures. He easily ranked in the top 5 percent for maximum power generation of all the masters I had ever coached. We also found, however, that he couldn't sustain the power output for even a few seconds and that his anaerobic endurance was relatively poor — he couldn't stay anaerobic very long. Maximum power generation wasn't holding him back at all. I subsequently set up a program for him that would improve his anaerobic endurance and lactate tolerance.

You also may have reached a conclusion about your strengths and weaknesses that is not true. By pursuing the wrong course of training, you're expending both time and energy and may still end up with very little to show for your trouble.

Of course, your weaknesses may never become strengths, but you must always be trying. The trick is to improve the weaknesses without letting the strengths deteriorate. That's what I want to teach you do in the planning chapters of this book. For now, let's discover where your strengths and weaknesses lay.

There are two general categories of assessment that should be done each year to see where your training needs to be focused during the Base and Build periods of training. Performance assessment is done on the bike and self-assessment is done with paper and pencil. There are three times during the season to conduct an assessment:

• At the end of the last Race period of the season, complete a performance assessment to establish a high fitness baseline.

• At the start of the Base period, do both performance and self-assessment to determine what is needed for training in the coming months.

• At the end of the Base period, repeat the performance assessment to measure progress before starting the Build period.

I will cover these training periods in detail in Chapter 7.

By the end of this chapter, you'll score yourself in terms of performance, physiology, proficiencies and mental skills. From this, you will be able to compare your capabilities to the specific demands of cycling and customize a training program specific to your needs.

Some athletes are not keen on testing, preferring instead to make decisions intuitively. That may work for some, but for most it often results in guessing and jumping to inaccurate conclusions. By completing all of the assessments included here, you'll be on the road to training more effectively than you've ever done before. Imagine what that could mean for your next race season.

PERFORMANCE ASSESSMENT

POWER TESTING

Tests done on the bike are usually the best indicators of racing performance. With a SRM Powermeter, a CompuTrainer, or in a laboratory, measure your maximum power and average sustained power. The accompanying CompuTrainer Power Test describes how this is done with a CompuTrainer. With a SRM Powermeter, perform the test on the road in the same way. The course should be 0.2 miles (352 yards or 320 meters) and either flat or slightly uphill. Mark the start and finish points so you can find it in the future for re-tests.

If you can conduct the test in a lab, the applicable protocol will probably be something called a "Wingate Power Test." The technician should be able to explain what the results mean. The technician will probably not be able to relate the information to other cyclists, however.

Laboratory performance test in progress. The equipment in this test measures aerobic capacity, the body's ability to use oxygen to produce work, and also determine lactate threshold.

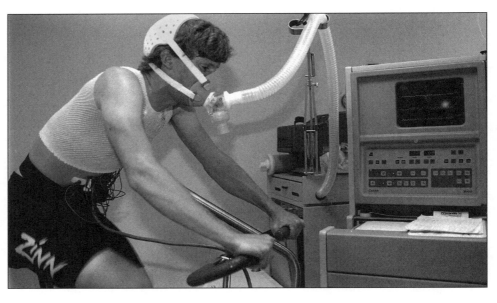

Test 5.1

Power test on CompuTrainer

POWER TEST ON COMPUTRAINER

COMPUTRAINER SET-UP

1. You will need one or two assistants to record information and possibly to spot.

2. Warm-up equipment for 5-10 minutes and calibrate. Re-insert Nintendo stereo

jack into handlebar control unit.

3. Set "Program" to "Road Races/Courses" program 70.

4. Indicate a course of 0.2 miles length.

5. Input your body weight plus bike weight.

6. Turn "Drafting" off.

TEST

1. Following your warm-up, take two or three practice starts of 8-12 seconds each to determine best gear to start test in. The start is with the rear wheel stopped. If rear wheel slips, tighten and recalibrate.

2. During the test you may stand or sit and shift gears at any time. If you are a large or powerful rider, you want a spotter on either side of the bike to prevent tipping over. You may also bolt your CompuTrainer to a sheet of plywood to prevent tipping.

3. When ready to start the test, stop your rear wheel and have an assistant press F1 on the handlebar control unit.

4. At the sound of the gun, sprint the 0.2-mile course as fast as you can. It will probably take 25-40 seconds.

5. Early in the test, your assistant should carefully watch "Watts" on the TV monitor to determine maximum power output.

6. At the completion of the test, record maximum watts and average watts.

7. Recover by spinning in a light gear and resistance for several minutes.

Once you've completed the power test, use Table 5.1 to help you decide what the results mean.

Ranking	Score	Senior Men		Senior Women		Master Men	
		Maximum	Average	Maximum	Average	Maximum	Average
Excellent	5	950+	665+	760+	530+	800+	560+
Good	4	800-949	560-664	640-759	450-529	680-799	475-559
Average	3	650-799	455-559	520-639	360-449	550-679	385-474
Fair	2	500-649	350-454	400-519	280-519	425-549	300-384
Poor	1	<500	<350	<400	<280	<425	<300

Table 5.1
Power ranges of cyclists.
All measurements in watts.

The Training Bible

The heavily muscled legs of a sprinter create great power instantaneously.

Don't be disheartened if your maximum is lower than expected. You need to realize that this is a weakness and that you must work on the ability to quickly generate force against the pedals if you're going to improve. A low average power is a warning to improve lactate tolerance. I will discuss how to improve both force and lactate tolerance in later chapters. If you score four or five for both, the quick application of force and lactate tolerance are among your strength areas. We'll need to keep looking for your weakness.

Average power output will vary more throughout the year than will maximum power. Testing in the winter, for example, you may find average power rel-

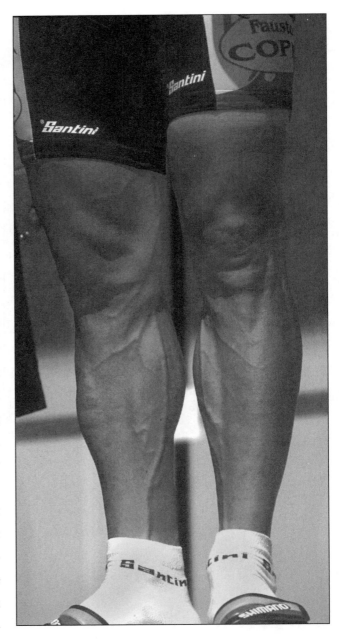

atively lower than in the summer when race fitness is high. That's because you quickly lose the ability to tolerate lactate (winter), when the body no longer experiences it.

Divide maximum power by body weight in pounds to establish a ranking score that is a good indicator of your potential for climbing. As you'll see later, good climbers have a high power-weight index — for obvious reasons. Gravity quickly separates the mountain goats from the plow horses. A low power-weight index means either that you need to build greater force generation or lose excess weight.

The climber's legs (middle pair) aren't as bulky as the sprinter's, but the power generated per pound of body weight is very high.

Graham Watson photo

Ranking	Score	Senior Men/Women	Masters Men
Excellent	5	6.0+	5.0+
Good	4	5.0-5.9	4.0-4.9
Average	3	4.0-4.9	3.0-3.9
Fair	2	3.0-3.9	2.0-2.9
Poor	1	<3.0	<2.0

Table 5.2
Power-weight index. Maximum power in watts divided by body weight in pounds.

LACTATE THRESHOLD TESTING

The lactate threshold test can be done with a CompuTrainer or SRM Power-meter. Most laboratory testing facilities at hospitals, clinics and universities also conduct a very sophisticated ergometer stress test that measures aerobic capacity and determines lactate threshold. Some may even sample blood to determine lactate profiles as described in Chapter 4. Expect to pay dearly for a lab test.

In the scientific world, there are several different definitions for the point at which lactate threshold is reached. I've found that labs frequently use the most conservative of these definitions. That conservative approach yields a low threshold heart rate and power level for a racer. If you're a master, the lab technicians may also be reluctant to allow you to continue the test until fatigue sets in, choosing instead to stop the test prematurely. Be sure to work out these issues before scheduling a lab test.

If you're new to racing, or have coronary risk factors such as a history of heart disease in your family, high cholesterol, high blood pressure, a heart murmur or dizziness after exercise, then you should only conduct this test in a laboratory under the close supervision of a physician.

It is possible to conduct the lactate threshold test using a magnetic-load trainer or stationary bike. To use a magnetic trainer, you will need a handlebar computer sensor for the rear wheel. Power outputs will not be known, but you can measure speed, instead. Accurate and reliable stationary bikes are hard to find for such precise measurement. Look for one that digitally displays power or speed. Do not use a health-club bike that shows speed or power with a needle or sliding gauge. These are far too inaccurate.

If using an SRM Powermeter, use a magnetic trainer and follow the Compu-Trainer protocol.

Test 5.2

Lactate threshold test on CompuTrainer.

LACTATE THRESHOLD TEST ON COMPUTRAINER

....

COMPUTRAINER SET-UP

1. You will need an assistant to record information.
2. Warm-up equipment for 5-10 minutes and calibrate. Re-insert Nintendo stereo jack into handlebar control unit.
3. Set "Program" to "Road Races/Courses" program 70.
4. Program a course to 10 miles long, though you won't use all of it.
5. Input body weight plus bike weight.
6. Turn "Drafting" off.

TEST

1. Throughout the test, you will hold a predetermined power level (plus or minus 5 watts) as displayed on the TV screen. Start at 100 watts and increase by 20 watts every minute until you can no longer continue. Stay seated throughout the test. Shift gears at any time.
2. At the end of each minute, tell your assistant how great your exertion is using the guide on the following page (place this where it can be seen):

6		13	Somewhat hard
7	Very, very light	14	
8		15	Hard
9	Very light	16	
10		17	Very hard
11	Fairly light	18	
12		19	Very, very hard
		20	

3. Your assistant will record your exertion rating and your heart rate at the end of the minute and instruct you to increase power to the next level.

4. The assistant will also listen closely to your breathing to detect when it becomes labored. This point is defined as the "VT" or ventilatory threshold.

5. Continue until you can no longer hold the power level for at least 15 seconds.

6. The data collected should look something like this:

Power	Heart Rate	Exertion	
100	110	9	
120	118	11	
140	125	12	
160	135	13	
180	142	14	
200	147	15	
220	153	17	"VT"
240	156	19	
260	159	20	

7. Compare VT heart rate/power with an exertion rating in the range of 15-17 to determine lactate threshold. To help confirm this, realize that athletes are seldom able to go more than five minutes beyond their lactate thresholds on this test. You now have an estimate of lactate threshold to compare with other indicators, including time-trial heart rates and subsequent retests.

Test 5.3

Lactate threshold test on stationary bike.

LACTATE THRESHOLD TEST ON STATIONARY BIKE

1. Test must be done with a stationary bike that accurately displays speed (or watts).
2. Select "manual" mode.
3. You will need an assistant to record information.
4. Warm-up equipment for 5-10 minutes.

TEST

1. Throughout the test, you will hold a predetermined speed or power level. Start at 15 mph (or 100 watts) and increase by 1 mph (or 20 watts) every minute until you can no longer continue. Stay seated throughout the test. Shift gears at any time.
2. At the end of each minute, tell your assistant how great your exertion is using this guide (place this where it can be seen):

6		13	Somewhat hard
7	Very, very light	14	
8		15	Hard
9	Very light	16	
10		17	Very hard
11	Fairly light	18	
12		19	Very, very hard
		20	

3. Your assistant will record your exertion rating and your heart rate at the end of the minute and instruct you to increase speed (watts) to the next level.
4. The assistant will also listen closely to your breathing to detect when it becomes labored. This is the "VT" or ventilatory threshold.
5. Continue until you can no longer hold the speed (watts) for at least 15 seconds.
6. The data collected should look something like this:

Speed	Watts	Heart Rate	Exertion
15	100	110	9
16	120	118	11
17	140	125	12
18	160	135	13
19	180	142	14

20	200	147	15	
21	220	153	17	"VT"
22	240	156	19	
23	260	159	20	

7. Compare VT heart rate with an exertion rating in the range of 15-17 to determine lactate threshold. To help confirm this, realize that athletes are seldom able to go more than five minutes beyond their lactate thresholds on this test. You now have an estimate of lactate threshold that you can use to compare with other indicators, including time-trial heart rates and subsequent retests.

Testing for lactate threshold will reveal two elements of your race fitness — power at lactate threshold and speed-endurance. It also locates your lactate threshold heart rate — a key element of your training when using a heart rate monitor. In order to derive the full benefit of a workout, you should regulate the intensity of that workout using lactate threshold heart rate as a guide.

Power at lactate threshold is a good indicator of performance and will allow you to train the muscular system with the SRM Powermeter or CompuTrainer. Speed-endurance is important in criteriums and during the sustained, high intensity efforts of road races. Most race-fit athletes can last four or more minutes beyond their lactate threshold in this test. If you're unable to achieve that, then speed-endurance is a weakness. This is nearly always the case with tests completed at the start of the winter Base period.

Ranking	Score	Senior men	Senior women	Master men
Excellent	5	350+	280+	300+
Good	4	300-349	240-279	255-299
Average	3	250-299	200-239	210-254
Fair	2	200-249	160-199	170-209
Poor	1	<200	<160	<170

Table 5.3

Lactate threshold power. Power (watts) achieved at lactate threshold during testing.

The lactate threshold test also serves as an excellent baseline of your fitness. By graphing the results from two or more serial tests, you can see changes in fitness throughout the year. Construct a graph by plotting heart rate on the vertical axis versus power on the horizontal axis. The Conconi Test — developed by Italian physiologist Francesco Conconi in the early 1980s — applied the method to Francesco Moser's

Table 5.4

Anaerobic endurance. Time (in minutes and seconds) to test cessation beyond lactate threshold during testing.

Ranking	Score	Minutes
Excellent	5	5:00+
Good	4	4:00-4:59
Average	3	3:00-3:59
Fair	2	2:00-2:59
Poor	1	<2:00

training program in preparation for his attempt on the world hour record. The test relies on the establishment of the lactate threshold heart rate as the point at which the line on such a graph deflects or bends downward. I've found very few athletes who have an obvious deflection in their graph.

Figure 5.1 illustrates the tracings of a lactate threshold test performed on December 18 and again on March 11, following 12 weeks of Base training. Notice that the tracing for the March 11 test has shifted to the right and slightly down. This shows that the athlete has a lower heart rate at any given power level. That is one effective way of measuring progress. Another is that power has increased for every given heart rate. While the lactate threshold heart rate, indicated by "0" and "X," has not changed in 12 weeks, power, and therefore speed, has.

Figure 5.1

Lactate threshold tests compared. Improvement of fitness following 12 weeks of training as shown by a shift of the tracing to the right and down.

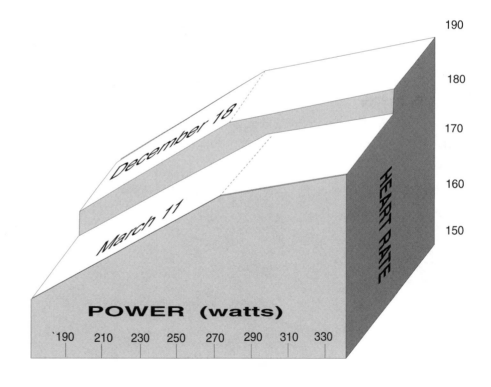

SELF-ASSESSMENT

If you have the equipment to conduct the performance assessment tests you now have a good idea of some of your strength and weakness areas. Chances are, however, that you don't have access to sophisticated equipment. We can still get a pretty good notion of your capabilities by asking the right questions and, of course, answering honestly. Even if you were able to do the performance testing, there are three other areas of racing fitness that you should examine at the start of every training year: Natural abilities, proficiencies and mental skills. Before reading any further, complete the three profiles on the following pages. Then I'll tell you what your scores mean.

PROFICIENCIES PROFILE

....

Read each statement below and decide if you agree or disagree with it as it applies to you. Check the appropriate answer. If unsure, go with your initial feeling.

A=Agree   D=Disagree

A   D

___ ___ 1. I'm quite lean compared with others in my category.

___ ___ 2. I'm more muscular and have greater total body strength than most others in my category.

___ ___ 3. I'm usually capable of single-handedly bridging big gaps that take several minutes.

___ ___ 4. I'm capable of enduring relentless suffering for long periods of time, perhaps as long as an hour.

___ ___ 5. I can climb long hills out of the saddle with most others in my category.

___ ___ 6. I can hop and jump my bike better than most.

___ ___ 7. I can spin at cadences in excess of 140 rpm with no difficulty.

___ ___ 8. I look forward to the climbs in races and hard group workouts.

___ ___ 9. I'm comfortable in an aerodynamic position: aero' bars, elbows close, back flat.

___ ___10. I have a lot of fast-twitch muscle based on my instantaneous sprint speed, vertical jump or other indicator.

___ ___11. While I suffer, I never "blow up" on climbs even when the tempo increases.

___ ___12. In a race, I can ride near my lactate threshold (heavy breathing) for long periods of time.

___ ___13. In an individual time trial, with the exception of turn arounds and hills, I
can stay seated the entire race.

___ ___14. In a pack sprint, I feel aggressive and physically capable of winning.

___ ___15. When standing on a climb, I feel light and nimble on the pedals.

*SCORING: For each of the following sets of questions count the number of "Agree" answers
you checked.*

<u>Question numbers</u>   <u>Score</u>

1, 5, 8, 11, 15: Number of "agrees" _____ Climbing _____

2, 6, 7, 10, 14: Number of "agrees" _____ Sprinting _____

3, 4, 9, 12, 13: Number of "agrees" _____ Time trial _____

MENTAL-SKILLS PROFILE

Read each statement below and choose an appropriate answer from these possibilities:

1=Never   2=Rarely   3=Sometimes   4=Frequently   5=Usually   6=Always

____ 1. I believe my potential as an athlete is excellent.

____ 2. I train consistently and eagerly.

____ 3. When things don't go well in a race, I stay positive.

____ 4. In hard races, I can imagine myself doing well.

____ 5. Before races, I remain positive and upbeat.

____ 6. I think of myself more as a success than as a failure.

____ 7. Before races, I'm able to erase self-doubt.

____ 8. The morning of a race, I awake enthusiastically.

____ 9. I learn something from races when I don't do well.

____10. I can see myself handling tough race situations.

____11. I'm able to race close to my ability level.

____12. I can easily picture myself training and racing.

____13. Staying focused during long races is easy for me.

____14. I stay in tune with my exertion levels in races.

____15. I mentally rehearse skills and tactics before races.

____16. I'm good at concentrating as a race progresses.

___17. I make sacrifices to attain my goals.

___18. Before an important race, I can visualize doing well.

___19. I look forward to workouts.

___20. When I visualize myself racing, it almost feels real.

___21. I think of myself as a tough competitor.

___22. In races, I tune out distractions.

___23. I set high goals for myself.

___24. I like the challenge of a hard race.

___25. When the race gets hard, I concentrate even better.

___26. In races, I am mentally tough.

___27. I can relax my muscles before races.

___28. I stay positive despite late starts or bad weather.

___29. My confidence stays high the week after a bad race.

___30. I strive to be the best athlete I can be.

SCORING: Add up the numerical answers you gave for each of the following sets of questions.

Question numbers			Score
2, 8, 17, 19, 23, 30:	Total _____	Motivation	_____
1, 6, 11, 21, 26, 29:	Total _____	Confidence	_____
3, 5, 9, 24, 27, 28:	Total _____	Thought habits	_____
7, 13, 14, 16, 22, 25:	Total _____	Focus	_____
4, 10, 12, 15, 18, 20:	Total _____	Visualization	_____

Total	Ranking	Score
32-36	Excellent	5
27-31	Good	4
21-26	Average	3
16-20	Fair	2
6-15	Poor	1

NATURAL-ABILITIES PROFILE

Read each statement below and decide if you agree or disagree with it as it applies to you. Check the appropriate answer. If unsure, go with your initial feeling.

A=Agree **D=Disagree**

A   D

___ ___ 1. I prefer to ride in a bigger gear with a lower cadence than most of my training partners.

___ ___ 2. I race best in criteriums and short road races.

___ ___ 3. I'm good at sprints.

___ ___ 4. I'm stronger at the end of long workouts than my training partners.

___ ___ 5. I can squat and/or leg press more weight than most in my category.

___ ___ 6. I prefer long races.

___ ___ 7. I use longer crank arms than most others my height.

___ ___ 8. I get stronger as a stage race or high volume training week progresses.

___ ___ 9. I comfortably use smaller gears with higher cadence than most others I train with.

___ ___ 10. I have always been physically quicker than most other people for any sport I've participated in.

___ ___ 11. In most sports, I've been able to finish stronger than most others.

___ ___ 12. I've always been physically stronger than most others I've played sports with.

___ ___ 13. I climb best when seated.

___ ___ 14. I prefer workouts that are short but fast.

___ ___ 15. I'm confident of my endurance at the start of long races.

SCORING: For each of the following sets of questions, count the number of "agree" answers you checked.

<u>Question numbers</u>   <u>Score</u>

1, 5, 7, 12, 13: Number of "agrees" _____   Strength   _____

2, 3, 9, 10, 14: Number of "agrees" _____   Speed   _____

4, 6, 8, 11, 15: Number of "agrees" _____   Endurance   _____

NATURAL ABILITIES

Some were born to be cyclists. Their parents blessed them with the physiology necessary to excel on two wheels. Others were born to be soccer players or pianists. Many of us who are cyclists have chosen to race a bike regardless of our genetic luck. Passion for the sport means a lot and helps overcome many physiological weaknesses.

Success in any sport is determined by the right mix of three basic abilities:

- Endurance
- Strength
- Speed

For example, an Olympic weight lifter must generate a tremendous amount of strength, needs a fair amount of speed and very little endurance. A pole vaulter needs tremendous speed, a moderate amount of strength and little endurance. A marathon runner doesn't need much strength, only a little speed, but great endurance. Every sport is unique in terms of the mix of these three elements and, therefore, requires unique methods of training.

Road cycling puts a premium on endurance, but strength for climbing hills and speed for sprinting are also important elements of the formula. This unique combination of abilities is one of the reasons that cycling is such a difficult sport for which to train. A cyclist can't just put in a lot of miles to develop huge endurance and disregard strength and speed. It takes a mix of all three abilities to excel.

The Natural Abilities Profile you completed provides a snapshot of your individual capabilities for the three elements of fitness for cycling. A score of four or five for one of the abilities indicates a strength area. If all of your scores are four or five you undoubtedly have been a good athlete in many sports. A score of 3 or less indicates a weakness, one that may partly be due to heredity and partly to training. You can't change your genes, but you can change your training, if it's needed. That's what you'll find out in the next chapter.

PROFICIENCIES

There are three proficiencies that determine success in cycling:

- Climbing
- Sprinting
- Time trialing

It's an unusual cyclist who scores a four or five on each of these. Body size and shape, aerobic capacity potential and muscle type often determine which of these you will be good at. Just because you are a good sprinter, however, doesn't mean that you should neglect climbing. What value is it to have a tremendous sprint but be unable to climb and so arrive at the finish well after winners? You must work to improve your weaknesses. Any proficiency in which you scored a three or less needs work. Just how much work you need depends on the types of races you plan to be doing. We'll explore that issue in the next chapter.

MENTAL SKILLS

Mental skills are the most neglected aspect of racing for serious cyclists at all levels. I've known talented riders who, except for their lack of confidence, were capable of winning or always placing well, but were seldom contenders. Their heads were holding them back.

More than likely, you scored a four or five in the area of motivation. I always see this in the athletes I coach. If you didn't, then it may be time to take a long look at why you train and race.

A highly motivated and physically-talented rider who is confident, has positive thought habits, can stay focused during a race and has the ability to visualize success is practically unbeatable. A physically-talented athlete without these mental qualities hopes to finish with the peloton.

If you are weak in this area, other than working closely with a good sports psychologist, one of the best courses of action is to read a book by one of them. Here are some books I've found to be helpful in improving mental skills:

Elliott, Richard. *The Competitive Edge*, TAFNEWS, 1991.

Loehr, James. *Mental Toughness Training for Sports*, Stephen Greene Press, 1982.

Loehr, James. *The New Mental Toughness Training for Sports*, Penguin Books, 1995.

Lynch, Jerry. *Thinking Body, Dancing Mind*, Bantam Books, 1992.

Orlick, Terry. *Psyching for Sport*, Leisure Press, 1986.

Orlick, Terry. *Psyched to Win*, Leisure Press, 1992.

SUMMARY

You've now evaluated yourself in several key areas. To compile the results mark your score for each on the Cyclist Assessment form on page 57. All of those with a score of four or five are strength areas. Scoring a three or less indicates a weakness.

For each item, briefly comment on what you learned about yourself. Later on we'll come back to this form to help design your training plan for the year.

CYCLIST ASSESSMENT

SEASON GOALS FOR 199_

1. _____

2. _____

3. _____

	SCORE (5=BEST)	COMMENTS

POWER TEST

Maximum Power ? 1 2 3 4 5 _____

Average Power ? 1 2 3 4 5 _____

Power-Weight Index ? 1 2 3 4 5 _____

LACTATE THRESHOLD TEST

Lactate Threshold Power ? 1 2 3 4 5 _____

Speed-Endurance ? 1 2 3 4 5 _____

NATURAL-ABILITIES PROFILE

Endurance ? 1 2 3 4 5 _____

Strength ? 1 2 3 4 5 _____

Speed ? 1 2 3 4 5 _____

To improve weaknesses: _____

_____

PROFICIENCIES PROFILE

Climbing ? 1 2 3 4 5 _____

Sprinting ? 1 2 3 4 5 _____

	SCORE (5=BEST)	**COMMENTS**
Time trialing	? 1 2 3 4 5	_____

To improve weaknesses: _____

_____

MENTAL-SKILLS PROFILE

Motivation	? 1 2 3 4 5	_____
Confidence	? 1 2 3 4 5	_____
Thought habits	? 1 2 3 4 5	_____
Focus	? 1 2 3 4 5	_____
Visualization	? 1 2 3 4 5	_____

To improve weaknesses: _____

_____

TRAINING OBJECTIVES TO ACHIEVE GOALS

1. _____

2. _____

3. _____

4. _____

5. _____

REFERENCES

Bouchard, C. and G. Lortie. Heredity and endurance performance, *Sports Medicine*, vol. 1, pp. 38-64, 1984.

Costill, D. Predicting athletic potential: The value of laboratory testing, *Sports Medicine Digest*, vol. 11 (11), P. 7, 1989.

Daniels, J. Physiological characteristics of champion male athletes, *Research Quarterly*, vol. 45, pp. 342-348, 1974.

Expert Level Coaching Manual, USA Cycling, Inc., pp. 49-77, 1995.

Friel, J. *CompuTrainer Workout Manual*, 1994.

Noakes, T.D. Implications of exercise testing for prediction of athletic performance: A contemporary perspective, *Medicine and Science in Sports and Exercise*, vol. 20 (4), pp. 319-330, 1988.

Sharkey, B. *Coaches Guide to Sport Physiology*, Human Kinetics, 1986.

Chapter 6

RACING ABILITIES

I can't believe that out of 100,000 sperm cells,
you were the quickest.

— STEVEN PEARL

The trend in American racing in the last 10 years has been away from road racing as the number of criteriums has increased. Many parts of the country have also seen a drop in time trials. This has caused many American cyclists to become criterium specialists. By training only for short, fast events, it's difficult to be competitive at occasional road races and time trials. The criterium specialist's fitness may be lacking in several areas.

This chapter will look at what you need to perform well at road races, time trials and criteriums by developing a more complete level of fitness based on your individual strengths and weaknesses discovered in the last chapter. I will discuss the steps needed to prepare for stage races in Chapter 10.

LIMITERS

There are aspects of your fitness that are holding you back when it comes to racing. We discovered some of these weaknesses in the last chapter. While it would be nice to eliminate all of your weaknesses and have only strengths, that is neither likely nor really all that necessary. More than likely, only one or two of these shortcomings stand between you and better race results. These key weaknesses are your "limiters."

Peak performance is a consequence of matching your individual strengths with the requirements of an event. This is similar to comparing your lottery number to the winning number and finding out that you had five of the six numbers right — close, but no million-dollar prize.

Racing is like this. Having two of the three qualities necessary to race at the front isn't good enough. The one you're missing is the limiter. By correcting it, regardless of your other weaknesses, you're a contender. So it's really not weaknesses that should concern you, it's the limiters.

What you should closely watch for in this chapter is what are the necessary requirements are to race well in the types of races you do, and which of those requirements you are missing. Later I'll show you how to strengthen your limiters.

BASIC RACING ABILITIES

In Chapter 5, I mentioned the three basic abilities required in all sports: endurance, strength and speed. Different types of races, from hilly or flat to long or short, require different mixes of these abilities. The basic abilities are the ones with which an athlete should start his or her training year. They also should be the foundations of the novice cyclist's development in the sport for the first two or three years.

It may help to understand where this discussion is going if you see the basic racing abilities as the corners of a triangle. While endurance, strength and speed sound simple enough, it may also be helpful to explain how those terms are used here.

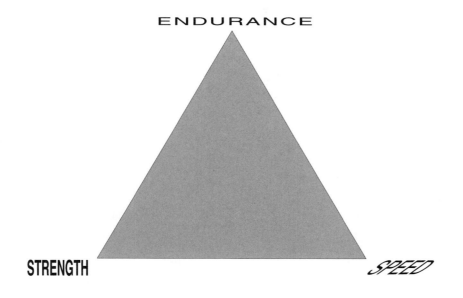

Figure 6.1
Basic abilities triangle.

ENDURANCE

Endurance is the ability to continue working despite the onset of fatigue. Within the context of this book, it implies an aerobic level of exertion. Endurance is specific to the event. A one-hour race does not require the endurance to ride for five hours.

As with other aspects of fitness, endurance is typically developed by starting with general endurance training and progressing to more specific training. This means that an aerobic endurance base is built first in the winter months by developing the capabilities of the cardiorespiratory system, usually with cross-training activities such as skiing or running. For those of you strongly committed to riding your bikes year-round, consider cyclo-cross since it combines running with cycling and lets you hone your handling skills. Later in the winter, training becomes more specific as the length of the longest rides are extended to a minimum of two hours or the duration of the longest race, whichever is longer.

For the novice cyclist, endurance is the key to progress. This ability has to be nurtured before others are emphasized.

STRENGTH

Strength, or force, is the ability to overcome resistance. In cycling, strength comes into play on hills and when riding into the wind. You also develop strength by progressing from general to specific work during the training year. It makes sense to emphasize weight lifting early in the year so as to build the musculature necessary to drive the bike. This is general training — no bike is involved. Later on, training becomes more specific when strength is further refined with hill training on the bike.

SPEED

Speed is the ability to move quickly. Much of that ability is largely genetic. In other words, you are either born to be exceptionally fast, or you aren't. Athletes with world-class speed have been found to have a high percentage of fast twitch muscles which are capable of rapid movement, but fatigue quickly.

In the realm of cycling, the ability to comfortably turn the cranks at a high cadence, in excess of 140 rpm, is typical of athletes with great natural speed. While heredity plays a major role in such movement, a less naturally talented cyclist can develop this ability by improving his or her economy — quick movement with little wasted energy. This comes from practicing at near one's cadence limits with low resistance while allowing muscles to relax at the right instances. For example, the quadriceps muscle group must be activated while quickly driving the pedal down. But if it fails to relax at the bottom of the stroke, the cyclist's butt is lifted off of the saddle causing the rider to bounce. Bouncing is not a very economical way to pedal.

ADVANCED RACING ABILITIES

The triangle diagrammed in figure 6.1 may be further refined. The basics of endurance, strength and speed make up the corners, but each of the sides of the triangle also represents a more refined ability. These are the abilities the advanced athlete will emphasize in the later periods of training, once the basics have been covered.

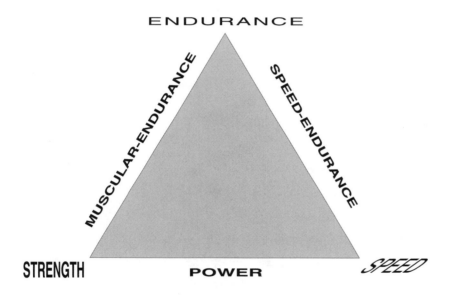

Figure 6.2
Advanced racing abilities triangle.

MUSCULAR-ENDURANCE

Muscular-endurance is the ability of muscles to sustain a high load for a prolonged time. It is the combination of strength and endurance abilities. In the world of cycling, muscular-endurance is the ability to repeatedly turn a relatively high gear at a relatively high cadence. For the road cyclist, this is a critical ability.

POWER

Power is the ability to apply maximum force in the shortest time possible. It results from having high levels of the basic abilities of strength and speed. Other than short, steep hills and short road sprints, power falls primarily in the realm of the track sprinter.

SPEED-ENDURANCE

Speed-endurance is the ability to resist fatigue at high speed. In advanced athletes, it is the blending of speed and endurance. Speed-endurance is a primary ability for races in which long sprints determine success. A rider with the ability to maintain sprint speed for several hundred meters can often dictate the outcome of a race either as a strong lead-out or as a solo effort.

TRAINING OF ABILITIES

As you can see from this brief discussion of the abilities of racing, there are training patterns that progress from the general to the very specific. Figure 6.3 illustrates this concept. At the start of the training year, much of the work is general in nature, meaning that it may not include a bicycle or may involve riding in an unusual fashion, as when doing drills. Strength training serves as a good example of the progression from general to specific. Early in the training year, weight workouts take up a large portion of training time. Later in the winter, you can cut back weight room training as you begin to increase the number of hilly rides — especially in a high gear with low cadence. Eventually, the athlete may progress to hill repeats or hill intervals, and, finally, to racing on hilly courses — the most specific of strength-related work.

Figure 6.3

General to specific training emphasis throughout the training year.

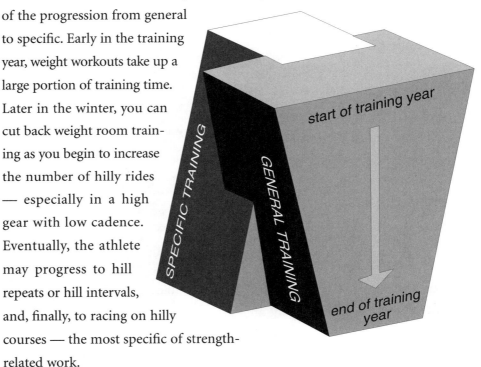

Each ability has a unique method of training associated with it throughout the season. Here is a brief and simplified summary of how to train each ability from the start of the season through the end. Chapter 8 will provide details of how to blend all of the abilities, and Chapter 9 will furnish workout menus and the criteria for selecting workouts for each of these abilities.

ENDURANCE

Endurance training starts in early winter with aerobic cross-training activities such as Nordic skiing or in-line skating. These modes of training will provide enough stress to the heart, lungs and blood to improve their endurance qualities. By mid-winter, the program calls for a gradual phasing-in of on-bike training and the gradual elimination of cross-training. An increase the length of late-winter or early-spring rides to a point where they are at least as long as the longest race of the upcoming season should also occur. By this point, you have already established a good level of stamina and you begin to favor high-intensity workouts over endurance training. During the Transition period from the end of the race season to the beginning of the Base period, you can maintain a minimum level of endurance with cross-training.

STRENGTH

Strength development begins in early winter with training in the weight room. If you have followed the schedule, you should have attained maximum strength by mid-winter. At this point, you should shift your emphasis toward improving your power and muscular-endurance. Depending on the weather, late winter is the best time to begin riding in the hills. Later, hill work may evolve into hill intervals and repeats, depending on your weaknesses. A rider can work to maintain strength throughout the season with weight room training and hill work. This is especially helpful for women and masters.

Martha Pomares training in the mountains. Riding in the hills, especially while in the saddle, develops cycling-specific strength.

SPEED

Speed drills throughout the winter, enhance the ability to pedal quickly and economically. These are best done on a trainer with low resistance. Rollers are good for developing leg speed in a more dynamic environment. Associated with speed are bike handling skills such as jumps and hops — skills that will come in handy in close quarters sprinting. Throughout the late winter and spring, you should do form sprints weekly to further refine this ability. In the summer, weekly jumps will maintain speed.

MUSCULAR ENDURANCE

Muscular-endurance work begins in mid-winter with sustained efforts of several minutes in the heart rate 3 zone. By late winter, it gradually progresses to interval training in the heart rate 4 and 5a zones. The work intervals gradually get longer as the recovery intervals shorten. By spring, the athlete is riding up to an hour in the 4 and 5a zones. The effort is much like "controlled" time trialing and tremendously effective in boosting both aerobic and anaerobic fitness with little risk of overtraining. Throughout the Race period, muscular-endurance is maintained.

Darren Baker time trialing at the 1995 Tour DuPont. Muscular-endurance is the most common limiter in the time trial.

POWER

Power may be the most misunderstood aspect of training in cycling. Most athletes do sprints with brief recovery periods to try to help their power. They are really working on speed-endurance. You can improve power with brief sprints at near maximum exertion followed by long recovery intervals. Natural sprinters love these workouts. Those with little power — riders possessing great endurance and little speed or strength — find power workouts painful and dread doing them. For these cyclists the blending of speed and strength training into power development means the difference in having an effective jump at the start of sprints.

Sprint training is best done with a partner.

SPEED-ENDURANCE

Speed-endurance training includes aerobic capacity-developing intervals and lactate tolerance repetitions. At the start of the Build period of training, the experienced athlete should phase into interval training to bring his or her aerobic capacity to a peak. During the last weeks of the Build period, lactate tolerance work trains the body to dissipate lactate from the blood and to buffer its usual effects. Speed-endurance training is quite stressful and should not be a part of the novice cyclist's regimen. Both speed and endurance should be well established with at least two years of training before regularly attempting these workouts. The likely results of too much speed-endurance work too soon are burnout and overtraining.

ABILITY REGIONS

At the start of this chapter, I lamented the demise of road races and cautioned against becoming a criterium specialist. In this section, it may sound as if I'm encouraging you to specialize. I'm not. My purpose here is to show you how to blend the six abilities just discussed to produce optimal performance for specific types of races. Your strengths will favor success in some of these, but it is likely that you will still need to improve limiters for complete mastery. It will also help you to begin seeing how strengths and limiters are blended into a comprehensive training program.

To understand the requirements of various types of races, it is helpful to further refine the triangle as in figure 6.4.

Figure 6.4

Racing abilities regions

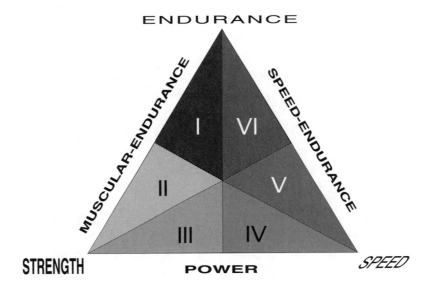

Note that the triangle is divided into six regions, each representing a specific set of ability requirements. By now, you should be able to position yourself within one of the regions based on your known strengths. For example, if endurance is your number one ability and strength is second, then you are a region I cyclist — high in muscular-endurance with a tendency toward endurance. If two or all three of the natural abilities are equal for you, then your proficiencies may help define your region. Sprinters usually fit into the speed regions (IV-V), climbers into the strength regions (II-III) and time trialists into the endurance regions (I-VI).

Races may also be divided into these same six regions based on their type, distance and terrain. If you are a region I cyclist, then you will do best in region I races. The ability regions triangle also helps you decide what to work on in order to perform better in any of the other regions.

Following is a race description by ability regions and a prioritizing of the abilities you must train for each type. Obviously, your strengths will require less training time than your limiters. Chapter 8 will teach you how to blend the training of the various abilities, and Chapter 9 will provide detailed workouts to support each of these ability requirements.

The priorities of training that are listed here for each region do not imply an order of training, but rather an emphasis in training. Given that you have time and energy constraints placed on your training, it is necessary to decide what is most important in order to properly focus. If any of the first three abilities in a given list is a personal weakness, you must elevate it to priority 1. The last three abilities in each priority list have limited value for the type of race for which you're training. Do not avoid these areas, but do assign them less training time and energy. If a strength area falls into one of the last three abilities, you need place only minor emphasis on it. Realize that you can't be good at everything. We are working within the concept of limiters. Determine what's holding you back and then correct that weakness.

REGION I

Region I includes the long, flat to rolling races that are so common in the northwestern European countries of the Netherlands and Belgium. In the U.S., races of more than 100 miles are becoming harder to find. Wind direction, team tactics and mental tenacity go a long way toward determining the outcome of those races. Riders with excellent endurance and time trialing proficiency are likely to emerge victorious. These races are also likely to come down to a pack sprint.

Also included in this region are time trials that are 30 kilometers or longer. Indeed, time trialing proficiency is critical to performance in region I races. If your weakness is time trialing, you need to put a great deal of emphasis on muscular-endurance training in order to race well. Good time trialists have exceptional lactate thresholds relative to their aerobic capacities and maximum power outputs. They develop the ability to ride comfortably in an aerodynamic position and minimize wasted energy in pedaling. They also have superior ability to concentrate despite great suffering.

ENDURANCE

MUSCULAR-ENDURANCE

I

STRENGTH

The Training Bible

Udo Bölts suffers during a long time trial in the 1994 Giro d'Italia. Region I races, such as this, require exceptional endurance, muscular-endurance and strength.

Region I ability training priorities are:

Primary importance

1. Endurance

2. Muscular-endurance

3. Strength

Secondary importance

4. Speed-endurance

5. Speed

6. Power

REGION II

Region II races include time trials of about 15 to 30 kilometers and road races of less than three hours. Hills are usually the element that determines outcomes. These are the most common road races in U.S. cycling at this time.

Climbing is a central proficiency skill for region II. What makes for a champion climber? Typically, they are less than two pounds of body weight for every inch of height. They are capable of generating more than a thousand watts of power and can sustain 70 percent of their maximum for several minutes. This requires a high lactate threshold-power output and a very high aerobic capacity. Natural climbers have an economical climbing style and are especially nimble on the pedals when out of the saddle on a climb.

Priorities for region II training are:

Primary importance

1. Strength

2. Muscular-endurance

3. Endurance

Secondary importance

4. Power

5. Speed

6. Speed-endurance

Franco Vona climbs the Passo del Stelvio in the 1994 Giro d'Italia. Region II races favor climbers.

REGION III

Region III in road racing is found only in short prologues of stage races. These are generally individual time trials on hilly courses taking less than 20 minutes to complete. As such, there is no need for the road racer to train for these events. The stage racer must simply grin and bear the agony.

STRENGTH III **POWER** *SPEED*

REGION IV

Region IV is in the domain of the track racer, especially the match sprinter. Training for this region is not within the scope of this book.

STRENGTH IV **POWER** *SPEED*

REGION V

Region V includes short criteriums that are typical of many masters, women and juniors races. These are 45 minutes or less and have a high requirement for speed and speed-endurance. You must also realize that while this is a short event with much sprinting, that it is still an endurance race. Don't disregard the development of this primary ability.

Short criteriums attract riders who are good sprinters. They usually have great total body strength and a capacity to produce extremely high power outputs instantaneously. This power is often marked by the ability to produce vertical jumps in excess of 22 inches. Champion sprinters have the dynamic balance of a gymnast and can turn the cranks at extremely high cadences. In close-quarters sprints, they race aggressively with no thought given to "what would happen if …" They are confident of their ability to win the close one.

Priorities for region V training are:

<u>Primary importance</u>

1. Speed

2. Speed-endurance

3. Endurance

<u>Secondary importance</u>

4. Power

5. Strength

6. Muscular-endurance

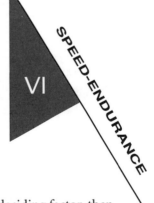

REGION VI

Region VI races are long criteriums and circuit races. This is the most common type of race in the U.S. Notice that the primary quality of criterium racing is still endurance. Success in criteriums, however, requires less endurance ability than does road racing. The ability to maintain speed and repeatedly sprint out of corners is necessary for success as are superb bike handling skills like cornering, bumping and balancing.

If in a particular race, a hill or hills are the deciding factor, then strength may replace speed as a success characteristic.

Priorities for region VI training are:

<u>Primary importance</u>

1. Endurance

2. Speed-endurance

3. Speed

<u>Secondary importance</u>

4. Muscular-endurance

5. Strength

6. Power

REFERENCES

Bompa, T. *Theory and Methodology of Training*, Kendall/Hunt Publishing, 1994.

Brunner, R. and B. Tabachnik. *Soviet Training and Recovery Methods*, Sport Focus Publishing, 1990.

Freeman, W. *Peak When It Counts*, TAFNEWS Press, 1991.

Maglischo, E. *Swimming Faster*, Mayfield Publishing Co., 1982.

Martin, D.E. and P.N. Coe. *Training Distance Runners*, Leisure Press, 1991.

Sleamaker, R. *Serious Training for Serious Athletes*, Leisure Press, 1989.

Part IV

Planning

TRAINING A HALF-CENTURY AGO

Modern European Training Methods
BY JACK HEID
As it appeared in Cycling Almanac, 1951

No one can tell you exactly how to train. It is something you have to work out according to the time at your disposal and the roads and companionship available. However, there are some basic things that you can make your training plans around, which you can copy from my present training methods that I assure you I copied from the European "masters" who have taught me to the point that I feel I have the ability to stay with many of them.

No matter how much training you do on the road with 70 gear or lower, you cannot go stale. You must get in the hours and the mileage. There is no substitute for it. Great riders like Harris and Coppi, who have entirely different actual racing styles, attest to this. Road riders here sit on their bikes all day and do 150 miles one day and the other they rest in the woods doing calisthenics and much deep breathing.

For my track training, I first get on the track and ride around slowly for 5 minutes to warm up. Then we get into a group and for about one-half hour change off pace every 500 yards (about one lap of the track) traveling at 20 mph. Then we all take a 15-minute rest and then go out taking turns leading out for sprints of 250 yards. We have three or four of these 15-minute turns, always resting off the track between. The same can be done on a piece of road measured off for 250 yards.

Developing a jump can be practiced afterwards by coming to an almost dead stop and jumping hard to get up top speed, then rolling slowly to a stop and duplicating this procedure. Don't do too much in one day if you don't feel like it — don't ever force yourself in training.

Chapter 7

Planning to Race

It wasn't raining when Noah built the ark.

— Howard Ruff

Why do you train? Is it to enjoy fresh air, the companionship of friends, travel to exotic places, and the feeling of fitness? Or is it to prepare for the peak experience of racing near your limits?

Certainly all of these play a part in getting you out the door and onto a saddle, but since you're reading this book, I suspect the latter choice is correct. All of us want to see how well we can perform, to get new glimpses of our potential, to push the limits of fitness, and to bask in the glow of success.

This chapter will lay the groundwork for chapters 8 and 9, in which you will develop your own personalized training plan.

TRAINING SYSTEMS

Cyclists typically gravitate to one of three training systems in order to prepare for racing. Each has produced champions. Most athletes don't consciously select a system — it just happens. They roll out of the driveway every day and then do what they feel like once on the road, or they meet with a group and let the top riders determine the day's workout.

The three training systems most common to cyclists are:

- Race into shape,
- Always fit, and
- Periodization.

RACE INTO SHAPE

The most common training system used by cyclists is racing into shape. It traces its roots back to the days of wool jerseys and nail-on cleats. Even in the age of the SRM, floating pedal systems, and titanium components, racing into shape is still the system used by most cyclists. It's easy to do — there are only two steps.

Step 1 involves building a large aerobic base by pedaling 1,000 miles easily. Nearly every rider I talk with knows this number and speaks of it with quiet reverence. Interestingly, the thousand-mile goal does work well for some athletes. But it doesn't work for everyone. For some, it is way too much, and for others it is simply not enough.

Once you have established aerobic endurance, step 2 commences: Race. The idea is that by going to a race every weekend, and club races at mid-week, a high level of fitness will result.

There are some good reasons to train this way. The most important being that the fitness so developed is specific to the demands of racing. What could be more similar to racing, than racing? There are, however, a couple of problems. Training this way is very unpredictable. It's just as likely that great fitness will occur at the wrong time as at the right time. The other problem is that there is no planned rest. Racing into shape frequently leads to overtraining.

ALWAYS FIT

In warmer climates such as Florida, Southern California, and Arizona, cyclists often try to stay in racing shape year round. The cooler weather and availability of training races throughout the winter entice them to keep a constant level of fitness by doing the same training rides every week. Due to weather constraints, athletes in other parts of the country never even consider this system. That's a good reason why sloppy weather and frigid temperatures are probably an advantage for training.

The greatest issues facing the always-fit trainer are boredom and burnout. After 220 to 250 days of high-level training, an athlete becomes toast. Burnout is not a pretty sight. All interest in training, racing and life in general vanishes. It sometimes takes months to regain enthusiasm for riding, if it's regained at all. (Chapter 17 will discuss burnout in detail.)

Another problem has to do with physiology. After about 12 weeks of training in the same way, improvement ceases. And since fitness is never stagnant, if it's not improving, it must be getting worse. Trying to maintain fitness at a high level all the time really means trying to minimize losses. It just doesn't work.

PERIODIZATION

Periodization is the system used by most successful athletes today, and the one I propose you use. The rest of Part IV describes how to incorporate it into your training.

In Chapter 3, I described periodization. You may recall that this is just a way of combining training and time management. It's arranging the pieces of the training puzzle into a pattern of multi-week periods that carefully brings fitness to a peak when the most important races occur while avoiding overtraining and burnout.

Periodization, however, is not without challenges. It requires long-range planning. It really can't be done by the seat of the pants unless the athlete has been following such a plan for several years and knows instinctively what to do and when to do it.

Flexibility, or lack of it, may be the biggest obstacle facing a cyclist using periodization. Once a rider has outlined a plan, there is often a reluctance to vary from it. Successful periodization requires flexibility. I've never coached an athlete who got through an entire season without a cold, work responsibilities, or a visit from aunt Bessie getting in the way of the plan. That's just the way life is. An annual training plan should always be written in pencil to allow for changes due to unforeseen and unavoidable complications.

Remember that in the next chapter, when you sit down to write your training plan.

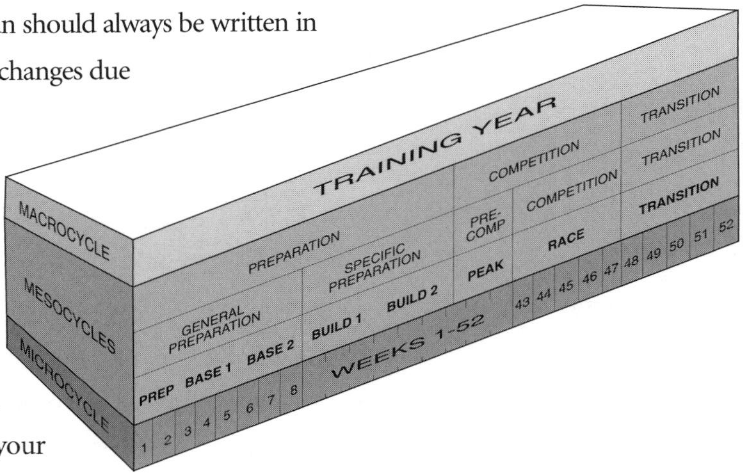

Figure 7.1

The training year divided into mesocycles and microcycles.

Another problem with periodization is all the scientific mumbo-jumbo that goes along with it. The language of periodization seems to confuse many, including coaches. Figure 7.1 illustrates the terms as used for blocks of time in periodization. For the purposes of this book, when referring to specific mesocycle periods, the bold terms in Figure 7.1 are used: Preparation, Base, Build, Peak, Race, and Transition.

TRAINING PERIODS

The reason for dividing the season into specific periods in a periodization plan is that this division allows for emphasis on specific aspects of fitness, while maintaining others developed in earlier periods. Trying to improve all aspects of training at the same time is impossible. No athlete is capable of handling that much simultaneous stress. Periodization also allows for two of the training principles discussed in Chapter 3 — progressive overload and adaptation.

Figure 7.2 diagrams the process of periodization, describes the focus of each mesocycle period, and suggests a time frame for each period.

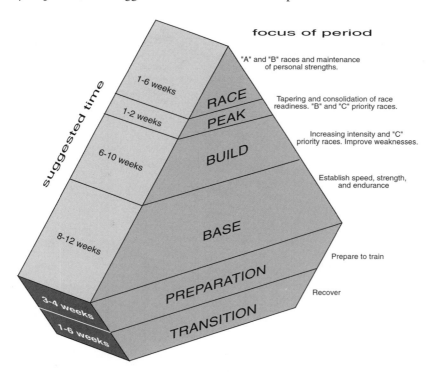

focus of period

"A" and "B" races and maintenance of personal strengths.

Tapering and consolidation of race readiness. "B" and "C" priority races.

Increasing intensity and "C" priority races. Improve weaknesses.

Establish speed, strength, and endurance

Prepare to train

Recover

suggested time

1-6 weeks — RACE
1-2 weeks — PEAK
6-10 weeks — BUILD
8-12 weeks — BASE
3-4 weeks — PREPARATION
1-6 weeks — TRANSITION

Figure 7.2
Using training periods to peak at pre-selected times.

If you add up the suggested times for each period you'll find a range of 20-40 weeks — well short of a year. The reason for this is that I've found cyclists perform best when they peak two or three times during a year. Multi-peak seasons allow for rest

The Training Bible

and recovery more frequently, are less likely to cause burnout or overtraining, and keep training and racing fun. If you do things right — instead of losing fitness as a long race season progresses — each subsequent peak is higher than the last. In the next chapter, I'll teach you how to design such a multi-peak season.

In the remainder of this chapter, I'll introduce you to each period in detail. Every aspect of Periodization is described along with suggestions for how to train the racing abilities discussed in the last two chapters. As you read about the period, turn to Figure 7.3 to see how volume and intensity blend in this hypothetical season. While this doesn't look exactly the way yours will, it probably comes close. The elements common to most periodization plans are an increase in volume at the start of the training year followed by an increase in intensity as volume declines. Notice that there are reduced volume recovery weeks scheduled periodically throughout the Base and Build periods. These are important — don't pass them up.

Accompanying each description is a diagram that illustrates the mix of racing abilities for that period. The portion of the pie chart devoted to each ability is not exact. The amount of time spent working on each aspect of fitness will vary with the individual's strengths and weaknesses. Use the pie chart only as a rough guide of how to proportion training time.

Figure 7.3

Hypothetical training year divided into periods showing the interplay of volume and intensity.

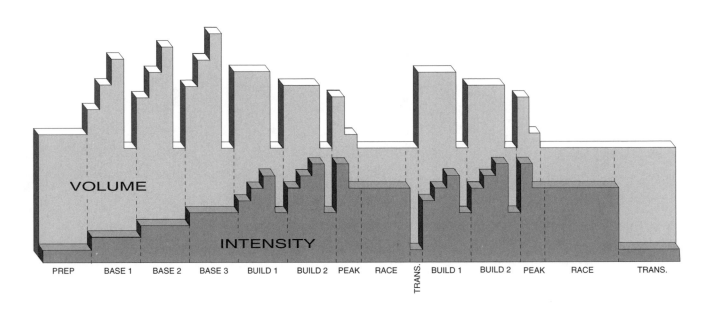

PREP　BASE 1　BASE 2　BASE 3　BUILD 1　BUILD 2　PEAK　RACE　TRANS.　BUILD 1　BUILD 2　PEAK　RACE　TRANS.

PREPARATION PERIOD

The preparation period generally marks the start of the training year and is included only if there has been a long transition following the end of the racing season. It is usually scheduled for the late fall or early winter, depending on when the last race was and the length of the transition.

The purpose of this period is to prepare the athlete's body for the periods to follow. It's a time of training to train. Workouts are low intensity with an emphasis on aerobic endurance, especially in the form of cross training. Activities such as running, cross-country skiing, snowshoeing, swimming, and in-line skating will maintain or improve cardiorespiratory fitness. The total volume of training is low when compared with most other periods.

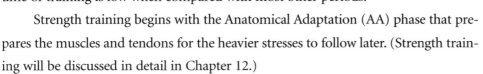

Figure 7.4

PREPARATION

Strength training begins with the Anatomical Adaptation (AA) phase that prepares the muscles and tendons for the heavier stresses to follow later. (Strength training will be discussed in detail in Chapter 12.)

Speed work in the form of drills, usually done on an indoor trainer or rollers, reawakens the legs to spinning fluidly in smooth circles.

BASE PERIOD

The Base period is the time to establish the basic fitness abilities of endurance, strength and speed. Base is generally the longest period of the season lasting eight to 12 weeks. Some athletes are careless with Base training — ending it too soon. That is a mistake. It is essential that the basic abilities have a strong foothold before launching high intensity training.

In the warm-winter states, there may be races available during this period. I usually recommend that these be avoided. They are often demoralizing since some riders are in good shape (the always-fit ones), and you won't be, if you're following this plan. If you must do one of these races, treat it as a workout and do not take the results seriously. Remember that it is OK to abandon the race. These races are of no consequence for your season ahead.

Since this is such a long period and there will be many changes taking place in your fitness throughout, the Base period is divided into three four-week segments: Base 1, Base 2, and Base 3. The volume of training grows in each base period as cross training phases into on-bike training. Intensity rises slightly (see Figure 7.3).

Figure 7.4a

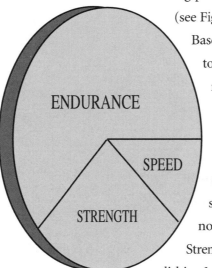

BASE 1

Base 1 marks the start of steady increases in volume to boost aerobic endurance and increase the body's resiliency to large workloads. In the more northern latitudes, you accomplish most of this through cross training. Even those in the warm-winter states, should consider cross training instead of spending all of their time on a bike. It's a long season, and many of the elements of fitness developed now can be accomplished off the bike.

Strength training in Base 1 places an emphasis on establishing Maximum Strength (MS) with the use of high resistance loads and low repetitions. The shift to these greater loads should be gradual so as not to cause injury.

Speed work continues just as in the Preparation period with drills that empha-

Even in the warm-weather states such as Arizona, training in some way other than on the road bike during the early Base period will reduce the risk of burnout later.

size high cadence on a trainer or rollers.

In Base 2, on-bike endurance work begins to replace cross training as the volume rises. As the road rides become longer, the companionship of a group helps the time to pass faster. Be careful, however, not to ride with groups that turn these endurance rides into races. This time of year you will find many "Christmas Stars" — riders who are in great race shape in the winter, but aren't around when the serious racing starts in the summer.

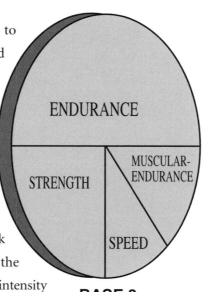

Figure 7.4b

BASE 2

You should plan your road workouts each week on rolling courses that place controlled stress on the muscular system. A rolling course is one that keeps intensity in the lower zones and allows cadences of 80 rpm and higher while seated. Staying in the saddle is important for these workouts to develop greater hip extension strength for the next period.

Weight-room training becomes power-oriented with lower workloads than in Base 1, and should incorporate explosive movement. Also, speed work moves outside, weather permitting. Otherwise, indoor workouts continue. Whenever possible, use the road to refine your sprinting form.

Muscular-endurance training is also introduced in Base 2, with tempo training based on heart rate or power output (see Chapter 4 for details)

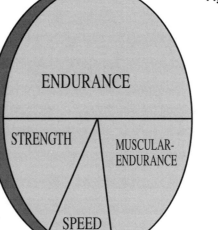

Figure 7.4c

BASE 3

Base 3 marks a phasing in of higher-intensity training with the introduction of hill work. In Base 2, rolling courses ridden in the saddle complemented the weight-room workouts by creating greater hip extension strength. Now you should seek out serious hills with long climbs, riding them mostly in the saddle.

The total weekly volume of training progresses to the highest point of the season in Base 3, with aerobic endurance rides on the road accounting for about half of all training time. The longest workouts now should be at least as long as your longest race of the season. Group rides are still the best way to get in these long rides. Some in the group may be ready for higher-intensity training and so these rides typically are becoming faster. While it's OK to occasionally put the hammer down in a sprint for the city limits sign, don't turn these into races. Be patient and sit in. Your purpose is to get as fast as you can with low-heart-rate rides before turning up the heat in the next period. Later in the season, you'll be glad you held back.

Muscular-endurance training, both on the bike and in the weight room, is increased. These workouts should now take you to the lactate threshold intensity training zones.

Speed work, done as form sprints, must now be on the road.

BUILD PERIOD

A multi-peak season will include two or more Build periods. This is shown in Figure 7.3. As you can see, Build 1 maintains the volume of training at a relatively high level, although less than that achieved in three of the previous eight weeks. That means when it is time to return to Build 1, following the first Race period, you will re-establish your endurance.

The Build period is marked by the introduction of speed-endurance training. Just as with strength, hill work, and muscular-endurance training, this should be done cautiously to avoid injury.

There will probably be races throughout this period. These should normally be low-priority, and you can regard them as a substitute for speed-endurance training. Speed-endurance workouts may also include intervals and fast group rides.

During Build 1, endurance work is reduced, but is still a prominent focus of training. You will be much better served by doing your long, easy endurance rides during this period with one or two teammates rather than with a large group. Use the group rides for the development of muscular-endurance and speed-endurance. It is important to avoid overtraining during this phase of training. Now is the time it can easily happen. Pay close attention to your fatigue level during group rides. If you feel dead in the saddle, don't work hard with the group. Either

Figure 7.4d

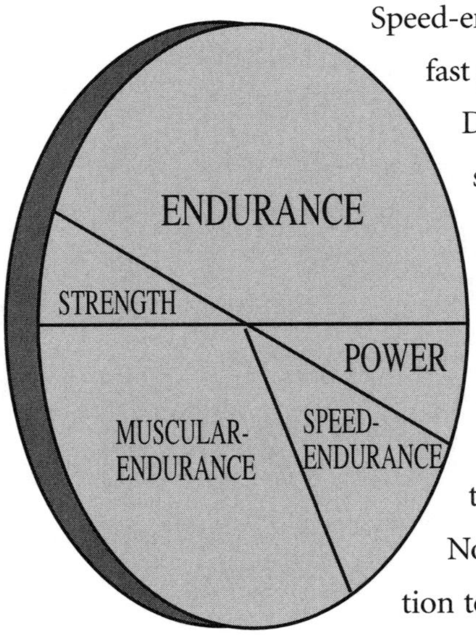

ENDURANCE
STRENGTH
POWER
MUSCULAR-ENDURANCE
SPEED-ENDURANCE

BUILD 1

sit-in, getting as much of a free ride as you can, or turn off and ride alone. Be smart. You're not doing this to impress your friends. Save that for the races.

Strength training in the weight room is cut back to one or two days a week now as the duration of these sessions gets shorter. For the athlete limited by strength, hill work continues. This may be in the form of muscular-endurance or speed-endurance intervals done on a hill. Chapter 9 will offer suggestions for such workouts.

Speed-endurance workouts can be done with one or two other riders of about your ability. Muscular-endurance training is best alone to prepare you for the focus needed in time trialing and to keep you in the narrow threshold training zones.

Power may now replace speed work. Power training can be incorporated into other workouts, such as speed-endurance sessions. If so, incorporate the power training portion of your routine early in the workout when the legs are still fresh. Don't make the mistake that many make in doing power training at the end of workouts. Reserve that for speed-endurance and muscular-endurance.

Build 2 slightly decreases the volume of training while increasing the intensity. Notice that intensity in Figure 7.3 is increased each of the three weeks just as volume increased in the Base period. By now you should be experiencing increasing levels of fatigue and need to continue being cautious with anaerobic intensity. If unsure about whether you should do a certain workout, be wise and leave it out. The mere fact that you're questioning it is enough reason to do so. When in doubt — leave it out.

Training in Build 2 emphasizes intensity to a greater extent than in the previous four weeks. Speed-endurance and muscular-endurance sessions become longer with decreasing recovery intervals. At this point, muscular-endurance should be long, continuous exertions just as in time trialing.

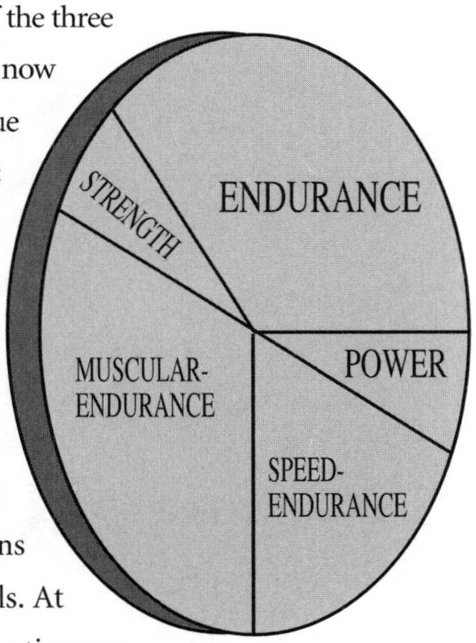

Figure 7.4e

BUILD 2

Weight room training is now down to once a week and follows a maintenance plan that alternates power and muscular-endurance training every two or four weeks. Riders for whom strength is not a priority may stop weight training in this period. I recommend, however, that masters and women continue, but the choice is up to you.

Power training may continue as in Build 1.

Figure 7.4f

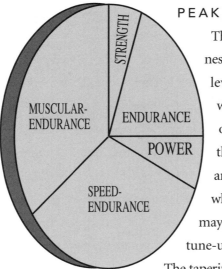

PEAK

A time to test the legs: Peaking for the spring races produces the greatest fitness level of the young season.

PEAK PERIOD

The Peak period is when you consolidate racing fitness. It is time to reduce volume and keep intensity levels high while emphasizing recovery between workouts. It is now best to train at high intensity only twice each week with one at mid-week and the other on the weekend. The idea is to be rested and ready to push the limits of the fitness envelope when it's time for a quality workout. These workouts may also be "B"- or "C"-priority races that serve as tune-ups for the "A"-priority races to follow.

The tapering brings added rest which sometimes causes athletes to question whether they are doing enough. If you've designed your season correctly and followed the plan, you will be ready. And, even if you aren't ready, there's nothing you can do about it now.

RACE PERIOD

This is what you've been waiting for. The fun time of the year is starting. Now all that's needed is to race, work on strength areas, and recover. The races will provide adequate stress to keep your systems working at a maximum level. Your anaerobic fit-

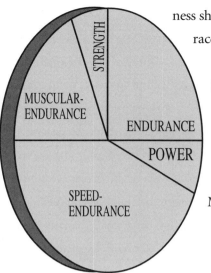

RACE

ness should stay high. In weeks when there are no races, a race-effort group ride is the best option.

Up until now, you've been working on your limiters. Now is the time to take your strength areas to a new level by emphasizing them. If muscular-endurance is a strength, time trial at mid-week. If you're a strong sprinter, work on that each week. If climbing is your forte, then climb every week. Make your strength as strong as possible.

Figure 7.4g

Luc Leblanc, Richard Virenque and Armand De Las Cuevas break away on Mont Ventoux in the 1994 Tour de France. The second race peak of the season, in July or early August for many racers, produces higher levels of fitness.

Figure 7.4h

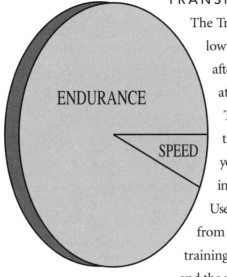

ENDURANCE

SPEED

TRANSITION

The transition period is a time of easy workouts and no training regimentation.

TRANSITION PERIOD

The Transition period is a time of rest and recovery following a Race period. This should always be included after the last race of the year, but may also be inserted at mid-season to prevent burnout later in the year. The Transition period should have little regimentation or structure. My only admonition is to do what you feel like doing during this period, as long as it is low intensity and low volume. Cross training is a good idea. Use this time to recharge your "batteries." The time away from your bike will pay off with higher motivation for training and racing, the healing of minor muscle trauma, and the reduction of psychological stress.

REFERENCES

Bompa, T. *Periodization of Strength*, Veritas Publishing, Inc, 1993.

Bompa, T. *Theory and Methodology of Training*, Kendall Hunt Publishing, 1994.

Freeman, W. *Peak When It Counts*, TAFNEWS, 1989.

Rogers, J. Periodization of training, *Endurance Training Journal*, vol. 2, pp. 4-7, 1992.

Sleamaker, R. *Serious Training for Serious Athletes*, Leisure Press, 1989.

VanHandel, P.J. Periodization of Training, *Bike Tech*, vol. 6(2), pp. 6-10, 1987.

VanHandel, P.J. Training for Cycling I, *Conditioning for Cycling*, vol. 1(1), pp. 8-11, 1991.

VanHandel, P.J. Training for Cycling II, *Conditioning for Cycling*, vol. 1(2), pp. 18-23, 1991.

Chapter 8

THE TRAINING YEAR

A man who carries a cat by the tail, learns something he can learn in no other way.

— MARK TWAIN

In this chapter, you'll begin designing an annual training plan. The best time of year to do this is four to six weeks following the end of your last Race period, when you're ready to start the Preparation period. If you've purchased this book after your season has already begun, it's still a good idea to plan where you're going the rest of the year. Better late than never.

I'm about to take you through a simple six-step process of annual planning that will have you on the way to a better season before you even turn a crank. This will require some writing, so you'll need a pencil. Don't work in ink, as you'll need to make changes later. The Annual Training Plan worksheet is in appendix A. You should make a copy of the appropriate one before starting to work.

The danger in following a methodical process to arrive at a training plan is that you'll be so engrossed in procedures and numbers that you'll forget to think in a realistic way. The purpose is not simply to write a plan; the purpose is to race better than ever before. At the end of a successful season, you'll realize how important having a written plan was.

Writing and following an annual training plan is somewhat like climbing a mountain. Before you take the first step, it's a good idea to know where the peak of the mountain is and how you plan to get there. It also helps if you know what problems you're likely to encounter along the route, so you're prepared to deal with them. While ascending the mountain, you'll stop occasionally to look at the peak and check your progress. You may decide to change the route based on new conditions such as bad weather or unexpected crevasses. Arriving at the peak you'll be elated, but looking back down you will remember all of the problems you overcame along the way and how the plan gave you direction.

Remind yourself throughout this chapter that you're not writing an annual plan to impress anyone or simply to feel organized. The purpose is to create a useful and dynamic guide for your training. You will refer to the plan regularly to make decisions as your training progresses. The plan will help you to keep an eye on the goal and not get lost in "just going to races." A training plan is dynamic in that you'll frequently modify it as new situations arise.

THE ANNUAL TRAINING PLAN

It's time to get started planning. The six steps you'll complete in this chapter are

Step 1: Determine season goals   Step 4: Prioritize races

Step 2: Establish supporting objectives   Step 5: Divide year into periods

Step 3: Set annual hours   Step 6: Assign weekly hours

In Chapter 9, you will complete the annual plan by assigning weekly workouts based on abilities. This probably sounds like a lot to accomplish. It is, but the system I've set out here will make it easy to do.

Figure 8.1 is a working copy of the Annual Training Plan for the year 1997. Appendix A has worksheets for years 1997-2002. You should complete the appropriate worksheet in this and the next chapter. Notice that there are several parts to the Plan. At the top left of the page are spaces for Annual Hours, Season Goals, and Training Objectives. Down the left side are rows for each week of the year with the week number and date of the Monday of each week indicated. There is a column to list the Races, their priorities (Pri), the Period, weekly Hours, and Details for each week. The small boxes down the right side will be used to indicate categories of workouts by abilities as listed at the top of the page. Chapter 9 will explain this last part.

Fig. 8.1 Annual Training Plan: 1997

Athlete:

Annual Hours:

Season Goals:

1

2

3

Training Objectives:

1

2

3

4

5

								Strength Phase	Endurance	Strength	Speed	Muscular End	Speed Endur	Power	Testing
Wk#	**Monday**	**Races**		**Pri**	**Period**	**Hours**	**Details**								
01	Jan 6														
02	Jan 13														
03	Jan 20														
04	Jan 27														
05	Feb 3														
06	Feb 10														
07	Feb 17														
08	Feb 24														
09	Mar 3														
10	Mar 10														
11	Mar 17														
12	Mar 24														
13	Mar 31														
14	Apr 7														
15	Apr 14														
16	Apr 21														
17	Apr 28														
18	May 5														
19	May 12														
20	May 19														
21	May 26														
22	Jun 2														
23	Jun 9														
24	Jun 16														
25	Jun 23														
26	Jun 30														
27	Jul 7														
28	Jul 14														
29	Jul 21														
30	Jul 28														
31	Aug 4														
32	Aug 11														
33	Aug 18														
34	Aug 25														
35	Sep 1														
36	Sep 8														
37	Sep 15														
38	Sep 22														
39	Sep 29														
40	Oct 6														
41	Oct 13														
42	Oct 20														
43	Oct 27														
44	Nov 3														
45	Nov 10														
46	Nov 17														
47	Nov 24														
48	Dec 1														
49	Dec 8														
50	Dec 15														
51	Dec 22														
52	Dec 29														

WORKOUTS

STEP 1: DETERMINE SEASON GOALS

Let's start with the destination: What racing goals do you want to accomplish this season? It could be to upgrade, to place in the top five at the district road race, or to finish a stage race. Studies have shown that clearly defined goals improve one's ability to achieve them. A successful mountain climber always has the peak in the back of his or her mind. If you don't know where you want to go, by the end of the season you will have gone nowhere.

Don't get goals confused with wishes and dreams. The athletes I train sometimes dream about what they wish to accomplish, and I encourage them to do so. Dreaming is healthy. Without dreams there is no vision for the future, no incentive. Dreams can become realities. But wishes and dreams take longer to accomplish than one season. If you can achieve it this season, no matter how big it is, it's no longer a dream — it's a goal.

Let's be realistically optimistic. If you had trouble finishing club rides in the past season, winning a stage race this season is a wish, not a goal. "But," you say, "if you don't set high goals you never achieve anything." That's true, but the problem with wishes is that since you know down deep you really aren't capable of achieving it this season, there's no commitment to the training required. A challenging goal will stretch you to the limits, and may require you to take some risks, but you can imagine yourself accomplishing it in the next few months. Ask yourself: "If I do everything right, can I imagine success with this goal?" If you can't even conceive of achieving it now, you're wasting your time. If you can, it's a good goal. Otherwise, it's just another dream.

There are four principles your goals must adhere to:

Principle 1: Your goal must be *measurable*. How will you know if you're getting closer to it? How do business people know if they're achieving their financial goals? By counting their money, of course. Rather than saying "get better" in your goal statement, you might say, "complete a 40k time trial in less than 58 minutes."

Principle 2: Your goal must be under *your* control. A successful person doesn't set goals based on other people. "If Jones misses the break, win XYZ race," is not a goal that demands your commitment. "Make the winning break at the Boulder Road Race," however, gets your juices flowing.

Principle 3: Your goal must *stretch* you. A goal that is too easy or too hard is the same as having no goal. For a category 3 racer, winning the Core States

National Pro Championship this year is more than a stretch, even though it's a great dream. On the other hand, "finish the club's 8-mile time trial" isn't much of a challenge. But upgrading to category 2 would, perhaps, be an excellent stretch.

Principle 4: Whatever your goals, you must state them in the *positive*. Whatever you do while reading this paragraph, *don't think about pink elephants*. See what I mean? Your goal must keep you focused on what you want to happen, not what you want to avoid. Guess what happens to people who set a goal such as "Don't lose the Podunkville Criterium." You got it, they lose because they didn't know what they were *supposed* to do.

The goal should also be racing-outcome oriented. For example, don't set a goal of climbing better. That's an objective, as we'll see shortly. Instead, commit to winning the Mount Evans Road Race, or whatever. Table 8.1 offers examples of racing-oriented goals to help you.

> Examples of Goals
>
> Goal: Top 10 finish in district category 3 road race.
>
> Goal: Break one hour in 40 km time trial in August.
>
> Goal: Finish in top five in two out of three "A"-priority criteriums.
>
> Goal: Upgrade to category 2.
>
> Goal: Ranked in top five in district in category 3 B.A.R.
>
> Goal: Finish in top three in masters nationals road race.
>
> Goal: Place in top 25 in category 3 G.C. at Mike Nields Stage Race.

Table 8.1
Goal setting

After this goal, you may have one or two others that are important to you. Give them the same consideration you did the first goal. Stop at three goals so things don't get too complicated in the coming months. All of your goals should be listed at the top of the Annual Training Plan.

STEP 2: ESTABLISH TRAINING OBJECTIVES

In Chapter 5, you determined your strengths and weaknesses. After doing this you completed the "Cyclist Assessment" form in that chapter. Look back at that form now to refresh your memory: What are your strengths and weaknesses?

You may remember that in Chapter 6, I described the concept of limiters. These are your key race-specific weaknesses holding you back from being success-

Table 8.2

Training objectives

Limiters and Training Objectives by Goal

Goal: Top 10 finish in district category 3 road race.

Training Objectives:

1. Improve muscular-endurance: Complete a sub-57-minute 40 km TT in June.

2. Improve climbing: Squat 320 pounds by end of Base 1.

Goal: Break one hour in 40 km time trial in August.

Training Objectives:

1. Improve focus: Feel more focused in tempo workouts and races by July 31 (subjective measurement).

2. Improve muscular-endurance: Increase lactate threshold power to 330 watts by end of Base 3.

Goal: Finish in top five in two out of three "A"-priority criteriums.

Training Objectives:

1. Improve speed-endurance: Increase speed score on Natural Abilities Profile by end of Base 3.

2. Improve sprinting: Increase average watts to 700 on power test by end of Base 3.

Goal: Upgrade to category 2.

Training Objectives:

1. Improve climbing: Increase power-to-weight index by 10% by end of Base 3.

2. Improve training consistency: Complete all "BT" workouts in Build period.

Goal: Ranked in top five in district in category 3 B.A.R.

Training Objectives:

1. Improve speed: Spin at 140 rpm and remain in contact with the saddle (no bouncing) by February 12.

2. Improve speed-endurance: Continue for four minutes beyond 165 heart rate on lactate threshold test by end of first Build 2 period.

Goal: Finish in top three in masters nationals road race.

Training Objectives:

1. Improve sprint: Produce 950 watts on max power test by end of Base 3.

2. Improve climbing: Climb Rist Canyon in 28 minutes by May 31.

Goal: Place in top 25 in category 3 G.C. at Mike Nields Stage Race.

Training Objectives:

1. Improve muscular-endurance: Climb Poudre Canyon six times in 10 weeks prior to race.

2. Improve time trialing: Lower 8-mile TT self-test to 19:12 by April 15.

ful in certain races. In Chapter 6, I explained abilities required for different types of races. By comparing your weaknesses with the race's requirements, you will know your limiters. For example, a hilly race requires good strength and climbing proficiency. A weakness in either of these areas means you have a limiter for hilly races. You must improve in that area if you're to be successful in hilly races.

Read your first season goal. Do any of your weaknesses (score of 3 or lower on the Cyclist Assessment) present a limiter for this goal? If so, you'll need to train to improve that specific weakness. Under "Training Objectives" list the limiter. In the coming weeks of the Annual Training Plan, you'll work on improving this weakness. Chapter 9 will show you how to do that. The challenge for now is knowing when you have improved a limiter — in other words, being able to measure progress.

There are several ways to measure progress. Chapter 5 presented several tests you could conduct, but races and workouts also serve as good progress indicators. Table 8.2 provides examples of training objectives for limiters associated with specific goals. You should write your training objectives for each goal in a similar manner so you know how to determine when progress is being made. Notice that time limits are set for each objective. To accomplish the goal, you must meet the training objective by a certain time of the season. Too late is as good as never.

By the time you are done with this part of the Annual Training Plan, you will probably have three to five training objectives listed. These are short term standards against which you will measure progress.

STEP 3: SET ANNUAL TRAINING HOURS

The number of hours you train in the coming season — including on the bike, in weight room, and cross training — partly determine the stress load you carry. It is a balancing act: Too high an annual volume will probably result in overtraining; too low and you begin to lose endurance. Setting annual training hours is one of the most critical decisions you will make about training.

Before discussing how to arrive at this number, I'd like to make a case for training based on time rather than on distance. Training by miles encourages you to repeat the same courses week after week. It also causes you to compare your time on a given course today with what it was last week. Such thinking is counterproductive. Using time as a basis for training volume allows you to go wherever you want, so long as you finish within a given time. Your rides are more enjoyable due to the variety and lack of concern about today's average speed.

How do you determine annual hours if you haven't kept track of time in the past? Most cyclists keep a record of the miles they've ridden. If you have such a record divide the total by what you guess the average speed to have been — 18 miles per hour would be a reasonable guess. If you've also cross trained and lifted weights, estimate how many hours you put into those activities in the past year. By adding all of the estimates together, you have a ball park figure for your annual training hours. Looking back over the last three years you can easily see trends in training volume. If so, did you race better in the high volume years or worse? There were undoubtedly other factors in your performance at those times, but this may help you to decide what the training volume should be for the coming season.

Even without records of annual miles or hours trained, you may be able to produce an estimate. That will give you a starting point.

Table 8.3 offers a rough guideline of the annual hours typical of cyclists by racer category. This should not be considered a "required" volume. I know of many riders with 10 or more years of racing who put in fewer miles than those suggested here for their category and yet race quite well. The volume of training is primarily responsible for developing endurance. With endurance already established by years of riding, you can shift your emphasis toward intensity.

Limiting the number of hours an athlete trains produces better results than struggling through an overly ambitious volume. If you have a full time job, a family, a home to maintain, and other responsibilities, be realistic — don't expect to train with the same volume as the pros. Training *is* their job.

If, however, you have not been competitive in the past, and fall well below the suggested annual hours for your category, it may be wise to consider increasing your volume to the lower figure in your category range so long as this is not more than a 15 percent increase. Otherwise, increases in your annual hours from year to year should be in the range of five to 10 percent.

Many professional business people have limitations imposed on their training time by travel

Table 8.3

Training hours

Annual Training Hours by Racer Category	
Category	Hours/Year
Pro	800-1200
1-2	700-1000
3	500-700
4	350-500
5/junior	200-350

and work responsibilities. Determining annual hours in this case is based strictly on what is available.

Write your annual training hours at the top of the Annual Training Plan. Later you'll use that figure to assign weekly training hours.

STEP 4: PRIORITIZE RACES

For this step you need a list of the races you will be doing. If the race schedule hasn't been published yet, go back to last year's race calendar and guess which days they'll be on. Races nearly always stay on the same weekends from year to year.

On the Annual Training Plan, list all of the races you intend to do by writing them into the "Races" column in the appropriate date rows. Remember that the date indicated is the Monday of that week. This should be an inclusive list of tentative races. You may decide later on not to do some of them, but for now assume you'll do them all.

The next step is to prioritize the races into three categories — A, B, and C — using the criteria below. If your team is well organized, the team manager may have some input on the priorities of the season. Better check with him or her before going beyond this point.

A Races

Pick out the three or four races most important to you this year. A stage race counts as one race and two A races on the same weekend count as one race. An A race isn't necessarily the one that gets the most press or has the biggest prize purse. It could be the Nowhereville Road Race, but if you live in Nowhereville, that could be *the* big race of the year *for you*.

The A races are the most important on the schedule and all training will be designed around them. The purpose of training is build to and peak for the A races.

It's best that these races be clumped together in four or five weeks or widely separated by six or more weeks. For example, two of the races may fall into a three week period in May and the other two could be close together in August. Then again, two may occur in May, one in July, and the other in September. The idea is that in order to come to a peak for each of these most important races, a period of several weeks will be needed. During this time between A races you will still race, but won't be in top form.

It's best that the single most important race of the year (the "Mother of All A Races") comes near the end of the season when your fitness is likely to be at the highest level possible.

If your A races aren't neatly spaced or grouped as I've described here, don't worry. Season priorities are not determined by the calendar, but rather by goals. A schedule, however, that doesn't conveniently space the races makes planning and coming to a peak much more difficult, as you will shortly see.

In the "Pri" column write in "A" for all of your A-priority races.

B Races

These are important races at which you want to do well, but they're not as critical as the A races. You'll rest for a few days before each of them, but not build to a peak. There may be as many as 12 of these, and as with the A events, stage races count as one as do two B races on the same weekend.

In the Pri column write in "B" for all of these races.

C Races

You now have up to 16 weeks dedicated to either A or B races. That's most of the season. All the other races on the list are C-priority. C races are done for experience, as hard workouts, as tests of progress, for fun, or as tune ups for A races. You will "train through" these races with no peaking and minimal rest before each one. It's not unusual to decide at the last moment not to do one of these low-priority events. If your heart isn't in it, you'd be better off training that day.

Be careful with C races. They are the ones in which you're most likely to crash or go over the edge into a state of overtraining, since you may be tired and have low motivation to perform well. They are also usually associated with haphazard racing and confused incentives. Every race should have a meaning in your schedule, so decide before a C race what you want to get out of it.

The more experienced you are as a racer, the fewer C races you should do. Conversely, juniors and category 4 and 5 riders should do several to gain experience.

STEP 5: DIVIDE YEAR INTO PERIODS

Now that the times in the year when you want to be in top form are known, periods can be assigned. The last chapter described the six training periods of the year. To refresh your memory, Table 8.4 summarizes each.

Period	Duration	Training Focus
Preparation	3-4 weeks	General adaptation with weights, cross training and on-bike drills.
Base	8-12 weeks	Establish strength, speed and endurance. Introduce muscular-endurance and hill work.
Build	6-10 weeks	Develop muscular-endurance, speed-endurance and power.
Peak	1-2 weeks	Consolidate race readiness with reduced volume and race tune ups.
Race	1-6 weeks	Race, refine strengths and recover.
Transition	1-6 weeks	Rest and recover.

Table 8.4
Periodization summary

Find your first A race on the schedule and in the "Period" column write in "Race." This first Race period extends throughout your clumping of A races and could be as long as six weeks. Count (up the page) two weeks from "Race" and write in "Peak." Now work backwards four weeks from Peak and indicate "Build 2." Using durations as indicated in Table 8.4, do the same for Build 1, Base 3, Base 2, Base 1, and Prep. The first peak of the year is now scheduled.

Go to your second A race and write in "Race" as you did above. Count backwards two weeks and write in "Peak" again. Then count back four weeks for Build 2 and another four for Build 1. It's not necessary to repeat the Base period unless you have had two four- to six-week Race periods with four or less weeks between them, and have a third Race period planned late in the season.

It's unlikely that the Build-Peak period between your two Race periods will work out to be exactly 10 weeks. Once you have the second Peak period scheduled, if you have six weeks remaining, plan on a three-week Build 2 and a three-week Build 1. If there are seven weeks you could schedule a four-week Build 1 and a three-week Build 2, depending on your needs. There may only be time for one Build, in that case, make it Build 1, which does a better job of maintaining your endurance.

It's also a good idea to schedule a one- or two-week transition after your first Race period to allow for recovery and to prevent burnout later in the season. This always pays off with higher enthusiasm for training and greater fitness for late-season races. Following the last Race period of the season, schedule a Transition period.

If this step in the planning process seemed confusing, you may want to look ahead to Chapter 11 where case studies with easy and not-so-easy annual plans are described. These may help to clear up the confusion.

STEP 6: ASSIGN WEEKLY HOURS

Throughout the season there is a sine wave pattern of increasing and decreasing volume. Figure 7.3 in the last chapter illustrates this. The purpose of that pattern is to make sure your endurance is maintained, but to permit increases in intensity without overly stressing your body's systems. In this step, you'll write in the weekly training hours using Table 8.5 as a guide.

Now that you know annual hours and have divided the year into periods, you're ready to assign weekly training hours. Find your annual hours column in Table 8.5. In that column are weekly hours in half-hour increments. On the left side of the table are all of the periods and weeks. By reading across and down, determine the number of hours for each week and write those in under "Hours" on the Annual Training Plan.

You've now completed the Annual Training Plan with the exception of the workouts portion. That's the next chapter.

REFERENCES

Bompa, T. Physiological intensity values employed to plan endurance training, *New Studies in Athletics*, vol. 3(4), pp. 37-52, 1988.

Bompa, T. *Theory and Methodology of Training*, Kendall Hunt Publishing, 1994.

Costill, D., et al. Adaptations to swimming training: Influence of training volume, *Medicine and Science in Sports and Exercise*, vol. 23, pp. 371-377, 1991.

Maglischo, E. *Swimming Faster*, Mayfield Publishing Co., 1982.

Martin, D. and P. Coe. *Training Distance Runners*, Leisure Press, 1991.

Matveyev, L. *Fundamentals of Sports Training*, Progress Publishing, 1981.

Stucker, M. *Training for Cycling*, unpublished manuscript, 1990.

USA Cycling, *Expert Level Coaching Manual*, USA Cycling Inc., 1995.

VanHandel, P.J. The science of sport training for cycling I, *Conditioning for Cycling*, vol. 1(1), pp. 8-11, 1991.

Table 8.5 Weekly Training Hours

Period	Week	200	250	300	350	400	450	500	550	600	650	700	750	800	850	900	950	1000	1050	1100	1150	1200
Prep	All	3.5	4.0	5.0	6.0	7.0	7.5	8.5	9.0	10.0	11.0	12.0	12.5	13.5	14.5	15.0	16.0	17.0	17.5	18.5	19.5	20.0
Base 1	1	4.0	5.0	6.0	7.0	8.0	9.0	10.0	11.0	12.0	12.5	14.0	14.5	15.5	16.5	17.5	18.5	19.5	20.5	21.5	22.5	23.5
	2	5.0	6.0	7.0	8.5	9.5	10.5	12.0	13.0	14.5	15.5	16.5	18.0	19.0	20.0	21.5	22.5	24.0	25.0	26.0	27.5	28.5
	3	5.5	6.5	8.0	9.5	10.5	12.0	13.5	14.5	16.0	17.5	18.5	20.0	21.5	22.5	24.0	25.5	26.5	28.0	29.5	30.5	32.0
	4	3.0	3.5	4.0	5.0	5.5	6.5	7.0	8.0	8.5	9.0	10.0	10.5	11.0	12.0	12.5	13.5	14.0	14.5	15.5	16.0	17.0
Base 2	1	4.0	5.5	6.5	7.5	8.5	9.5	10.5	12.5	12.5	13.0	14.5	16.0	17.0	18.0	19.0	20.0	21.0	22.0	23.0	24.0	25.0
	2	5.0	6.5	7.5	9.0	10.0	11.5	12.5	14.0	15.0	16.5	17.5	19.0	20.0	21.5	22.5	24.0	25.0	26.5	27.5	29.0	30.0
	3	5.5	7.0	8.5	10.0	11.0	12.5	14.0	15.5	17.0	18.0	19.5	21.0	22.5	24.0	25.0	26.5	28.0	29.5	31.0	32.0	33.5
	4	3.0	3.5	4.5	5.0	5.5	6.5	7.0	8.0	8.5	9.0	10.0	10.5	11.5	12.0	12.5	13.5	14.0	15.0	15.5	16.0	17.0
Base 3	1	4.5	5.5	7.0	8.0	9.0	10.0	11.0	12.5	13.5	14.5	15.5	17.0	18.0	19.0	20.0	21.0	22.5	23.5	25.0	25.5	27.0
	2	5.0	6.5	8.0	9.5	10.5	12.0	13.5	14.5	16.0	17.0	18.5	20.0	21.5	23.0	24.0	25.0	26.5	28.0	29.5	30.5	32.0
	3	6.0	7.5	9.0	10.5	11.5	13.0	15.0	16.5	18.0	19.0	20.5	22.0	23.5	25.0	26.5	28.0	29.5	31.0	32.5	33.5	35.0
	4	3.0	3.5	4.5	5.0	5.5	6.5	7.0	8.0	8.5	9.0	10.0	10.5	11.5	12.0	12.5	13.5	14.0	15.0	15.5	16.0	17.0
Build 1	1	5.0	6.5	8.0	9.0	10.0	11.5	12.5	14.0	15.5	16.0	17.5	19.0	20.5	21.5	22.5	24.0	25.0	26.5	28.0	29.0	30.0
	2	5.0	6.5	8.0	9.0	10.0	11.5	12.5	14.0	15.5	16.0	17.5	19.0	20.5	21.5	22.5	24.0	25.0	26.5	28.0	29.0	30.0
	3	5.0	6.5	8.0	9.0	10.0	11.5	12.5	14.0	15.5	16.0	17.5	19.0	20.5	21.5	22.5	24.0	25.0	26.5	28.0	29.0	30.0
	4	3.0	3.5	4.5	5.0	5.5	6.5	7.0	8.0	8.5	9.0	10.0	10.5	11.5	12.0	12.5	13.5	14.0	15.0	15.5	16.0	17.0
Build 2	1	5.0	6.0	7.0	8.5	9.5	10.5	12.0	13.0	14.5	15.5	16.5	18.0	19.0	20.5	21.5	22.5	24.0	25.0	26.5	27.0	28.5
	2	5.0	6.0	7.0	8.5	9.5	10.5	12.0	13.0	14.5	15.5	16.5	18.0	19.0	20.5	21.5	22.5	24.0	25.0	26.5	27.0	28.5
	3	5.0	6.0	7.0	8.5	9.5	10.5	12.0	13.0	14.5	15.5	16.5	18.0	19.0	20.5	21.5	22.5	24.0	25.0	26.5	27.0	28.5
	4	3.0	3.5	4.5	5.0	5.5	6.5	7.0	8.0	8.5	9.0	10.0	10.5	11.5	12.0	12.5	13.5	14.0	15.0	15.5	16.0	17.0
Peak	1	4.0	5.5	6.5	7.5	8.5	9.5	10.5	11.5	13.0	13.5	14.5	16.0	17.0	18.0	19.0	20.0	21.0	22.0	23.5	24.0	25.0
	2	3.5	4.0	5.0	6.0	6.5	7.5	8.5	9.5	10.0	11.0	11.5	12.5	13.5	14.5	15.0	16.0	17.0	17.5	18.5	19.0	20.0
Race	All	3.0	3.5	4.5	5.0	5.5	6.5	7.0	8.0	8.5	9.0	10.0	10.5	11.5	12.0	12.5	13.5	14.0	15.0	15.5	16.0	17.0
Tran	All	3.0	3.5	4.5	5.0	5.5	6.5	7.0	8.0	8.5	9.0	10.0	10.5	11.5	12.0	12.5	13.5	14.0	15.0	15.5	16.0	17.0

The Training Bible

VanHandel, P.J. The science of sport training for cycling II, *Conditioning for Cycling*, vol. 1(2), pp. 18-23, 1991.

VanHandel, P.J. Planning a comprehensive training program, *Conditioning for Cycling*, vol. 1(3), pp. 4-12, 1991.

Chapter 9

Planning Workouts

If you haven't tried these things, you should.
These things are fun, and fun is good.

— Dr. Seuss

The heart of any cycling program is quality time on the road. These hard workouts are what most athletes think of when the subject turns to training. For many, simply riding fast all the time is what gets them in shape. These cyclists believe that if the workout doesn't cause pain just short of childbirth, then it didn't accomplish anything. While athletes who train this way often race well, workouts based on such beliefs don't produce consistent and predictable race results, and often lead to burnout or overtraining.

If there's one thing you're getting out of this book so far, I hope it's that training should be purposeful and precise to meet your unique needs. Haphazard training brings results initially, but to reach the highest level of racing fitness, carefully planned workouts are necessary. Before starting any training session, from the easiest to the hardest, you must be able to answer one simple question: What is the purpose of this workout?

WORKOUT CATEGORIES

In the last four chapters, I've described a system of planning based on strengths and weaknesses. In this chapter, you will complete the training plan by scheduling daily workouts determined by your limiters. To intelligently select workouts, it's important that you know what your limiters are. If you haven't read Chapters 5 and 6, do so before planning workouts. Knowing what you need to work on will make your plan purposeful and precise.

You are not going to schedule every workout of every week on your plan. With the exception of endurance-maintenance workouts, you will only be determining the "break through" (BT) workouts. These are the ones that provide the stress to start the adaptive process described earlier. Active recovery workouts, the ones you do between the BTs, will not be scheduled now, but will be a part of your weekly plan, as you will soon see.

You should base these workouts on the abilities listed at the top of the Annual Training Plan (see fig. 8.1). Notice that there are two categories of workouts added to the abilities we've discussed before: "Strength Phase" and "Testing." It may be helpful before you start this planning step to review all of the workout columns listed.

STRENGTH PHASE

In this column you will schedule weight room workouts. This is an often neglected aspect of training for cycling, especially for riders whose limiter is strength. It has been my experience that measurable results on the bike are more evident from this type of training than any other in athletes who lack the ability to apply force to the pedals. They are always amazed at how strong they feel riding in the spring after a winter of weights.

The details of the five strength phases are discussed in Chapter 12, but with a little information you can complete the Strength Phase column now by penciling in the abbreviations for the various phases. Here's how to determine the duration of each phase. If you're a bit confused, flip ahead to Chapter 11 for examples of completed Annual Training Plans.

Anatomical Adaptation (AA)

If you have not included strength work in your workouts over the last six weeks, include six weeks of AA at the outset of your training year, usually during the Preparation period. If there are less than six weeks since weight training stopped, assign four weeks of AA.

Maximum Strength (MS)

If strength or climbing proficiency is a limiter, schedule the next six weeks to MS. Otherwise, just four weeks of MS.

Power-Endurance (PE)

If sprinting proficiency, maximum power, average power or power-to-weight index is a limiter, assign the next six weeks to PE. If none of these power markers are limiters, write in four weeks for PE.

Muscular-Endurance (ME)

If time trialing, lactate threshold power or speed-endurance is a limiter, schedule eight weeks of ME. If none of these are limiters, plan on six weeks of ME. Muscular-endurance takes longer to develop than the other strength qualities.

Maintenance (PE and ME)

For the remainder of the season, alternate two weeks of PE with four weeks of ME phases. Maintenance may start as early as the first Build period, but could begin as late as the first Peak period. Riders in their twenties with good strength may omit strength training from their schedules at this time. During the week of A races schedule no weight training.

ENDURANCE

Racing on the roads is primarily an endurance sport. The ability to continue working despite the onset of fatigue is what sets road racers apart from track racers. For this reason, the Endurance column will be the most selected on the form. You will work on endurance in some form nearly every week of the year, for once you have lost endurance, the time required to fully restore it is exorbitant. That's not to say that there won't be fluctuations in your endurance throughout the season. Following an extended Race period, your endurance is likely to wane, and you must work to rebuild before you are able to attain another peak.

STRENGTH

This strength column refers to on-bike strength workouts while the Strength Phase column is off-bike workouts. If you don't live in a vertically-challenged region, use hills for on-bike strength training. Later on in the workout menu section of this chapter, I'll refer to hills by percentage grades. Here's a guide to help you select the proper types of hills for specific workouts.

2-4% grade: Slight hill. In a car on a 2% grade you may not even know there's a grade. You could easily ride these hills in the big chainring. Often described as "gently rolling hills."

4-6% grade: Moderate hill. These hills get your attention in races, but are seldom determining factors. You could ride them in the big chainring, but may drop down to the small chainring.

6-8% grade: Steep hill. These are the steepest hills you generally find on state and federal highways. Such hills, especially if they're long, often determine winners and losers. These are usually climbed in the small chainring.

8-10% grade: Very steep hill. These hills are always a determiner in a race. Climbed only in the small chainring. A workout on such a hill is challenging for riders of all abilities.

Hills play a major part in developing strength and power.

10%+ grade: Extremely steep hill. These hills are most often found in remote areas or in the mountains. In more populated areas, they are usually quite short. Everyone climbs in the small chainring. Some riders have difficulty just getting over them. They make you cry for your mother.

If you do live in a vertically challenged environment — the plains of Kansas or Florida's — don't despair. The real benefit of hills is that they offer greater resistance. You can achieve the same result with big gears and head winds while sitting up, or on a good indoor trainer. Highway overpasses offer short hills of about 4 percent. Multilevel parking garages are great simulated mountains — just remember to ask the attendant's permission first.

SPEED

Do not get speed confused with speed-endurance. While working on speed you are *not* doing intervals or hammering on group rides. The purpose of workouts in this column is always on improving mobility — the ability to handle the bike efficiently and effectively while turning the cranks quickly and smoothly. In the Base period, many of these workouts will be drills on a trainer or rollers that exaggerate the mechanics of pedaling in order to become more fluid and supple. On the road, speed training involves form sprints, high-cadence pedaling and the handling skills necessary for sprinting.

Connie Carpenter in the striped race leader's jersey climbing the Wall of the Morgul-Bismarck course in the 1984 Coors Classic.

Bernard Hinault in the Vail Criterium of the 1986 Coors Classic wearing the striped race leader's jersey.

Great muscular-endurance is the hallmark of most of cycling's champions.

Greg LeMond starts the 1990 Tour de France prologue in the yellow jersey.

Miguel Indurain wearing the yellow jersey at Luz-Ardiden in the 1994 Tour de France.

MUSCULAR-ENDURANCE

Muscular-endurance is the ability to turn a relatively high gear at a relatively high cadence for a long time, as in time trialing. As one of the primary ingredients of road racing fitness, you need to emphasize this approach throughout the training year regardless of your limiters. All of the legendary champion road cyclists — Merckx, Hinault, LeMond, Carpenter, Indurain and Longo — had great muscular-endurance. It will be developed starting in the Base period and continue in various forms right through the Race periods.

SPEED-ENDURANCE

Speed-endurance is sometimes called anaerobic endurance since it involves training to continue working hard even though the body is crying out for relief. Long sprints and short climbs are the usual times for this to occur. If it is known to be a limiter (which is the case for nearly every athlete), schedule workouts for this area at the start of the first Build period. Speed-endurance training is excellent for improving aerobic capacity.

POWER

For the rider whose limiter is power, these workouts mean the difference between success and failure in criteriums that require the ability to accelerate quickly out of corners and to contest field sprints. Workouts for power are dependent on speed and strength, so these abilities must be improved first.

TESTING

Throughout the Base and Build periods, make regular progress checks about every fourth week. It's important to regularly know how your abilities are developing in order to make adjustments to training. Test details will be discussed later in this chapter.

ABILITY WORKOUTS BY PERIOD

The following will help you complete the workouts section of the Annual Training Plan. I'll start with the recovery and rest weeks since those are usually neglected, but are in some ways the most important.

If there is any confusion on how to mark the Annual Training Plan, see the examples in Chapter 11.

R & R WEEKS

Reserve every fourth week during the Base and Build periods for recovery and rest from the accumulated fatigue of the previous three weeks. Without such regular unloading of fatigue, fitness won't progress for long. You've already partially incorporated R & R by assigning reduced weekly hours during the fourth weeks of Base and Build. Now we'll assign the workouts to those low-volume weeks.

For each of the R & R weeks, place an "X" under the Speed and Testing columns. Other than one strength session, that's all for those weeks. The idea is to recover from the collected stress, feel rested by week's end, maintain speed and strength, and test progress once rested. In the Build period, there may be a B or C race at week's end in place of a test.

Later in this chapter (under Testing), I'll describe the tests you will do during R & R weeks.

Now you're ready to complete workouts for the other weeks of the year. A "Workout Menu" near the end of the chapter will be used at a later time to fill in the details of what you schedule here.

PREPARATION PERIOD

Place an X in the Endurance and Speed columns for each week of the Preparation period. Endurance training during this period concentrates on improving the endurance characteristics of the heart, blood and lungs. Cross training accomplishes the same result and also limits the number of times each week that you're on an indoor trainer.

BASE 1

Again, mark the Endurance and Speed columns for each week of the Base 1 period. During this period, endurance training shifts slightly toward more time on the bike and less in cross training modes. Weather, however, is often the determining factor for the type of endurance training done now. A mountain bike is an excellent alternative during this period when the roads and weather don't cooperate. A good indoor trainer, especially CompuTrainer, is also an excellent way to train throughout the Base period when you can't get on the roads.

BASE 2

Place an X in the Endurance, Speed, and Muscular-Endurance columns for each week of the Base 2 period. As you will see in the Workout Menu, you should conduct muscular-endurance workouts at moderate heart rates and power outputs during this period. Endurance training should be mostly on the road by now. You will be doing some Strength work in the form of endurance rides on rolling courses staying in the saddle on the uphill portions. This is such an integral part of endurance training, however, that we won't mark strength.

BASE 3

Mark the Endurance, Strength, Speed, and Muscular-Endurance columns for each week of the Base 3 period. Training volume comes to a crescendo during this period. Intensity has also risen slightly with the addition of hill work.

BUILD 1

Schedule workouts for Endurance and Muscular-Endurance for each week of the Build 1 period. Also select your greatest limiter and mark that column. If unsure which limiter to schedule, choose Strength. If you don't select Power or Speed-Endurance, also mark Speed. A criterium may take the place of a Speed-Endurance or Power workout. Road races and time trials are substituted for Strength and Muscular-Endurance. Early season races in this period are best as C-priority. Schedule each Build 1 period on your Annual Training Plan in this same way.

BUILD 2

Check off Endurance and Muscular-Endurance for each week of the Build 2 period. Then mark two of your limiters. If unsure, or if you have only one limiter, mark Strength and Speed-Endurance. Speed will be maintained either with Speed-Endurance or Power training. If there are B or C races scheduled during this period, substitute them for workouts. A criterium takes the place of either a Power or Speed-Endurance workout. Depending on the terrain, you may substitute a road race or time trial for a Strength or Muscular-Endurance workout. The week of B-priority races, schedule only one limiter. Remember that you're training through C-priority races. Mark all Build 2 periods on your plan in the same manner.

PEAK

Place an X in the Muscular-Endurance column and that of your next greatest limiter for each week of the Peak period. If unsure of your next limiter, select Speed-Endurance. You may substitute races for workouts using the same criteria as in the Build period. C races in the Peak period are excellent tune-ups for the approaching A races as they get you back into a racing mode again. If there are no races, but you have a hard club ride available, that should be your Speed-Endurance training. There should only be two high intensity workouts each week.

Mark all Peak periods in this same way.

RACE

During each week of this period either race or complete a race-effort group ride. If there is no group ride or race available, substitute a Speed-Endurance workout. Also mark Speed and your strongest ability other than endurance. If unsure about your strength, mark Muscular-Endurance. All Race periods should be marked just as the first one was.

TRANSITION

Mark Endurance and Speed, but keep in mind that this is a mostly unstructured period. By "mostly," I mean that your only purpose is to stay active, especially in sports that you enjoy other than cycling. These are often team games such as soccer, basketball, volleyball or hockey. Such sports require some endurance and also encourage quick movement. Don't become a couch potato, but also don't train seriously.

WORKOUT MENU

The following are workouts listed by ability area, just as at the top of the Annual Training Plan (Figure 8.1). Following the description of each workout is the suggested training period or periods in which to incorporate it. The workouts are listed in a progressive manner, meaning that the easiest, or least stressful, come first and they progressively get harder. It's best to follow this sequence as you continue to refine the ability.

This menu is hardly an exhaustive list of workouts. You can do many more simply by modifying some of the characteristics. You may also create others from scratch, based on conditions known to be in a given race. Combining workouts often provides a comprehensive race simulation, but be careful not to try to accomplish so much in a single session that all benefits are diluted. It's best to limit a multiple-benefit workout to two combinations.

Each workout is preceded by an alpha-numeric code which may be used as a scheduling shorthand. Chapter 15 will discuss training journals and provide a weekly scheduling format where such shorthand will come in handy.

The intensity level of the workouts listed here are based on Table 9.2. Individual indicators of intensity are discussed in greater detail in Chapter 4.

Table 9.2
Workout Intensity

Zone	Purpose	RPE	Heart rate (%LTHR)*	Power (%LTP)**
1	Recovery	6-9	65-81	25-39
2	Aerobic	10-12	82-88	40-79
3	Tempo	13-14	89-93	80-87
4	Threshold	15-16	94-100	88-99
5a	Threshold	17	100-102	100-104
5b	Aerobic capacity	18-19	103-105	105-149
5c	Anaerobic capacity	20	106+	150+

* %LTHR is percent of lactate threshold heart rate

**%LTP is percent of lactate threshold power

ENDURANCE WORKOUTS

E1. Recovery. Done in the 1 zone using the small chain ring on a flat course. Do these the day after a BT workout. Best if done alone. May also be done on an indoor trainer or rollers, especially if flat courses are not available. Cross training is appropriate for recovery in Preparation, Base 1, and Base 2 periods. An excellent time to do a recovery spin is in the evening on a day when you've done intervals, sprints, a hard group ride, hills or a race. Spinning for 15-30 minutes on rollers or a trainer hastens recovery for most experienced riders. Novices are better taking the time off. These workouts are not scheduled on the Annual Training Plan, but are an integral part of training throughout the season. (Periods: All)

E2. Aerobic. Used for aerobic maintenance and endurance training. Stay primarily in the 1 and 2 zones on a rolling course up to 4% grades. Remain seated on the uphill portions to build greater strength while maintaining a comfortably high cadence. Can be done with a disciplined group or on an indoor trainer by shifting through the gears to simulate rolling hills. Cross training is effective during Preparation and Base 1. (Periods: All)

E3. Fixed Gear. Set up your bike with a gear that is appropriate for your strength level using a small chain ring (39-42) and a large cog (15-19). If you are in your first two years of training, don't do this workout. Start by riding flat courses and gradually add rolling hills. Intensity should be mostly in the 2-3 zones. This workout is multi-ability including endurance, strength, and speed — all elements required of Base training. (Periods: Base 2, Base 3)

STRENGTH (FORCE) WORKOUTS

F1. Moderate Hills. Select a course that includes several hills of up to 6% grade that take up to three minutes to ascend. Stay seated on all climbs pedaling from the hips. Cadence at 70 rpm or higher. Stay in the 1-4 zones on this ride. (Periods: Base 3)

F2. Long Hills. Ride a course including long grades of up to 8% that take six or more minutes to climb. Remain mostly seated on the hills and keep your cadence at 60 rpm or higher. Go no higher than 5a zone. Concentrate on bike position and smooth pedaling. (Periods: Base 3, Build 1)

F3. Steep Hills. Ride a course that includes 8% or steeper hills that take less than two minutes to climb. You can do repeats on the same hill with 3-5 minutes of recovery between climbs. Be sure to warm-up thoroughly. Intensity may climb to 5b several times with recoveries into the 1 zone. Climb in and out of the saddle. Maintain a cadence of 60-70 rpm. Stop the workout if you cannot maintain at least 60 rpm. Do this workout no more than twice per week. Do not do this workout if you have knee problems. (Periods: Build 1, Build 2, Peak, Race)

SPEED WORKOUTS

S1. Spin-ups. On a downhill or on an indoor trainer set to light resistance, for one minute gradually increase cadence to maximum. Maximum is the cadence you can maintain without bouncing. As the cadence increases, allow your lower legs and feet to relax — especially the toes. Hold your maximum for as long as possible.

Recover for at least three minutes and repeat several times. These are best done with a handlebar computer that displays cadence. Heart rate and power ratings have no significance for this workout. (Periods: Preparation, Base 1, Base 2, Base 3)

S2. Isolated Leg. With a light resistance on trainer or downhill, do 90% of work with one leg while the other is "along for the ride." Spin with a higher than normal cadence. Change legs when fatigue begins to set in. Can also be done on a trainer with one foot out of the pedal and resting on a stool while the other works. Focus on eliminating "dead" spots at top and bottom of stroke. Heart rate and power ratings have no bearing on this workout. (Periods: Base 1, Base 2)

S3. Cornering. On a curbed street with a clean surface and 90-degree turns, practice cornering techniques: lean both bike and body into turn, lean body while keeping bike upright, and keep body upright while leaning bike. Avoid streets with heavy traffic. Practice several speeds with different angles of approach. Include two or three sprint efforts into the turn. Heart rate and power ratings are not important for this workout. (Periods: Base 3, Build 1, Build 2)

S4. Bumping. On a firm, grassy field practice making body contact with a partner while riding slowly. Increase speed as skill improves. Also include touching overlapped wheels. (Periods: Base 3, Build 1, Build 2)

Thomas Craven, Lance Armstrong, George Hincapie, Fred Rodriguez, Djamolidin Abdujaparov and the peloton riding shoulder to shoulder in the 1995 Tour DuPont. Close-quarters racing is a skill that must be developed in novice riders.

S5. Form Sprints. Early in a ride, do 6-10 sprints on a slight downhill or with a tail wind. Each sprint lasts about 15 seconds with a five-minute recovery. These sprints are done for form, so hold back a bit on intensity. Heart rate is not an accurate gauge. Power/RPE should be in the 5b zone. Stand for the first 10 seconds while running smoothly on the pedals building leg speed. Then sit for 5 seconds and maintain a high cadence. Best done alone to avoid "competing." (Periods: Base 3, Build 1, Build 2, Peak, Race)

S6. Sprints. Within an aerobic ride, include several 10- to 15-second, race-effort sprints. These can be done with another rider or with a group. Designate sprint primes such as signs. Employ all of the techniques of form sprints, only now at a higher intensity. Power/RPE should be 5c zone. Heart rate is not a good indicator. There should be at least five minutes recovery between sprints. (Periods: Build 1, Build 2, Peak, Race)

MUSCULAR-ENDURANCE WORKOUTS

M1. Tempo. On a mostly flat course, or on an indoor trainer, ride in the 3 zone for an extended time without recovery. Avoid roads with heavy traffic and stop signs. Stay in an aerodynamic position throughout. Start with 20 to 30 minutes and build to 75 to 90 minutes by adding 10 to 15 minutes each week. This workout may be done two or three times weekly. (Periods: Base 2, Base 3)

M2. Cruise Intervals. On a relatively flat course, or an indoor trainer, complete three to five work intervals that are six to 12 minutes long. Build to the 4 and 5a zones on each work interval. If training with a heart rate monitor, the work interval starts as soon as you begin pedaling hard — not when you reach the 4 zone. Recover for two or three minutes after each. Recovery should be into the 2 zone. The first workout should total about 20 minutes of work intervals if on a trainer, or 30-40 minutes if on the road. Stay relaxed, aerodynamic, and closely listen to your breathing. (Periods: Base 3, Build 1, Build 2, Peak, Race)

M3. Hill Cruise Intervals. Same as M2 cruise intervals, except that you do them on a long 2-4% grade. These are good if strength is a limiter. (Periods: Build 1, Build 2, Peak, Race)

M4. Motorpaced Cruise Intervals. Same as M2 cruise intervals, except that you do this as a motorpaced workout. Whenever doing motorpace use only a motorcycle for pacing. Do not use a car or truck. Not only do they make the workout too easy, they also make it more dangerous. Be sure the driver of the motorcycle has experience with motorpaced workouts and will always be thinking about your safety. Discuss the workout details with the driver before starting. (Periods: Build 1, Build 2, Peak)

M5. Criss-Cross Threshold. On a mostly flat course with little traffic and no stops, ride 20 to 40 minutes in the 4 and 5a zones. Once you have reached the 4 zone, gradually build effort to the top of the 5a zone taking about two minutes to do so. Then begin backing off slightly and slowly drop back to the bottom of the 4 zone taking about two minutes again. Continue this pattern throughout the ride. Complete three or four cruise interval workouts before doing this workout. (Periods: Build 2, Peak)

M6. Threshold. On a mostly flat course with little traffic and no stops, ride 20 to 40 minutes non-stop in the 4 and 5a zones. Stay relaxed, aerodynamic, and closely listen to your breathing throughout. Don't attempt a threshold ride until you've completed at least four cruise interval workouts. This workout definitely should be included in your training. (Periods: Build 2, Peak)

M7. Motorpaced Threshold. Same as M6 threshold, except done as a motorpaced workout. (Periods: Build 2, Peak, Race)

SPEED-ENDURANCE (ANAEROBIC) WORKOUTS

A1. Group Ride. Ride how you feel. If tired, sit in or break off and ride by yourself. If fresh, ride hard going into the 5b zone several times. (Periods: Build 1, Build 2, Peak, Race)

A2. SE Intervals. After a good warm-up, on a mostly flat course with no stop signs and light traffic, do five work intervals of three- to six-minutes duration each. Build to the 5b zone on each. If unable to achieve the 5b zone by the end of the third work interval, stop the workout. You aren't ready. Recover to the 1 zone for the same time as the preceding work interval. (Periods: Build 1, Build 2, Peak, Race)

A3. Pyramid Intervals. The same as SE intervals, except the work intervals are 1-, 2-, 3-, 4-, 4-, 3-, 2-, 1-minutes building to the 5b zone. The recovery after each is equal to the preceding work interval. (Periods: Build 1, Build 2, Peak, Race)

A4. Hill Intervals. Following a thorough warm-up, go to a 6-8% hill that takes three to four minutes to go up and do five climbs. Stay seated with cadence at 60 or higher rpm. Build to the 5b zone on each. Recover to the 1 zone by spinning down the hill and at the bottom for a total of three to four minutes depending on how long the climb is. (Periods: Build 2, Peak)

A5. Lactate Tolerance Reps. This is to be done on a flat or slightly uphill course or into the wind. After a long warm-up and several jumps, do four to eight repetitions of 90 seconds to two minutes each. Intensity is 5c zone. The total of all work intervals must not exceed 12 minutes. Recovery intervals are 2.5 times as long as the preceding work interval. For example, after a two-minute rep, recover for five minutes. Build to this workout conservatively starting with six minutes total and adding no more than two minutes weekly. Do this workout no more than once a week and recover for at least 48 hours after. If you are unable to achieve the 5c zone after three attempts, stop the workout. Do not do this workout if you are in the first two years of training for cycling. (Periods: Build 2, Peak)

A6. Hill Reps. After a good warm-up, go to a 6-8% hill and do four to eight reps of 90 seconds each. Stay seated for the first 60 seconds as you build to the 5b zone. In the last 30 seconds, shift to a higher gear, stand, and drive the bike to the top attaining the 5c zone. Recover completely for four minutes after each rep. If you are unable to achieve the 5c zone after three attempts, stop the workout. Do not do this workout if you are in the first two years of training for cycling. (Periods: Build 2, Peak)

POWER WORKOUTS

P1. Jumps. Warm-up well. Then early in a workout, on an indoor trainer or the road, do 15-25 jumps to improve explosive power. Complete three to five sets of five jumps each. Each jump is 10 to 12 revolutions of the cranks (each leg). Recover for one minute between efforts and five minutes between sets. Power/RPE should be zone 5c. Heart rate is not a good indicator of exertion for this workout. (Periods: Build 1, Build 2, Peak, Race)

P2. Hill Sprints. Early in the workout, after a good warm-up, go to a hill with a 4-6% grade. Do six to nine sprints of 20 seconds each. Use a flying start for each sprint taking 10 seconds to build speed on the flat approach while standing. Climb the hill for 10 seconds applying maximal force standing on the pedals with a high cadence. Recover for five minutes after each sprint. Power/RPE should be zone 5c. Heart rate is not a good indicator of exertion for this workout. (Periods: Build 1, Build 2, Peak)

P3. Crit Sprints. Warm-up and then go to a course with curbed corners, clean turns, and little traffic. Do six to nine sprints of 25-35 seconds duration including corners just as in a criterium. Recover to the 1 zone for five minutes after each. Can be done with another rider taking turns leading the sprints. (Periods: Build 2, Peak, Race)

TEST WORKOUTS

T1. Aerobic Time Trial. This is best on an indoor trainer with a rear-wheel computer pick-up, or on a CompuTrainer. May also be done on a flat section of road, but weather conditions will have an effect. After a warm-up, ride five miles with heart rate nine to 11 beats below lactate threshold heart rate. Use a standard gear without shifting. Record time. The conditions of this workout must be as similar as possible from one test to the next. This includes the amount of rest since the last BT workout, the length and intensity of the warm-up, the weather if on the road, and the gear used during the test. As aerobic fitness improves, the time should decrease. (Periods: Base 1, Base 2)

T2. Time Trial. After a 15- to 30-minute warm-up, complete an eight-mile time trial on a flat course. Go four miles out, turn around, and return to the start line. Mark your start and turn for later reference. Look for faster times as your speed-endurance and muscular-endurance improve. In addition to time, record average power/heart rate and peak power/heart rate. Keep the conditions the same from one time trial to the next as in the aerobic time trial. Use any gear and feel free to shift during the test. (Periods: Build 1, Build 2)

WEEKLY ROUTINES

Now that your Annual Training Plan is complete, the only issue left to decide is the weekly routine — on what day to do which workout and how long each is. That's no small thing. You could have the best possible plan, but if you do not blend workouts in such a way as to allow for recovery and adaptation, then it's all for nothing. The problem is that you must blend both long and short duration workouts with workouts that are of high and low intensity.

Chapter 15 will provide you with a weekly training journal on which to record the days' scheduled workouts and their results. For now, let's examine ways to determine each day's routine.

Figure 9.1

Weekly Training Patterns

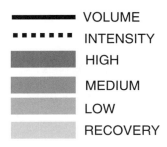

	VOLUME
	INTENSITY
	HIGH
	MEDIUM
	LOW
	RECOVERY

PREP

	M	T	W	Th	F	Sa	Su
Workout options by code	OFF E1	E2	S1	E2	OFF E1	E2	E2

BASE 1

	M	T	W	Th	F	Sa	Su
Workout options by code	OFF E1	E2	E2	E2	S1 S2	E2	E2

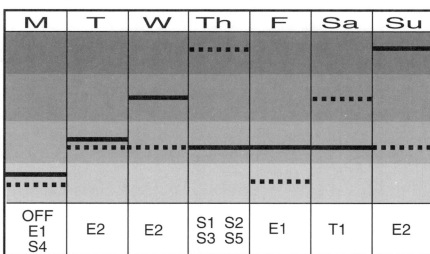

BASE 2

	M	T	W	Th	F	Sa	Su
Workout options by code	OFF E1	E3 M1	E2	E2	S1 S2	E2	E2

BASE 3

	M	T	W	Th	F	Sa	Su
Workout options by code	OFF E1 S4	M1 M2	E2	E3 S1 S3 S5	E2	F1 F2	E2

BASE R&R WEEK

	M	T	W	Th	F	Sa	Su
Workout options by code	OFF E1 S4	E2	E2	S1 S2 S3 S5	E1	T1	E2

BUILD 1

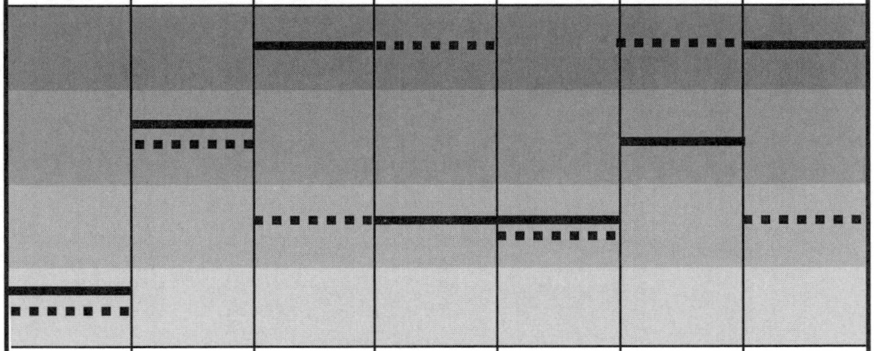

M	T	W	Th	F	Sa	Su
OFF E1 S4	M2 M3 F2 F3	E1 E2	P1 S6 A1 A2 A3	S3 S5	CRIT M4 A1	E1 E2

Workout options by code

BUILD 2

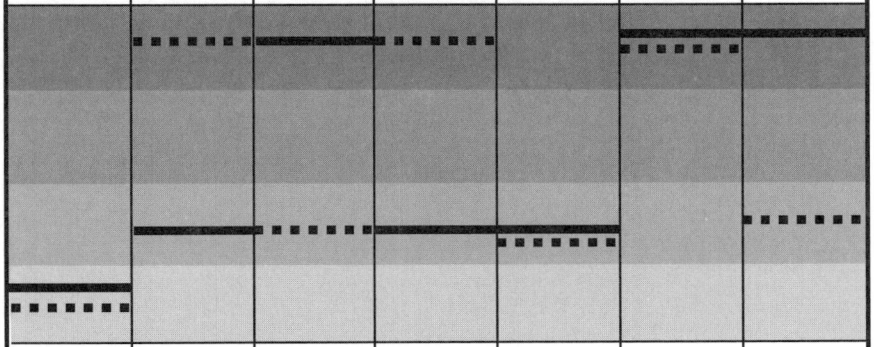

M	T	W	Th	F	Sa	Su
OFF E1 S4	M2 M3 M4 M5 M6 F3	E1 E2	S6 A5 A1 A6 A2 P1 A3 P2 A4 P3	S3 S5	RR M7 A1	E1 E2

Workout options by code

BUILD R&R WEEK

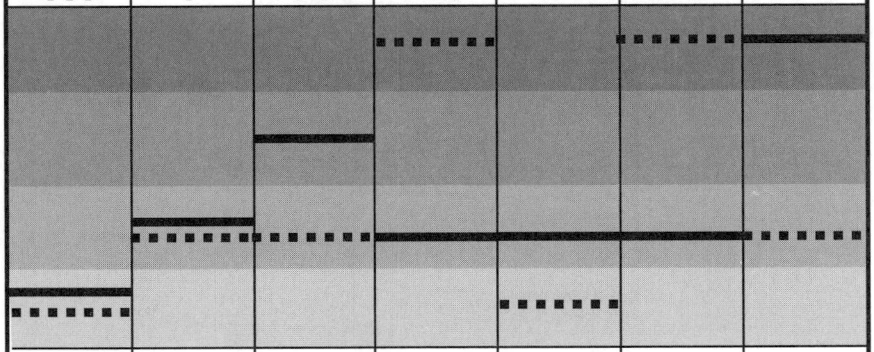

M	T	W	Th	F	Sa	Su
OFF E1 S4	E2	E2	S1 S2 S3 S5	E1	T2	E2

Workout options by code

M	T	W	Th	F	Sa	Su

PEAK

Workout options by code

OFF E1	E2	F3 A2 P1 M2 A3 P2 M3 A4 P3 M5 A5 S6 M6 A6	E1 E2	E2 S5	E2	CRIT M4 M7 A1 A2

M	T	W	Th	F	Sa	Su

RACE (A or B) on SUNDAY

Workout options by code

OFF E1	F3 M2 M3 A2 A3	E1 E2	S6 P1 P3	E1 E2 S5	S6 P1	RACE M7 A1

M	T	W	Th	F	Sa	Su

RACE (A or B) on SAT.

Workout options by code

OFF E1	E2	S6 P1 P3	E1 E2 S5	S6 P1	RACE M7 A1	E1 E2

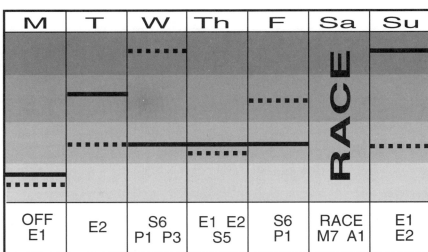

	M	T	W	Th	F	Sa	Su

RACE (A or B) on SAT. and SUN.

Workout options by code	OFF E1	E2	S6 P1 P3	E1 E2 S5	S6 P1	RACE	RACE

PATTERNS

Figure 9.1 illustrates a suggested pattern for blending volume and intensity for each week of the training periods plus the R & R and race weeks. Volume and intensity are indicated as high, medium and low, or recovery. Obviously, what is high for one cyclist may be low for another, so these levels are meaningful only to you. Recovery days may be active recovery (on the bike), or passive (complete rest) depending on your experience level.

Notice in the Base period that volume is high or medium, four times each week, while intensity is either medium or low, except for Base 3 when one high intensity day is included. Also note in the Build period that intensity increases and volume decreases. In Build 2 there are no moderate workouts — everything is either high or low. The reason for this is to allow for adequate recovery since there is so much high intensity during this period. In Build 2, both high volume and high intensity are combined once each week for the first time. Training in this period takes on many of the characteristics of racing.

Figure 9.1 also suggests a blending of volume and intensity for A- and B-race weeks. Of course, A-race weeks immediately follow a Peak period or a previous Race period week, so rest would be greater. B-race weeks would not necessarily have that advantage.

Workouts are suggested for each day by the alpha-numeric codes used in the "Workout Menu" section. Strength training has not been included in the suggested weekly patterns since some lift three times per week and others only twice. Also, some riders, such as masters, may lift year round, while others will stop once the racing begins. It is best to substitute a strength workout for an "E" or "EZ." Weights are best the day after a long or "BT" workout. Try to avoid doing weights the day before a "BT."

DAILY HOURS

In the Hours column of your Annual Training Plan, you've indicated the volume for each week of the season. All that remains is to decide how those hours should be spread during the week. Table 9.1 offers a suggested break down. In the left-hand column, find the hours you've scheduled for the first week of the season. By reading across to the right, the weekly hours are broken into daily amounts. For example, find 12:00 in the Weekly Hours column. To the right are seven daily hours — one for each day of the week. In this case, 3:00, 2:30, 2:00, 2:00, 1:30, 1:00 and Off. So, the long workout that week is three hours. You should do this as a continuous ride — not as two workouts of 1:30 each. The other daily hours may be divided between two workouts in the same day, especially in the Base period when volume is high. In fact, there are some advantages to working out two times a day, such as an increase in quality for each workout.

When it comes time to schedule hours for a given week, use Table 9.1 along with Figure 9.1 to assign high, medium and low volumes for each day of the week.

Table 9.1 Daily Training Hours

Weekly Hours	Long Ride	May be two-a-day workouts					
3:00	1:30	0:45	0:45	Off	Off	Off	Off
3:30	1:30	1:00	1:00	Off	Off	Off	Off
4:00	1:30	1:00	1:00	0:30	Off	Off	Off
4:30	1:45	1:00	1:00	0:45	Off	Off	Off
5:00	2:00	1:00	1:00	1:00	Off	Off	Off
5:30	2:00	1:30	1:00	1:00	Off	Off	Off
6:00	2:00	1:00	1:00	1:00	1:00	Off	Off
6:30	2:00	1:30	1:00	1:00	1:00	Off	Off
7:00	2:00	1:30	1:30	1:00	1:00	Off	Off
7:30	2:30	1:30	1:30	1:00	1:00	Off	Off
8:00	2:30	1:30	1:30	1:30	1:00	Off	Off
8:30	2:30	2:00	1:30	1:30	1:00	Off	Off
9:00	3:00	2:00	1:30	1:30	1:00	Off	Off
9:30	3:00	2:00	1:30	1:30	1:00	0:30	Off
10:00	3:00	2:00	1:30	1:30	1:00	1:00	Off
10:30	3:00	2:00	2:00	1:30	1:00	1:00	Off
11:00	3:00	2:00	2:00	1:30	1:30	1:00	Off
11:30	3:00	2:30	2:00	1:30	1:30	1:00	Off
12:00	3:00	2:30	2:00	2:00	1:30	1:00	Off
12:30	3:30	2:30	2:00	2:00	1:30	1:00	Off
13:00	3:30	3:00	2:00	2:00	1:30	1:00	Off
13:30	3:30	3:00	2:30	2:00	1:30	1:00	Off
14:00	4:00	3:00	2:30	2:00	1:30	1:00	Off
14:30	4:00	3:00	2:30	2:30	1:30	1:00	Off
15:00	4:00	3:00	3:00	2:30	1:30	1:00	Off
15:30	4:00	3:00	3:00	2:30	2:00	1:00	Off
16:00	4:00	3:30	3:00	2:30	2:00	1:00	Off
16:30	4:00	3:30	3:00	3:00	2:00	1:00	Off
17:00	4:00	3:30	3:00	3:00	2:00	1:30	Off
17:30	4:00	4:00	3:00	3:00	2:00	1:30	Off
18:00	4:00	4:00	3:00	3:00	2:30	1:30	Off
18:30	4:30	4:00	3:00	3:00	2:30	1:30	Off
19:00	4:30	4:30	3:00	3:00	2:30	1:30	Off
19:30	4:30	4:30	3:30	3:00	2:30	1:30	Off
20:00	4:30	4:30	3:30	3:00	2:30	2:00	Off
20:30	4:30	4:30	3:30	3:30	2:30	2:00	Off
21:00	5:00	4:30	3:30	3:30	3:30	2:00	Off
21:30	5:00	4:30	4:00	3:30	2:30	2:00	Off
22:00	5:00	4:30	4:00	3:30	3:00	2:00	Off
22:30	5:00	4:30	4:00	3:30	3:00	2:30	Off
23:00	5:00	5:00	4:00	3:30	3:00	2:30	Off
23:30	5:30	5:00	4:00	3:30	3:00	2:30	Off
24:00	5:30	5:00	4:30	3:30	3:00	2:30	Off
24:30	5:30	5:00	4:30	4:00	3:00	2:30	Off
25:00	5:30	5:00	4:30	4:00	3:00	3:00	Off
25:30	5:30	5:30	4:30	4:00	3:00	3:00	Off
26:00	6:00	5:30	4:30	4:00	3:00	3:00	Off
26:30	6:00	5:30	5:00	4:00	3:00	3:00	Off
27:00	6:00	6:00	5:00	4:00	3:00	3:00	Off
27:30	6:00	6:00	5:00	4:00	3:30	3:00	Off
28:00	6:00	6:00	5:00	4:00	3:30	3:30	Off
28:30	6:00	6:00	5:00	4:30	3:30	3:30	Off
29:00	6:00	6:00	5:30	4:30	3:30	3:30	Off
29:30	6:00	6:00	6:00	4:30	3:30	3:30	Off
30:00	6:00	6:00	6:00	4:30	4:00	3:30	Off
30:30	6:00	6:00	6:00	5:00	4:00	3:30	Off
31:00	6:00	6:00	6:00	5:00	4:00	4:00	Off
31:30	6:00	6:00	6:00	5:00	4:30	4:00	Off
32:00	6:00	6:00	6:00	5:30	4:30	4:00	Off
32:30	6:00	6:00	6:00	5:30	4:30	4:30	Off
33:00	6:00	6:00	6:00	5:30	5:00	4:30	Off
33:30	6:00	6:00	6:00	6:00	5:00	4:30	Off
34:00	6:00	6:00	6:00	6:00	5:30	4:30	Off
34:30	6:00	6:00	6:00	6:00	5:30	5:00	Off
35:00	6:00	6:00	6:00	6:00	6:00	5:00	Off

Table 9.1

Daily training hours

REFERENCES

Birkholz, D. (ed). *Training Skills*, United States Cycling Federation, 1991.

Bompa, T. Physiological intensity values employed to plan endurance training, *New Studies in Athletics*, vol. 3(4), pp. 37-52, 1988.

Borysewicz, E. *Bicycle Road Racing*, VeloNews, 1985.

Burke, E. *Serious Cycling*, Human Kinetics, 1995.

Daniels, J., et al. Interval training and performance, *Sports Medicine.* vol. 1, pp. 327-334, 1984.

Faria, I.E. Applied physiology of cycling, *Sports Medicine*, vol. 1, pp. 187-204, 1984.

Knuttgen, H.G., et al. Physical conditioning through interval training with young male adults, *Medicine and Science in Sports*, vol. 5, pp. 220-226, 1973.

Okkels, T. The effect of interval- and tempo-training on performance and skeletal muscle in well-trained runners, *Twelfth European Track Coaches Congress*, Acoteias, Portugal, pp. 1-9, 1983.

Maglischo, E.W. *Swimming Faster*, Palo Alto, CA: Mayfield Publishing Co., 1982.

Phinney, D., and C. Carpenter. *Training for Cycling*, Perigee Books, 1992.

USA Cycling, Inc. *Expert Level Coaching Manual*, USA Cycling, Inc., 1995.

VanHandel, P.J. Specificity of training: Establishing pace, frequency, and duration of training sessions, *Bike Tech*, vol. 6(3), pp. 6-12, 1987.

Zappe, D.H. and T. Bauer. Planning competitive season training for road cycling, *Conditioning for Cycling*, vol. 1(2), pp. 4-8, 1991.

Chapter 10

STAGE RACE TRAINING

It matters not whether you win or lose;
what matters is whether I win or lose.

— DARIN WEINBERG

For the serious cyclist, a stage race is often the most important event of the year. With a season made up mostly of one-hour crits and 60-or-so-mile circuit races, few riders are ready to take on five or more days of back-to-back races including time trials, 90-minute criteriums, 75-mile circuits and 100-mile road races in the mountains. Throw in the toughest competitors in the region, prize money and crowds, and it's easy to see why stage races are often the high point of the season and the ultimate measure of a road racer.

Separate stage races into two broad categories for training purposes — short events with four or fewer stages and long events with five or more stages. Short stage races require no specific preparation for the cyclist who frequently competes in two races on the same weekend. Long stage races, however, are a whole different game demanding exceptional raw endurance, muscular-endurance and usually strength for climbing. Combine that with the need to recover quickly in order to be ready for the next stage and it's easy to see why long stage races have such a high attrition rate. It's survival of the fittest.

Training to race well in a long stage race requires a focused six- to eight-week training program to prepare for the unique stresses. Stage races not only require a rider's fitness to be at peak, but recovery methods must also be perfected. All of

The Training Bible

this, of course, happens within the context of an on-going weekly race schedule.

It is important not to take race preparation lightly. The stress resulting from high volume, intensity and short recoveries threatens health, fitness, work performance and family relations. Overtraining is a definite possibility. Approach this training with great caution.

The start of stage 1 of the 1996 Tour DuPont, America's foremost stage race. Training for a long stage race requires six to eight weeks of concentrated preparation.

CRASH CYCLES

Training for a long stage race is much like doing a short-stage race several times in the weeks building to the event. High quality workouts are gradually brought closer together with the purpose of overloading the body's systems. That results in a delay in recovery, further increasing the stress load. This process is sometimes called "crashing" — a descriptive, if somewhat threatening title.

With the inclusion of a recovery week, there is a greater-than-normal training adaptation known as "supercompensation."

Two recent studies have measured supercompensation resulting from crash cycles. In 1992, a group of seven Dutch cyclists crashed for two weeks by increasing their training volume from a normal 12.5 hours per week to 17.5. At the same time, their intense training went from 24 to 63 percent of total training time. The immediate effect was a drop in all aspects of their fitness. But after two weeks of recovering, they realized a six-percent improvement in power, their time trial improved by an average of four percent, and they had less blood lactate at top speed compared with pre-crash levels. Not bad for two weeks of hard training.

A similar study in Dallas put runners through a two-week crash cycle with results similar to the Dutch study, plus an increase in aerobic capacities. Again, it took two weeks following the crash cycle to realize the gains. Other studies suggest an increase in blood volume, greater levels of hormones that cause muscle growth, and an improved ability to metabolize fat result from a high stress crash period and the following supercompensation.

Be careful with crashing. The risk of overtraining rises dramatically during such a build-up. If the typical signs of overtraining appear, such as a greatly changed resting heart rate or feelings of depression, cut back on the intensity of training immediately. High intensity training is more likely to magnify or cause overtraining than is low-intensity work.

Scott McKinley starts the Raleigh time trial of the 1996 Tour DuPont. In stage races, position on the general classification is often determined by time trial results.

PLANNING

Designing a stage race training plan is a complex task — almost as complex as designing an entire season. The key is to decide, just as you did when putting your Annual Training Plan together, what it takes to achieve your goals in the stage race and how those demands match with your own strengths and weaknesses. The key limiters for long stage races typically are endurance, muscular-endurance and strength for climbing. Speed, power and speed-endurance play a lesser part, depending on the number and relative importance of criteriums, which seldom play a role in the outcome on the general classification. The objective of winning a criterium stage, however, would increase the importance of speed-endurance in the preparation period. Otherwise, the amount of endurance work, muscular-endurance and strength training you do will determine your success.

For an A-priority stage race, start by finding out exactly what the stages will be, their order, how much time separates them, the terrain, and what the weather is likely to be — especially heat, humidity and wind. Then try to simulate these conditions as closely as possible during the build-up weeks.

Table 10.1 provides an eight-week stage race build-up emphasizing the above limiters.

This suggested plan assumes that base fitness is well built. That means you have been putting in adequate miles, hills, and strength training, if appropriate, for at least six weeks before starting.

The eight-week stage race preparation schedule looks like this:

Week 1	Build 1	Week 5	Build 2
Week 2	Build 1	Week 6	Recovery
Week 3	Recovery	Week 7	Peak
Week 4	Build 2	Week 8	Race

Notice that quality workouts are clumped together in two Build weeks of high volume and intensity and then followed by a week of recovery. The Build 1 period is not as intense as Build 2, so the first recovery period is only one week. A recovery week and a Peak week follow Build 2, allowing fitness to return and bloom.

Three-week cycles are used instead of the more typical four-week due to the greater accumulated stress and more frequent need for recovery. If there's any question about your readiness for a break through (BT) workout, don't do it. Better to be mentally and physically sharp, but somewhat undertrained, rather than the opposite. As always, when in doubt, do less intensity.

Also, note that the most intense workouts are clumped closer together in Build 2 than in Build 1. This is the basis of crash training — providing increasing dosages of high intensity within short spans of time and then allowing for complete recovery.

Weekly Training Patterns to Prepare for a Stage Race

Figure 10.1

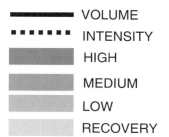

———— VOLUME
▪▪▪▪▪▪▪ INTENSITY
HIGH
MEDIUM
LOW
RECOVERY

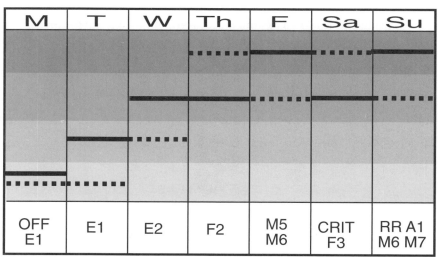

BUILD 1

	M	T	W	Th	F	Sa	Su
Workout options by code	OFF E1	E2	F1	M2	OFF E1	CRIT F2	RR A1 M1 M4

BUILD 2

	M	T	W	Th	F	Sa	Su
Workout options by code	OFF E1	E1	E2	F2	M5 M6	CRIT F3	RR A1 M6 M7

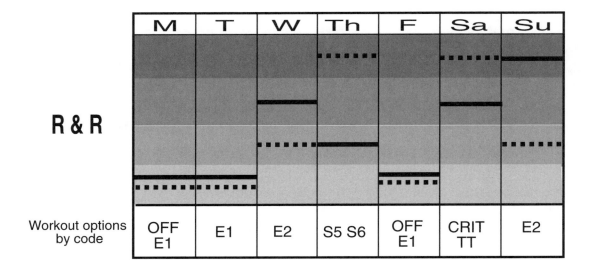

	M	T	W	Th	F	Sa	Su
R & R Workout options by code	OFF E1	E1	E2	S5 S6	OFF E1	CRIT TT	E2

	M	T	W	Th	F	Sa	Su
PEAK Workout options by code	OFF E1	E2	M6 M7	OFF E1	E2 (S6)	CRIT F3	E1

During the Build weeks, be sure to practice recovery techniques following each of the intense workouts. This includes massage, stretching, fuel replacement, elevating legs, high fluid intake, staying off your feet and extra rest (see Chapter 18 for a complete discussion of recovery methods). Find out what works best for you, and be ready to use the best options between stages when it comes time to race. Once you have built your fitness, quick recovery is the key to stage racing.

AFTERWARD

Following the stage race, while the glow of the accomplishment is still fresh, take one or two weeks to transition back into normal training. You've just had a major crash and the body needs to recover from it fully. As always, a Transition period should be a break from structured training that allows the mind and body to recover, rest, and refresh.

If you don't reduce training to allow the body to "catch-up" with all of the stress it has experienced, you are likely to wind up overtrained or burned out. Stage races *must* be treated with respect.

If your endurance was good going into the stage race, you're likely to find that once returning to training your fitness is greater than it was before. That's the supercompensation kicking in. If you finished all the stages, despite questionable endurance, recovery is likely to be longer than two weeks, and you may feel as if you lost fitness. That's called overtraining. This is a good reason not to attempt a stage race until you know you're ready.

REFERENCES

Biological response to overload training in endurance sports, *European Journal of Applied Physiology*, vol. 64, pp. 335-344, 1992.

Borysewicz, E. *Bicycle Road Racing*, VeloNews, 1985.

Costill, D., et al. Effects of repeated days of intensified training on muscle glycogen and swimming performance, *Medicine and Science in Sports and Exercise*, vol. 20(3), pp. 249-254, 1988.

Physiological changes in male competitive cyclists after two weeks of intensified training, *International Journal of Sports Medicine*, vol. 13(7), pp. 534-541, 1992.

Snell, P., et al. Changes in selected parameters during overtraining, *Medicine and Science in Sports and Exercise*, vol. 18, abstract #268, 1986.

Chapter 11

CASE STUDIES

*Few things are harder to put up
with than a good example.*

— MARK TWAIN

As the last few chapters have shown, there is not just one training plan that fits all athletes. Not only do individual abilities vary, but so do goals, time available, race schedules, experience, and on and on. By the time all of these variables are mixed, the resulting schedule could hardly be used by another rider. Training must match the individual's needs.

While it may have seemed easy to design a schedule, there is more to it than that. As I said earlier, training is as much an art as a science. What I've described so far is the science. The schedule you've written is largely based on scientific principles, and will undoubtedly serve your needs well. As you become more experienced at writing your own schedules, however, it will become apparent that bending or even breaking the rules is sometimes necessary to better fit your needs.

This chapter provides examples of designing the plan to match the individual rider's unique needs. The following plans were developed for four very different cyclists. The same steps you used were applied, but each of these athletes had a unique set of circumstances requiring bending the rules in some way.

Fig. 11.1 Annual Training Plan: 1997

Athlete: Tom Brown
Annual Hours: 350
Season Goals:

1. Top 50 finish in National Masters Road Race.
2. Top 25 at Provinicial Masters Road Race.
3. Top 15 G.C. for masters at Tumbler's Classic Stage Race.

Training Objectives:

1. Improve endurance: Start 90% of all workouts scheduled in 1997.
2. Improve confidence: Finish all races by August 4.
3. Improve confidence: Read "Mental Toughness..." by March 3 and use skills.
4. Improve confidence: Higher score on Mental Skills Profile by August 4.
5. Improve muscular-endurance: Increase power on LT test by May 25.

Figure 11.1
Tom Brown's training plan

WORKOUTS

Wk#	Monday	Races	Pri	Period	Hours	Details	Str	End	For	Spd Sk	Musc End	Anaer End	Pwr	Test
01	Jan 6			Prep	6:00	XC SKI	AA	X		X				
02	Jan 13			"	"	" "	"	X		X				
03	Jan 20			"	"	" "	"	X		X				
04	Jan 27			"	"	" "	"	X		X				
05	Feb 3			"	"	" "	"	X		X				
06	Feb 10			"	"	" "	"	X		X				
07	Feb 17			"	"	" "	MS	X		X				
08	Feb 24			"	"	" "	"	X		X				
09	Mar 3			Base 1	7:00		"	X		X				
10	Mar 10			"	8:30		"	X		X				
11	Mar 17			"	9:30		"	X		X				
12	Mar 24			"	5:00	*ATT	"		X					*
13	Mar 31			Base 2	7:30		PE	X		X	X			
14	Apr 7			"	9:00		"	X		X	X			
15	Apr 14			"	10:00		"	X		X	X			
16	Apr 21	Regina RR	C	"	5:00	*Race #ATT	"		X	*				#
17	Apr 28			Base 3	8:00		ME	X	X	X	X			
18	May 5			"	9:30		"	X	X	X	X			
19	May 12			"	10:30		"	X	X	X	X			
20	May 19	Saskatoon RR	C	"	5:00	*Race #LT Test	"		X	X	*			#
21	May 26			Build 1	9:00		"	X	X	X	X			
22	Jun 2			"	"		"	X	X	X	X			
23	Jun 9	Regina RR	C	"	"	*Race	"	X	X	X	*			
24	Jun 16			"	5:00	*TT Test	PE		X					*
25	Jun 23	Race Across Saskatchewan	B	Build 2	8:30	*Race	"	X	X		*	X		
26	Jun 30	Prince Albert S.R.	B	"	"	*Race	ME	X			*	*		
27	Jul 7			"	"		"	X	X		X	X		
28	Jul 14			"	5:00	*TT Test	"		X					*
29	Jul 21	Canada Cup RR	C	Peak	7:30	*Race	"				*	X		
30	Jul 28			"	6:00		PE				X	X		
31	Aug 4	Tumbler's Classic S.R.	A	Race	5:00	*Race	O				*	*		
32	Aug 11	Provincial Championships	A	"	"	*Race	O				*	X		
33	Aug 18			"	7:00		PE	X	X			X		
34	Aug 25	Nationals RR	A	"	5:00	*Race	O		X			*		
35	Sep 1			"	6:00		PE	X	X			X		
36	Sep 8	Harvest Century	B	"	"	*Race	O		X			*		
37	Sep 15			Tran	5:00		O	X		X				
38	Sep 22			"	"		O	X		X				
39	Sep 29			"	"		O	X		X				
40	Oct 6			"	"		O	X		X				
41	Oct 13			Prep	6:00	XC SKI	O	X		X				
42	Oct 20			"	"	" "	O	X		X				
43	Oct 27			"	"	" "	O	X		X				
44	Nov 3			"	"	" "	O	X		X				
45	Nov 10			"	"	" "	O	X		X				
46	Nov 17			"	"	" "	O	X		X				
47	Nov 24			"	"	" "	O	X		X				
48	Dec 1			"	"	" "	O	X		X				
49	Dec 8			"	"	" "	O	X		X				
50	Dec 15			"	"	" "	O	X		X				
51	Dec 22			"	"	" "	O	X		X				
52	Dec 29			"	"	" "	O	X		X				

CASE STUDY 1: SINGLE-PEAK SEASON

PROFILE

Tom Brown, 39, is a sales manager for an electronics retail store. He works six days weekly, averaging more than 50 hours a week. Married with two daughters, ages 8 and 10, Tom is in his third year of racing. He races with masters, mostly in road races as he is uncomfortable with the high speed cornering of criteriums. In his first two years, he was satisfied with simply finishing road races, but at the end of the previous season he began to see improvement, probably due to increased endurance.

Tom's greatest limiter for cycling is endurance, due primarily to many missed workouts in the past two years. His job promises to place fewer demands on his time this season, and he has a greater commitment to riding consistently now. With regular training, his endurance will undoubtedly improve.

The Mental Skills Profile pointed out that lack of confidence is a serious limiter for Tom. Even though he set goals around three of the biggest races he could participate in, he lacks confidence when talking about them. Testing revealed that he has the ability to achieve the goals, which seemed to bolster his self-esteem. He has been asked to read *Mental Toughness Training for Sports*, by James Loehr (Stephen Greene Press, 1982) and apply the techniques. In August, he will repeat the Mental Skills Profile.

His maximum power tested high, but his power at lactate threshold was relatively low. He is limited by low muscular-endurance, a major weakness when it comes to road racing.

PLAN

Due to the weather in Regina, Saskatchewan, where Tom lives, training in the winter is difficult at best. He prefers to cross country ski from October through February rather than ride an indoor trainer. He participates in a few ski races, mostly in the late winter, which in Regina extends into March. Winter is also the busiest time of year for his business, so he has less time to train then. His Annual Training Plan, illustrated in Figure 10.1, projects a longer-than-normal Preparation period for these reasons.

I encouraged Tom to train more than the six-hour weeks scheduled through the winter Preparation period whenever he could. As this will be mostly on skis, I suggested he get on the trainer once or twice each week to do speed drills.

Since the road racing season is so short in Regina, and all of Tom's A races are clumped near the end of the season, there is only one Peak period. Notice that in weeks 33 and 35 hours are increased and endurance workouts are included. This change to the usual Race period layout is to help prepare for a century in week 36. By that week his speed-endurance will be better suited for 50-mile road races than for 100-mile efforts, so the century will be done at a conservative speed.

CASE STUDY 2: LOTS OF TIME — AND LIMITERS

PROFILE

Lisa Harvey is a 27-year-old Category II who has been racing for four years. She works full time as an engineer with an aeronautics company in the Phoenix, Arizona, area. She usually puts in 45 hours per week on the job and has weekends off. She lives with a roommate and has few family or community-related commitments and is able to ride with few restrictions on her time. Her training in the past was free form — she did what she wanted, when she wanted, if she wanted. As a result, many of the basic abilities are weak.

Lisa has good power due primarily to her ability to turn the cranks at high cadence. She has always been a good sprinter. Her limiters are strength, climbing and muscular-endurance. Her endurance is not as bad as the other limiters, but nevertheless it needs improving as well.

PLAN

While someone of Lisa's age with few restrictions on her time should be able to train on a 500-annual hour basis, she has broken down frequently over the past two years with colds and sore throats. It may be due to her habit of piling on too many hard workouts without adequate rest. Diet is also suspect. She trained about 400 hours last year, based on her records, so she will start at the same level. Her ability to cope with a structured training regimen that includes frequent recovery and rest should allow her to avoid such problems. At the end of Base 2, we will evaluate her capacity for handling the workload to that point and increase the volume if it seems manageable.

Lisa has two Race periods planned, the first in June lasting five weeks, and the second in September. There will be a short Transition period following the first Race period to allow her to recover in order to reach a higher peak later on. With

Figure 11.2

Lisa Harvey's training plan

Fig. 11.2   Annual Training Plan: 1997

Athlete: Lisa Harvey

Annual Hours: 400

Season Goals:

1. Break 1:04 at State TT.
2. Finish in top 20 at La Vuelta S.R.
3. Finish in top 15 at State RR.

Training Objectives:

1. Improve climbing: Climb South Mountain in less than 32 minutes by May 25.
2. Improve muscular-endurance: Complete 40-min threshold workout by May 11.
3. Improve endurance: Complete at least five 10+ hour training weeks by Mar 16
4. Improve strength: Increase all max lifts by at least 15% by Feb 16.

WORKOUTS

Wk#	Monday	Races	Pri	Period	Hours	Details	Strength	Endurance	Speed Skills	Muscular Endurance	Anaerobic Endurance	Power	Testing
01	Jan 6			Base 1	10:30		MS	X	X				
02	Jan 13			"	5:30	*ATT	"		X				*
03	Jan 20			Base 2	8:30		"	X	X	X			
04	Jan 27			"	10:00		"	X	X	X			
05	Feb 3			"	11:00		"	X	X	X			
06	Feb 10			"	5:30	*Test max strngth	"		X				*
07	Feb 17			Base 3	9:00		PE	X	X	X	X		
08	Feb 24			"	10:30		"	X	X	X	X		
09	Mar 3			"	11:30		"	X	X	X	X		
10	Mar 10			"	5:30	*ATT	"		X				*
11	Mar 17			Build 1	10:00		ME	X	X	X	X		
12	Mar 24	Arrowhead RR	C	"	"	*Race	"	X	X	X	X	*	
13	Mar 31			"	"		"	X	X	X	X		
14	Apr 7			"	5:30	*Time Trial Test	"		X				*
15	Apr 14	Congress-Yarnell RR	C	Build 2	9:30	*Race	"	X	X		*	X	
16	Apr 21			"	"		"	X	X		X	X	
17	Apr 28	Fountain Hills RR	C	"	"	*Race	"	X	X		*	X	
18	May 5	Festival RR	C	"	5:30	* "	"		X		*		
19	May 12			Peak	7:30		PE		X	X	X		
20	May 19			"	6:00		"		X	X	X		
21	May 26	La Vuelta SR	A	Race	5:30	*Race	O		X		*	*	
22	Jun 2	Thunder Road TT	B	"	"	* "	ME		X		*	X	
23	Jun 9	Climb to the Stars TT	B	"	"	* "	"		X		*	X	
24	Jun 16	Grand Canyon State RR	B	"	"	* "	"		X		*	X	
25	Jun 23	Wupatki RR	A	"	"	* "	O		X		*	X	
26	Jun 30			Tran	"		O	X	X				
27	Jul 7	High Country RR	C	Build 1	10:00	*Race	PE	X	X	X	*		
28	Jul 14			"	"		"	X	X	X	X		
29	Jul 21			"	"		ME	X	X	X	X		
30	Jul 28			"	5:30	*Time Trial Test	"		X				*
31	Aug 4			Build 2	9:30		"	X	X		X	X	
32	Aug 11	Falcon Field Crit	C	"	"	*Race	"	X	X		X	*	
33	Aug 18	Road to Nowhere TT	B	"	5:30	* "	PE		X		*		
34	Aug 25			Peak	7:30		"	X	X		X		
35	Sep 1			"	6:00		ME	X			X		
36	Sep 8	State TT	A	Race	5:30	*Race	O		X		*	X	
37	Sep 15	State RR	A	"	"	* "	O		X		*	X	
38	Sep 22			"	7:30		ME	X		X	X	X	
39	Sep 29			"	6:00		"	X		X	X	X	
40	Oct 6	Mt Graham RR	C	"	5:30	*Race	"		X		*	X	
41	Oct 13			Tran	"		O	X		X			
42	Oct 20			"	"		O	X		X			
43	Oct 27			"	"		O	X		X			
44	Nov 3			"	"		O	X		X			
45	Nov 10			"	"		O	X		X			
46	Nov 17			"	"		O	X		X			
47	Nov 24			Prep	7:00		AA	X		X			
48	Dec 1			"	"		"	X		X			
49	Dec 8			"	"		"	X		X			
50	Dec 15			"	"	*ATT	"	X		X			*
51	Dec 22			Base 1	8:00		"	X		X			
52	Dec 29			"	9:30		"	X		X			

only seven weeks following this Transition to the start of the second Peak, Build 2 was shortened by one week. The recovery week was, of course, not removed. Build 1 was left intact, as her basic abilities need more time to develop.

In this seven-week Build period, there will undoubtedly be other races that weren't known of when she drafted the plan. She can substitute these for workouts.

The last Race period is five weeks finishing with a C race — the last race of the season. There's no reason with only three weeks remaining in the race season following the state road race in week 37 to try to build to a higher level of fitness. Therefore, Lisa's C race is being treated like an A race, except more endurance work is added in the preceding two weeks.

CASE STUDY #3: THREE RACE PEAKS
PROFILE

Sam Crooks, 37, is a dentist in Johnson City, Tennessee. He is married and has two children by a former marriage who sometimes spend the weekend with him and his wife. When the kids are visiting, Sam reduces his training and racing schedule in order to spend more time with them.

Sam is a Category III and has been racing for four years in both Category III and masters races. He mostly competes in criteriums. He is dedicated to racing and training and fits in workouts whenever he can around his busy schedule. This means training on lunch hours and before and after work. He rarely misses a workout.

Maximum power and speed are Sam's strong points, making him an excellent criterium racer, but his marginal endurance, climbing and muscular-endurance limit his performance when it comes to road races and time trials. He has what it takes to win the district masters criterium, but will be taken to his limits with his goals of a top-five finish in the Johnson City Stage Race and a top-20 at the Greenville Road Race.

PLAN

Sam has a long season with races starting in early March and extending into mid-October. His A races are widely separated with one in late May, a pair in July, and the last in October. Because of this spread, I scheduled Sam for three Race peri-

Figure 11.3

Sam Crooks training plan

Fig. 11.3   Annual Training Plan: 1997

Athlete: Sam Crocks
Annual Hours: 500
Season Goals:

1. Win District Masters Criterium.
2. Top-5 at Johnson City Stage Race.
3. Top-20 at Greenville Road Race.

Training Objectives:

1. Improve climbing strength: Increase squat by 20% by Jan. 12.
2. Improve muscular-endurance: A sub-57-minute 40k at District TT.
3. Improve endurance: Train on a 500-annual hour schedule.

WORKOUTS

Wk#	Monday	Races	Pri	Period	Hours	Details	Str						Test
01	Jan 6			Base 1	7:00	*ATT, Test squat	MS		X				*
02	Jan 13			Base 2	10:30		PE	X	X	X			
03	Jan 20			"	12:30		"	X	X	X			
04	Jan 27			"	14:00		"	X	X	X			
05	Feb 3			"	7:00	*ATT	"		X				*
06	Feb 10			Base 3	11:00		ME	X	X	X	X		
07	Feb 17			"	13:30		"	X	X	X	X		
08	Feb 24	Crossville RR	C	"	15:00	*Race	"	X	X	X	*		
09	Mar 3			"	7:00	*TT	"		X				*
10	Mar 10			Build 1	12:30	///1 Str Ph/wk///	"	X	X	X	X		
11	Mar 17	Anderson Crit	C	"	"	*Race	"	X	X	X		*	
12	Mar 24			"	"		"	X	X	X	X		
13	Mar 31	Korbel Crit	B	"	7:00	*Race	"		X		*		
14	Apr 7			Build 2	12:00		PE	X	X		X	X	
15	Apr 14	Raccoon Mt RR	C	"	"	*Race	"	X	*		*	X	
16	Apr 21	Athens Crit	C	"	"	*Race	ME	X	X		X	*	
17	Apr 28			"	7:00	*TT	"		X				*
18	May 5	McMinnville Crit	B	Peak	10:30	*Race	"	X			X	*	
19	May 12	Drummond Crit	C	"	8:30	* "	"				X	*	
20	May 19	Johnson City SR	A	Race	7:00	* "	O			X	*	*	
21	May 26	District TT	B	"	"	* "	PE			X	*	X	
22	Jun 2	Roann RR	C	Build 1	12:30	* "	"	X	X	X	*		
23	Jun 9	Crossville Crit	B	"	"	* "	ME	X	X		X	*	
24	Jun 16			"	7:00	*TT	"		X				*
25	Jun 23	Charleston Crit	C	Peak	10:30	*Race	"	X			X	X	
26	Jun 30	Murfreesboro Crit	B	"	8:30	* "	"				X	*	
27	Jul 7	District Crit	A	Race	8:00	* "	O	X		X	X	*	
28	Jul 14	Gaffney Crit	B	"	8:00	* "	PE	X		X	X	*	
29	Jul 21	Asheville RR	B	"	7:00	* "	"			X	*	X	
30	Jul 28	Greenville RR	A	"	"	* "	O			X	*	X	
31	Aug 4			Tran	"		O	X		X			
32	Aug 11			Build 1	12:30		ME	X	X	X	X		
33	Aug 18			"	"		"	X	X	X	X		
34	Aug 25			"	7:00	*TT	"		X				*
35	Sep 1			Build 2	12:00		PE	X	X		X	X	
36	Sep 8	Carolina Cup	B	"	"	*Race	"	X	X		X	*	
37	Sep 15			"	"		ME	X	X		X	X	
38	Sep 22	A to Z RR	B	"	7:00	*Race	"			X	*		
39	Sep 29	Apple Dash	C	Peak	10:30	*Race	"				*	X	
40	Oct 6			"	8:30		"				X	X	
41	Oct 13	Michelin Classic Crits	A	Race	7:00	*Race	O			X	X	*	
42	Oct 20			Tran	"		O	X		X			
43	Oct 27			"	"		O	X		X			
44	Nov 3			"	"		O	X		X			
45	Nov 10			"	"		O	X		X			
46	Nov 17			"	"		O	X		X			
47	Nov 24			"	"		O	X		X			
48	Dec 1			Prep	8:30		AA	X		X			
49	Dec 8			"	"		"	X		X			
50	Dec 15			"	"		"	X		X			
51	Dec 22			"	"		"	X		X			
52	Dec 29			Base 1	10:00		"	X		X			

ods. For his first race peak in late May, I decided to maintain his peak for the district time trial in week 21 since he needs to concentrate more on muscular-endurance training. A bit more focus on time trial training will help accomplish that.

The second Race period is followed by a one-week Transition, which comes fairly late in the season. This Transition period may be extended by another three to five days if Sam loses enthusiasm after completing the Greenville Road Race. With a break in the racing and 10 weeks until the next A race, that shouldn't present a problem.

In the second Race period, endurance workouts have been added to weeks 27 and 28, since he will be coming into two road races in weeks 29 and 30 — one is an A race, and endurance is one of his limiters. If the week 27 and 28 criteriums are on Saturdays, he will ride long on the two Sundays. If they're Sunday races, he'll do endurance rides following the races. He has increased his hours for these two weeks to allow for the longer rides.

The last Peak of the season (early October) will be preceded by a four-week Build 2 since the last race is a group of criteriums and we will want to emphasize speed-endurance coming into them. By that point, Sam will have solidly established endurance and muscular-endurance.

After such a long season, Sam may be in need of a longer Transition starting in October, so I've extended it to six weeks.

CASE STUDY #4: SUMMER BASE TRAINING
PROFILE

Randy Stickler, 25, is a college student living in Fort Collins, Colorado. He has been racing since he was 14 and has been on the National team participating as a Category I in several high profile races in the U.S. and in international competition. He carries a full load at Colorado State University majoring in watershed management. Classes and studying limit his available riding time during the week, but on the weekends time is available to train. In the summer, he will be doing an internship that keeps his time to ride somewhat restricted on weekdays.

Randy's greatest abilities are endurance, strength, muscular-endurance, power and climbing. With so much on his side, it's no wonder that he is a

Figure 11.4

Randy Stickler's training plan

Fig. 11.4   Annual Training Plan: 1997

Athlete: Randy Stickler

Annual Hours: 800

Season Goals:

1. Top 10 in G.C. at Bisbee Stage Race.
2. Top 3 at State Road Race Championship.
3. Top 3 in G.C. at Colorado Cyclist Stage Race.

Training Objectives:

1. Improve sprint: Average 800 watts on Power test by 4/20 and again by 9/14.
2. Improve speed-endurance: 5 min anaerobic on LT test by 4/20 and again 9/14.
3. Improve speed-endurance: Average 30 mph for 30 min of SE intervals by 6/8.

Wk#	Monday	Races	Pri	Period	Hours	Details	Strength	Endurance	Speed	Muscular	Power	Testing
01	Jan 6			Base 2	17:00		MS	X		X	X	*
02	Jan 13			"	20:00		PE	X		X	X	
03	Jan 20			"	23:00		"	X		X	X	
04	Jan 27			"	11:30	*ATT	"			X		*
05	Feb 3			Base 3	18:00		"	X	X	X	X	
06	Feb 10			"	21:30		"	X	X	X	X	
07	Feb 17			"	23:30		"	X	X	X	X	
08	Feb 24			"	11:30	*LT & Power Tests	ME			X		*
09	Mar 3	Boulder Crit Series	C	Build 1	20:30	*Race	"	X	X	X	X	*
10	Mar 10	Boulder Crit Series	C	"	"	* "	"	X	X	X	X	*
11	Mar 17			"	11:30	*TT	"			X		*
12	Mar 24	Boulder Crit Series	C	Build 2	20:30	*Race	"	X	X	X	X	*
13	Mar 31	Boulder RR	B	"	"	* "	"	X	X	X		*
14	Apr 7			"	11:30	*TT	O			X		*
15	Apr 14			Peak	13:30	*TT, LT & Power	"			X	X	*
16	Apr 21	Bisbee SR	A	Race	11:30	*Race	"		*	X	*	*
17	Apr 28			Tran	11:30			X	X			
18	May 5	Sunburst Circuit & Crit	C	Build 1	20:30	*Race		X		*	*	
19	May 12	Pueblo Crit	C	"	"	* "		X		X	*	
20	May 19			"	"			X		X	X	
21	May 26	Ironhorse RR	B	"	11:30	*Race				X	*	
22	Jun 2	Meridian Crit	C	Peak	13:30	* "				X	*	
23	Jun 9	State RR Champs	A	Race	11:30	* "			X	X		
24	Jun 16			"	"				X	X		X
25	Jun 23	Mt Evans Hill Climb RR	A	"	"	*Race			*	X		X
26	Jun 30			Tran	"			X	X			
27	Jul 7	Peak to Peak RR	C	Base 3	18:00	*Race		X	X	X	*	
28	Jul 14	Grand Junction RR/Crit	C	"	21:30	* "		X		X	*	*
29	Jul 21			"	23:30			X	X	X	X	
30	Jul 28	Hummel Crit	C	"	11:30	*Race				X		*
31	Aug 4	Coal Miner Crit	C	Build 1	20:30	* "		X		X	*	
32	Aug 11	Black Forest RR	B	"	"	* "		X		*	X	*
33	Aug 18			"	11:30	*TT				X		*
34	Aug 25			Build 2	19:00			X		X	X	X
35	Sep 1	Deer Creek HC	C	"	"	*Race		X	*	X	X	
36	Sep 8			"	11:30	*TT, LT & Power				X		*
37	Sep 15			Peak	17:00					X	X	
38	Sep 22			"	13:30					X	X	
39	Sep 29	Colorado Cyclist SR	A	Race	11:30	*Race			X	X	*	*
40	Oct 6			Tran	"			X	X			
41	Oct 13			"	"			X	X			
42	Oct 20			"	"			X	X			
43	Oct 27			"	"			X	X			
44	Nov 3			Prep	13:30		AA	X	X			
45	Nov 10			"	"		"	X	X			
46	Nov 17			"	"		"	X	X			
47	Nov 24			"	"		"	X	X			
48	Dec 1			"	"		"	X	X			
49	Dec 8			"	"		"	X	X			
50	Dec 15			Base 1	15:30		MS	X	X			
51	Dec 22			"	19:00		"	X	X			
52	Dec 29			"	21:30		"	X	X			

force to be reckoned with in every race he enters. He believes his limiter is speed-endurance, but since he determined that from early-winter testing, that concern is somewhat suspect. Nearly everyone has poor speed-endurance in the winter months. Randy's short sprint is excellent, but his longer sprints fade in races.

PLAN

Randy is capable of training about 1000 hours a year. However, with restrictions on his free time, I've limited the volume to only 800 hours. With the massive base he's built during 11 years of racing, that should not present any problems.

With his age and muscular strength as a strong ability, strength training will end the last week of March.

The first A race of the season for Randy will be the Bisbee Stage Race in late April, a five-day event that attracts a strong field. He will train through the Boulder Criterium Series and other races in March and early April using them in combination with a build up of intensity to peak for Bisbee. A top-10 placement in the general classification is well within his reach.

Following the Bisbee Stage Race, Randy will transition for one week to make sure he's recovered before preparing for the Colorado State Road Race Championship in week 23. With this race coming so soon after Bisbee, he should be in excellent form.

The greatest challenge in Randy's race schedule is maintaining race form for the three-day *Colorado Cyclist* Stage Race, at the very end of the season (week 39). With 14 weeks separating his last two A races, it's best to re-establish his basic fitness by repeating Base 3 training in July, even though that is an unusual time to work on base. The events during this period are all C races, so he can either train through them or even skip a few.

With no races in the three weeks preceding the *Colorado Cyclist* Stage Race it's important that Randy make best use of what are dwindling group rides at that time of year and race-intense workouts to peak his fitness.

Not having done any strength training since March, six weeks of AA-phase weight work will begin in week 44 following a four-week Transition period. During the six-week Preparatory period Randy will mountain bike, run and cross country ski, as the weather allows.

SUMMARY

I hope you noticed in each of these case studies I occasionally changed the procedures for designing a training plan as discussed in Chapters 8, 9 and 10. Life rarely presents you with races, work, vacations and other events spaced to neatly fit into annual plans. Don't be afraid to bend the rules a little so you can design a plan that exactly fits your needs.

Part V

⟡Other Aspects ⊙f Training

TRAINING A HALF-CENTURY AGO

Conditioning for Cycling
BY WILLIE HONEMAN
As it Appeared in American Bicyclist *magazine, June 1945*

Sleep eight to nine hours daily and try to make it a point of retiring and arising at about the same hour every day. Of course, when one races at night this may break up the routine, but otherwise try to follow this rule.

The question of food and what to eat is one that would take much space to cover. A good rule is to eat whatever foods appeal to you, but be sure they are of good quality and fresh. Avoid too many starchy foods, such as white bread, potatoes, pies, pastries, etc. Eat plenty of green and cooked vegetables.

Before a race meet, or road race, eat at least three hours before. If your appetite is good, and it should be, a good quality steak, cooked rare (when and if it can be had), spinach, or lettuce, toast, prunes, or some other fruit, black coffee, with a small quantity of sugar, makes up a good pre-race meal. If the time before a meet or race is limited, two soft-boiled eggs, toast, fruit and black coffee is another menu. Lamb chops may be a good substitute for the steak. Ovoid overeating. It is better to leave the table a little hungry than to overeat which will interfere with the proper digestion of your food.

Physical culture and exercise should be indulged in each morning to develop the arms, chest and to prevent getting too fat around the stomach. Small weights, or pulleys, can be used. Perform these exercises before an open window and practice deep breathing at the same time.

Chapter 12

STRENGTH

Most weightlifters are biceptual.

— JOHN ROSTONI

Cycling at all levels of competition is becoming more competitive every year. To stay ahead, or even just keep up with the competition, you need to have as much speed, endurance and strength as you can develop early in the season. Simply adding road miles may not be the best way to develop that raw fitness. Off-the-bike workouts are sometimes more effective for this. Strength training is a good example, especially in winter.

There was a time when endurance athletes avoided strength training like the plague. Today there are still reasons why some don't strength train. Many riders have a great fear of gaining weight. While there are those who have a tendency to increase their muscle mass, very few cyclists have a genetic predisposition to become hulking monsters, especially on an endurance-based program. If three or four extra pounds result from weight training, the increased power typically more than offsets the mass to be carried. For most riders, strength training does not cause appreciable weight changes. But since it's winter when most of them are lifting, and they are riding infrequently while eating at the rate they do during the racing season, fat accumulates and they blame it on weight training. By spring when the mileage goes back up, this will disappear.

Many cyclists simply hate the weight room. They would much rather be outside on the road doing lung-searing intervals or suffering through the last 10 miles of a hard club ride. Gyms once were intimidating places frequented by heavy-breathing Cro-Magnon types whose knuckles drag the ground. There may still be places like that, but for the most part things have changed. Today there are more petite housewives in pink leotards at the clubs than Neanderthals. Find a club that you feel comfortable going to and you actually may find strength training to be enjoyable.

In the last 10 years, American cyclists have become increasingly aware of what weight training can do for their racing performances. This is largely due to the success of former Eastern Bloc riders who lift weights and to reports of numerous research studies demonstrating the benefits of greater strength for endurance events. Today's cyclists are much more likely to visit a gym and reap the benefits with better race results.

STRENGTH TRAINING BENEFITS

Research has demonstrated positive gains in cycling-endurance performance resulting from strength increases. Nearly all the studies show that riders enjoy an increased "time to exhaustion" — meaning the subjects could ride farther at a given intensity level — after following a leg-strength program for a few weeks. The endurance improvements have typically ranged from 10 to 33 percent, depending on the intensity of the effort.

These studies don't generally find any improvement in aerobic capacity following a strength program. What may be happening is that the slow twitch muscles are stronger from weight training and able to carry more of the workload, thus sparing the fast twitch muscles. Since fast twitch muscles burn glycogen — a precious fuel in short supply — and produce lactate — a limiter to high intensity efforts — endurance benefits.

Whatever the mechanism of improvement may be, there is no longer any doubt that strength work will make you a better racer. Even if you were to improve your endurance by only 10 percent, think how much better you could race. You would be able to ride 10 percent faster or feel 10 percent stronger at the end of a long road race.

GETTING STARTED

There are two problems for the rider determined to improve his or her racing with greater strength. The first is that there are as many strength programs as there are athletes, coaches and cycling books. The average rider does not know which to follow. The second challenge is time. Given jobs, family and life in general, most riders just can't afford huge blocks of time in the gym. The program below is one pared down to fit into the "normal" athlete's busy lifestyle. While you might be able to squeeze in more gym time, the racing benefits would not be much greater.

The sport of body building has had an unusually heavy influence on strength training in the U.S. But for cyclists, using resistance exercise the same way body builders do is likely to decrease endurance performance. Body builders organize training to maximize and balance muscle mass while shaping their physiques for display. Function is not a concern. Endurance athletes' goals are far different, but all too often they learn the body builder's methods at their gym and follow them for lack of a better way.

The purpose of strength training for cycling is the application of force to the pedals. To accomplish this, the cyclist must improve the synchronization and recruitment patterns of muscle groups — not their size and shape. This means that resistance work must not only develop the muscles, but also the central nervous system that controls muscle use.

RULES TO LIFT BY

Based on comments from the athletes I train and their results over the years, I have slowly refined the weight training program I recommend. The basic rules of my program have stayed the same. Whatever program you follow as far as sets, reps and load, be sure to lift by these rules.

Rule 1: Focus on prime movers.

Prime movers are the muscle groups that do the major work on the bike. For example, a prime mover for cycling is the quadriceps muscle group. While having well-developed deltoids may look nice, they're only good for lifting your bike — not a common movement in road racing.

Rule 2: Use multi-joint exercises whenever possible.

Biceps curls are a single-joint exercise, involving only the elbow joint. This is the type of muscle-isolation exercise body builders do. Squats, a basic cycling exercise, include three joints — the hip, knee and ankle. This comes closer to simulating the dynamic movement patterns of the sport and also reduces time in the gym.

Rule 3: Mimic the positions and movements of cycling as closely as possible.

When doing leg presses on a leg press sled, place your feet in about the same relative position as if you were on your bike. You don't, for example, ride with your feet spread 18 inches and your toes turned out at 45 degrees.

Rule 4: Always include the "core" — abdominal and lower back.

The forces applied by your arms and legs must pass through the core of your body. If it is weak, much of the force is dissipated and lost. As you climb or during a sprint, it takes a strong core to transfer more of the force generated by pulling against the handlebars to the pedals. Weak abdominals and back muscles make for wimpy climbing and sprinting.

Rule 5: As the race season approaches make strength training more specific and less time intensive.

While a crucial period in developing force is during the winter Maximum Strength phase, the strength developed then must be converted to power and muscular endurance later — forms of strength usable in road racing. These latter two phases precede the start of the race season.

Rule 6: Keep the number of exercises low.

In order to concentrate on improving specific movements, put greater focus on sets and reps rather than the number of exercises. Following the initial Anatomical Adaptation phase, gradually reduce the number of exercises. The idea is to spend as little time in the weight room as possible and yet still improve race performance.

Rule 7: Strength training fitness precedes on-bike training within each season period.

Specific exercise demands in the weight room must come before the same or similar demands on the bike. For example, the Maximum Strength training phase should occur in the weeks just prior to the start of hill training on the bike. Power Endurance training with weights is best in the weeks just preceding interval training on the bike. In this way your muscles and tendons have been prepared for the workloads you will experience on the bike and you will be able to start stressful workouts such as hill repeats at higher levels of performance.

The following suggested strength program complies with the above guidelines. I designed it specifically for road cyclists. If you have been training like a body builder before, you may feel guilty at times using lighter weights, higher repetitions and only a few exercises. Stay with the program and I think you'll see improvements in your racing. You won't look much better in the mirror. But then again, that is not what you are after.

STRENGTH-TRAINING PHASES

There are five phases through which the cyclist should progress in approaching the most important races of the year. Here is an explanation of the phases listed in Table 12.1, Strength Training for Road Cycling.

Anatomical Adaptation (AA)

This is the initial phase of strength training that usually occurs in the late fall or early winter. Its purpose is to prepare the muscles and tendons for the greater loads of the next phase — Maximum Strength. More exercises are done at this time of year than at any other, since improved general body strength is a goal. Weight machines are convenient, but you should also use free weight training during this period. Circuit training can add an aerobic component to this phase.

In this phase, as in all others, the athlete should be able to increase loads by about five percent every four or five workouts.

Maximum Strength (MS)

As resistance is gradually increased and repetitions decreased, more force is generated. This phase is necessary to teach the central nervous system to easily recruit high numbers of muscle fibers. Be particularly careful not to cause injury during this phase, especially with free weight exercises such as the squat. Select your loads conservatively at the start of this phase and in the first set of each workout. You can gradually increase the loads throughout this phase.

It is tempting for some athletes to extend this phase beyond the recommended ranges in the table. Don't do it. Continuing this phase for several weeks is likely to result in muscle imbalances, especially in the upper leg, which may contribute to hip or knee injuries.

Power Endurance (PE)

The purpose of this phase is to develop the capacity to quickly recruit most of the fibers for a movement and to sustain their use. A race-situation example of this kind of recruitment would be attacking short, steep hills or a long finishing sprint.

Power is the ability to produce the greatest possible force in the shortest possible time. It may be expressed as power = force X velocity. This means that speed of movement is critical to improving power, so the lifting portions of all exercises are done with an explosive movement. Be careful not to move so quickly that you risk injury and always lower the weight under control. A proper warm-up is critical. As you lose the ability to move quickly, stop the exercise, regardless of the number of repetitions completed.

Muscular Endurance (ME)

ME is the heart of training for endurance sports and greatly benefits riders whose race endurance is lacking. The purpose is to extend the ability to manage fatigue at high load levels by increasing capillary density and the number and size of mitochondria — energy production sites within the muscles. This is also the longest phase as it takes time to bring about these physiological changes. You may also use circuit training during this phase.

Endurance Maintenance (EM)

Alternate between two-week Power Endurance and four-week Muscular Endurance phases throughout the remainder of the race season. This maintains the two critical types of endurance needed for racing. Stopping all resistance training at this point will cause a gradual loss of strength and performance throughout the season. Maintenance of strength is particularly important for women and masters.

Hip extension training (squats, step-ups or leg presses) is optional during the maintenance phase. If you find hip extension exercises help your racing, continue doing them. If, however, working the legs only deepens your fatigue level, cut them out. Continuing to work on core muscles and personal weakness areas will maintain your strength needs.

To properly time your peak, eliminate all strength training for the seven days leading up to A-priority races.

DETERMINING LOAD

Table 12.1 summarizes a suggested strength training program for the road cyclist. Perhaps the most critical aspect of this chart is the load you select during each phase. While it suggests a load based on the maximum you can lift for a single repetition (1RM), that is not always the best way to determine weight due to the possibility of injury, especially to the back, and of prolonged soreness eliminating most, if not all, training for two or three days.

Another way to decide how much weight to use is to initially estimate the load and then adjust as the phase progresses. Always start with less than you think is possible for the number of reps indicated. You can add more later, if you do it cautiously.

You can also estimate one-repetition maximums based on a higher number of reps done to failure. Start by doing a warm-up set or two. Select a resistance you can lift at least four times, but no more than 10. You may need to experiment for a couple of sets. If you do, rest for at least five minutes between attempts. To find your predicted one-repetition maximum, divide the weight lifted by the factor below that corresponds with the number of repetitions completed:

# of reps	Factor
4	.90
5	.875
6	.85
7	.825
8	.80
9	.775
10	.75

Another way of estimating your 1RM from a multiple lift effort is described in appendix B.

During the Maximum Strength phase, free weights are likely to bring greater results than machines, but if you use free weights also include them in the latter weeks of the AA phase. Free weights are preferable during the PE phase. Again, be cautious whenever using barbells and dumbbells, especially with rapid movement.

MISCELLANEOUS GUIDELINES

In carrying out a strength-development program there are several other factors to consider.

EXPERIENCE LEVEL

If you are in the first two years of strength training, emphasis must be on building movement patterns and bolstering connective tissue. Experienced athletes are ready to do more maximum strength and power development than novices.

DAYS PER WEEK

Table 12.1 suggests a range of days per week to lift weights based on the phase. The period of the season you are in will help you to further refine this number. During Base 3, Build 1 and Build 2, reduce the number of days of strength training per week by one. In the Peak and Race periods cut back to the minimum listed on the table. The week of A races, eliminate strength training altogether.

WARM-UP AND COOL DOWN

Before an individual strength workout, warm-up with about 10 minutes of easy aerobic activity. This could be running, rowing, climbing or cycling. Following a weight session, spin with a light resistance at a cadence of 90 or higher for 10 to 20 minutes on a stationary bike. Allow your toes to relax. Do not run immediately following a strength workout.

PHASING IN

As you move into a new phase of strength training, blend the prior and new phase for a week. For example, when going from AA to MS, the first week may have one AA workout and one MS workout. Otherwise you might devote half of each workout in the first week to AA and the other half to MS. You could also do one or two sets of MS training at the end of each AA exercise for a week.

EXERCISE ORDER

Exercises are listed in Table 12.1 in the order of completion to allow for a smooth progression and for recovery. In the AA and ME phases, proceed by completing the first set of all exercises before starting the second sets. For example, in AA, do the first set of squats followed by the first set of seated rows. In the other phases, all sets of each exercise are done to completion before progressing to the next exercise. This is called "horizontal progression." In some cases, you may do two exercises as a "superset" in the MS and PE phases — alternate sets between two exercises to completion. Supersetting will make better use of your time in the gym since you'll spend less time waiting for recovery of a specific neuromuscular group. This does not eliminate the need to stretch following each set, however.

RECOVERY INTERVALS

On the chart, notice that I have specified the time needed for recovery between sets. These recovery periods are important if you expect to derive any benefit from strength work. During this time, your heart rate drops as your short-term energy supply is rebuilt in preparation for the next set. Some phases require longer recovery intervals than others. During the recovery time stretch the muscles just exercised. See Chapter 13 for illustrations of stretches listed here.

Table 12.1

Strength training for road cycling

STRENGTH TRAINING FOR ROAD CYCLING

Phase	AA	MS	PE	ME	Endurance Maintenance PE	ME
Duration (weeks)						
Novice	8-10	3-4	3-4	6-8	2	4
Experienced	4-6	4-6	4-6	6-8	2	4
Days per week						
Novice	2-3	2	2	2	1	1
Experienced	3-4	2-3	2	2	1-2	1-2
Load (% of 1RM)						
Novice	40-60	80-90	30-50	30-50	30-50	30-50
Experienced	40-60	85-95	40-60	30-50	40-60	30-50
Sets						
Novice	3	3-4	3-4	2-4	1-3	1-3
Experienced	3-5	3-5	3-6	3-5	2-3	2-4
Repetitions	20-30	3-6	6-10	40-60	6-10	40-60
Recovery (in minutes)	1-1.5	2-4	2-5	0.5-1	2-5	0.5-1
Speed	Slow	Slow-Mod	Quick	Mod	Quick	Mod
Procedure*	Circuit	Horiz	Horiz	Circuit	Hor	Cir
Exercises**	123456789	12[35][67]	1[27][63]	12763	1[76]3	1763

(in order of completion)

*Circuit: Complete one set of exercise #1 and then do one set of exercise #2, etc. Horizontal: Complete all sets of exercise #1 before going to #2. Exception is supersetting (see "Exercises").

Exercises: 1-Hip extension (squat, step-up, or leg press), 2-Seated row, 3-Back extension, 4-Hip extension (different from #1), 5-Bench press or Push-up, 6-Personal weakness option*: Heel raise or Knee extension or Leg curl (can do all of these), 7-Crunch***, 8-Dead lift, 9-Lat pull. Brackets indicates pair of superset exercises, for example [27] means superset seated row and crunch

***Note. During the MS and PE phases continue AA load, sets, reps, rest and speed for these exercises.

RECOVERY WEEKS

Every third or fourth week should be a time of reduced training volume coinciding with your recovery weeks scheduled on the Annual Training Plan. You may accomplish this by reducing the number of strength workouts that week and/or by reducing the number of sets within workouts.

STRENGTH EXERCISES

SQUAT

1. Wear a weight belt during the Max Strength (MS) phase.

2. Stand with feet 6-8 inches apart, inside edge to inside edge, with toes pointed straight ahead.

3. Head up and back straight.

4. Squat until upper thighs are halfway to parallel to floor — about the same knee bend as at top of pedal stroke.

5. Knees point straight ahead staying over feet at all times.

6. Return to start position.

7. Stretches: Stork stand and Triangle

STEP-UP

1. Place left foot on a sturdy 13-15 inch high platform with toes pointing straight ahead.

2. Step up with right foot touching platform and immediately return to start position.

3. Complete all right leg reps before repeating with left leg stepping up.

4. Stretches: Stork stand and Triangle *(Please see the next page for illustration)*

Step-up

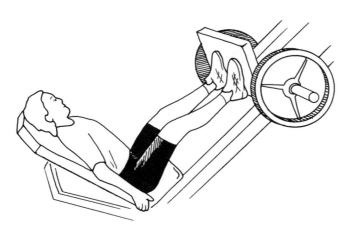

LEG PRESS

1. Place feet on middle portion of platform with the inside edges of feet 6-8 inches apart and feet parallel.

2. Press platform up until legs are straight, knees nearly locked.

3. Lower platform until knees are about 8 inches from chest.

4. Knees remain directly in line with feet throughout the movement.

5. Return to start position.

6. Stretches: Stork stand and Triangle

SEATED ROW

1. Grasp bar with arms fully extended and hands about 6 inches apart, inside edge to inside edge.
2. Pull bar toward lower chest keeping elbows close to body.
3. Minimize movement at the waist using the back muscles to stabilize position.
4. Return to start position.
5. Stretch: Pulldown

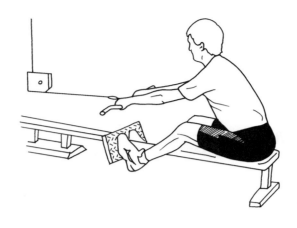

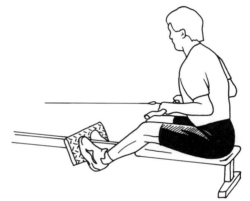

BACK EXTENSION

1. Start with head at lowest possible position.
2. Stop when back is parallel to floor.
3. Stretch: Squat

BENCH PRESS

1. Grasp bar with hands directly above shoulders.
2. Lower bar to nipple line and touch chest.
3. Keep elbows close to body.
4. Return to start position.
5. Stretch: Pulldown

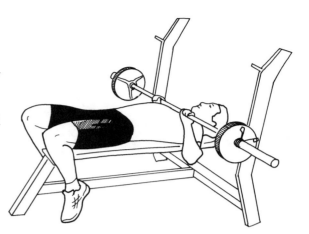

PUSH-UP

1. Hands directly below shoulders.
2. Back straight and head up.
3. Keeping body rigid lower body until chest touches floor.
4. Elbows in.
5. Return to start position.
6. Stretch: Pulldown

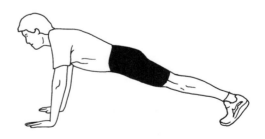

HEEL RAISE

1. Stand with toes on riser, heels on floor.

2. Feet are parallel and 6-8 inches apart, inside edge to inside edge.

3. Raise up onto toes.

4. Return to start position.

5. Stretch: Wall lean

KNEE EXTENSION

1. Start with knees fully extended and toes pointing slightly to outside.

2. Lower weight only about 8 inches (do <u>not</u> go all
   the way down).

3. Return to start position.

4. Stretch: Stork stand

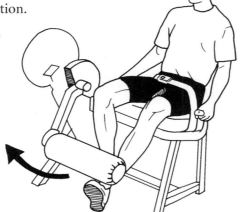

LEG CURL

1. Curl leg until calf touches thigh.

2. Return to start position.

3. Stretch: Triangle

CRUNCH

1. Knees bent at about 90 degrees.

2. Hands behind head for support only (do <u>not</u> pull on head).

3. Lift shoulders and upper back off of floor by curling torso.

4. Slowly return to start position.

5. Stretch: While on floor, arch back up and extend arms and legs.

DEAD LIFT

1. Wear a weight belt.

2. Stand with feet 6-8 inches apart, inside edge to inside edge, with toes pointed straight ahead.

3. Head up and back straight.

4. Grasp bar with hands just outside of thighs with an alternated grip (one hand over, one under the bar).

5. While looking up and keeping butt low, lower weight to near the floor until thighs are halfway to parallel to floor — about the same knee bend as at top of pedal stroke.

6. Return to start position.

7. Stretches: Stork stand and triangle

LAT PULL

1. Grasp bar with arms fully extended and hands about 6 inches apart, inside edge to inside edge.

2. Pull bar toward upper chest keeping elbows close to body.

3. Minimize movement at the waist using the back muscles to stabilize position.

4. Return to start position.

5. Stretch: Pulldown

REFERENCES

Bompa, T. *Periodization of Strength*, Veritas Publishing, Inc., 1993.

Bompa, T. *Power Training for Sports*, Mosaic Press, 1993.

Bompa, T. *Theory and Methodology of Training*, Kendall/Hunt Publishing Co., 1994.

Hickson, R.C., et al. Potential for strength and endurance training to amplify endurance performance, *Journal of Applied Physiology*, vol. 65, pp. 2285-2290, 1988.

Hickson, R.C., et al. Strength training effects on aerobic power and short-term endurance, *Medicine and Science in Sports and Exercise*, vol. 12, pp. 336-339, 1980.

Kraemer, W.J., et al. Compatibility of high-intensity strength and endurance training on hormonal and skeletal muscle adaptations, *Journal of Applied Physiology*, vol. 78(3), pp. 976-989, 1995.

Marcinik, E.J., et al. Effects of strength training on lactate threshold and endurance performance, *Medicine and Science in Sports and Exercise*, vol. 23(6), pp. 739-743, 1991.

McCarthy, J.P., et al. Compatibility of adaptive responses with combining strength and endurance training, *Medicine and Science in Sports and Exercise*, vol. 27(3), pp. 429-436, 1995.

Nelson, A.G., et al. Consequences of combining strength and endurance training regimens, *Physical Therapy*, vol. 70, pp. 287-294, 1990.

Sale, D.G., et al. Comparison of two regimens of concurrent strength and endurance training, *Medicine and Science in Sports and Exercise*, vol. 22(3), pp. 348-356, 1990.

Stone, M.H., et al. Health- and performance-related potential of resistance training, *Sports Medicine*, vol. 11(4), pp. 210-231, 1991.

Dear Joe,

I'm writing because of your recent story in VeloNews about weight training.

I have been riding for the last 52 years without ever missing a year of at least 1,000 miles. I began riding in 1943 as a junior (my first ABL of A card cost me a whopping 50¢). There were probably no more than 1,200 registered riders in the whole country then.

It's like you say, that back in those days, and for years after, pumping iron was never encouraged. So I didn't — until 1945 when I was in the Navy. After work I had a lot of idle time, so I went to the base gym and started working out with weights. I didn't know what the hell I was doing. I just "free-lanced" it all winter.

The next season, my fourth for racing, was the best I ever had and I know now that it was due to the strength training I did the previous winter. But because it wasn't supposed to be good for you (the thinking of the time) I didn't lift for about 30 years. A little late wouldn't you say? If I knew then...

Yours truly,
Bob Dunihue
Fort Collins, Colorado

Chapter 13

STRETCHING

I've tried relaxing, but — I don't know
— I feel more comfortable tense.

— HAMILTON CARTOON

Physiologically speaking, cycling is not a perfect sport. But then again, no sport is. One of the problems cycling causes is a shortening and tightening of muscles. Pedaling leg muscles lose elasticity since they don't go through a full range of motion — the leg stops both before reaching a full extension and complete flexion. *Rigor mortis* sets in, affecting the back, neck, arms and shoulders on rides lasting several hours with little change of position. Such tightness can hold you back.

A good example of how tight muscles limit your performance involves the hamstrings muscle on the back of the upper leg. Of all the tightness that can result from cycling, this may be the most debilitating. Tight hamstrings restrain the leg during the down stroke. They work to prevent the leg from straightening, and in doing so, reduce the force produced by the leg. In an attempt to alleviate the tension felt in the back of the leg, the affected cyclist will often lower his or her saddle. A saddle that is set too low further reduces force generation, which in turn reduces power output.

STRETCHING BENEFITS

Tight hamstrings can also contribute to a tight lower back which haunts some riders on long rides as they wonder when it might lock up, forcing them to abandon the race. Off the bike, this low back tightness may become lower-back pain.

A consistent and effective program of stretching can prevent such problems from occurring. Prevention is always more comfortable, less time consuming and cheaper than treatment.

Stretching plays a role in the prevention of such injuries. A study of 1,543 runners in the Honolulu Marathon found that those who stretched regularly following workouts had fewer injuries than those who didn't. It is noteworthy that in this same study those who stretched only *before* workouts had the highest rate of injuries.

Stretching following workouts also appears to aid the recovery process by improving muscle cells' uptake of amino acids, by promoting protein synthesis within muscle cells and by maintaining the integrity of muscle cells.

Stretching after a workout takes less than 15 minutes, and you can do it while downing a recovery drink and chatting with your training partners. This is the optimum time to work on flexibility, as the muscles are warm and supple.

Another important time to stretch is during strength workouts. The act of forcefully contracting muscles against resistance creates extreme tightness. As was described in the previous chapter, following each strength set you should stretch the muscles just used. Correctly doing a strength workout means spending more time in the gym stretching than lifting weights.

Stretching a little bit throughout the day is also beneficial to long-term flexibility and performance. While sitting at a desk working or reading, you can gently stretch major muscle groups such as the hamstrings and calves. Work on flexibility while watching television, standing in line, talking with friends and first thing in the morning while still in bed. After a while, you may make it such an integral part of your life that you no longer even think about stretching. It just happens. That's when your flexibility will be at its peak.

HOW TO STRETCH

Over the past 40 years, three stretching methods have gained (and sometimes lost) popularity. When I was in college in the 1960s, ballistic stretching was common. Bouncing movements were thought to be the best way to make muscles

Jane Marshall stretching.
Working a little on
flexibility daily may
improve long-term
performance.

longer. Later we learned that this technique had just the opposite effect — muscles resisted lengthening and could even be damaged by overly motivated stretchers. Today almost no one stretches this way.

In the 1970s, a Californian named Bob Anderson refined a stretching method and in 1980 released a book called *Stretching*. Anderson's approach involved static stretching with little or no movement at all. Stretch the muscle to a level of slight discomfort and then hold it in that position for several seconds. Static stretching remains the most popular style today.

Another method also surfaced about the same time as static stretching, but never received much exposure or support until recently. Several university studies going back to the early 1970s found it to be 10 to 15 percent more effective than static stretching. This approach, called "proprioceptive neuromuscular facilitation" has started to catch on over the last few years.

There are many variations on PNF stretching, some being quite complex. Here are the steps in one easy-to-follow version:

1. Static stretch the muscle for about 8 seconds.

2. Contract the same muscle for about 8 seconds. (Leave out the contraction step

when stretching between sets of strength training. Instead, hold static stretches for about 15 seconds.)

3. Static stretch the muscle again for about 8 seconds.

4. Continue alternating contractions with stretches until you have done four to eight static stretches. Always finish with a static stretch.

   You should find that the static stretches become deeper with each repeat as the muscles seem to loosen up.

   Using this PNF method, a stretch would take one to two minutes. The time is well worth it for the benefit received.

CYCLING STRETCHES

The following are stretches for cyclists. You may find that some are more important for you than others. These are the ones to focus on every day and every time you ride. You should also blend some of these with your strength training in the gym. Those are indicated here and also with the strength exercise drawings in the last chapter. I recommend following this stretching order at the end of a workout. You can do most of them while holding your bike for balance.

STORK STAND: QUADRICEPS.

1. While balancing against your bike or a wall, grasp your right foot behind your back with your left hand.

2. Static stretch by gently pulling your hand up and away from your butt.

3. Keep your head up and stand erect — do not bend over at the waist.

4. Contract by pushing against your hand with your foot, more gently at first.

5. Repeat with other leg.

6. Use this stretch in the weight room during the hip extension, dead lift and seated knee extension exercises.

TRIANGLE: HAMSTRING.

1. Bend over at the waist while leaning on your bike or a wall.

2. Place the leg to be stretched forward with the foot about 18 inches from the bike.

3. The other leg is directly behind the first. The farther back you place this leg, the greater the stretch.

4. With your weight on the front foot, sag your upper body toward the floor. You should feel the stretch in the hamstring of your forward leg.

5. Contract the forward leg by trying to pull it backwards against the floor. There will be no movement.

6. Repeat with other leg.

7. Use this stretch in the weight room during the hip extension, leg curl and dead lift exercises.

PULLDOWN: LATISSIMUS DORSI, TRAPEZIUS, PECTORALIS AND TRICEPS.

1. Hold onto your bike or a railing for balance with your weight resting on your arms.

2. Allow your head to sag deeply between outstretched arms to create a stretch in your lats.

3. To contract, pull down with your arms.

4. In the weight room do this stretch with seated lat pulls to chest, chest press and seated rows.

SQUAT: LOW BACK, CALVES, QUADRICEPS, GLUTEALS.

1. Using your bike for balance, squat down keeping your heels on the floor (this is easier with cycling shoes off).

2. Allow your butt to sag close to your heels as you rock forward. Hold this position for about 30 seconds.

3. There is no contraction for this stretch.

4. Do this stretch during back extension strength exercises in the weight room.

WALL LEAN: CALVES.

1. Lean against a wall with the leg to be stretched straight behind you and the other forward holding most of your weight.

2. Keep the heel of the rear foot on the floor with the toe pointed forward.

3. The farther forward your hips move the greater the stretch in your calf.

4. To contract the calf, push against the wall as if trying to push it away using your leg.

5. Repeat with other leg.

6. Use this stretch in the weight room during the heel raise exercise.

REFERENCES

Goldspink, D.F. The influence of immobilization and stretch on protein turnover of rat skeletal muscle, *Journal of Physiology*, vol. 264, pp. 267-282, 1977.

Holly, R.G., et al. Stretch-induced growth in chicken wing muscles: A new model of stretch hypertrophy, *American Journal of Physiology*, vol. 7, pp. C62-C71, 1980.

Vanderburgh, H. and S. Kaufman. Stretch and skeletal myotube growth: What is the physical to biochemical linkage? *Frontiers of Exercise Biology*, K. Borer, D. Edington and T. White, editors, Human Kinetics Publishers, pp. 71-84, 1983.

Wallin, D., et al. Improvement of muscle flexibility, a comparison between two techniques, *The American Journal of Sports Medicine*, vol. 13 (4), pp. 263-268, 1985.

Chapter 14

SPECIAL GROUPS

*Women who seek to be equal
with men lack ambition.*

— TIMOTHY LEARY

*It takes about 10 years to get
used to how old you are.*

— UNKNOWN

Half of the licensed cyclists in this country are under 30. Most are men,
and a few are teenagers. As a result, nearly all training information for
cycling is directed at the needs of senior men in their 20s. But everyday I talk with
women, masters or juniors whose interest, dedication and enthusiasm for racing
are no different from the young, senior men. The challenge for these special
groups is that they often cannot find answers to their questions regarding gender
and age differences.

For the most part, these groups should train the same as the senior men, but
there are a few exceptions. In this chapter, I will explore what research and experience say about the training needs of women, masters and juniors.

WOMEN

A couple of years ago, a particularly thorough female professional cyclist was interviewing me as a potential coach. One of the questions she asked was a good one: Is there any difference between the way men and women should train? My answer was simple: No. Perhaps it is too simple. There are some things women could do differently than men to improve their performance.

There is no getting around the obvious male-female differences. Hip width, short torsos relative to leg length and a low center of gravity all certainly affect the equipment a woman uses. There are other differences. Numerous studies have demonstrated that elite women athletes have aerobic capacities somewhat below that of elite men. The highest VO_2max ever recorded for a man was 94 ml/kg/min while the highest woman's aerobic power measured was 77 — both Nordic skiers. Absolute muscular power outputs of women are also well below those of men. Nothing new here.

In the real world of racing, there are actually more similarities between male and female athletes at comparable levels of sport than there are differences. Women are capable of training at the same volume levels as men, and they respond to training in essentially the same ways. Except for absolute magnitude of workload, there is not much difference in the way the two sexes should train. But there are a few opportunities for individual women to improve relative to their competition that men seldom, if ever, have. Here are five that may give you an edge.

QUANTITY VS. QUALITY

Even though women are fully capable of training at the same volume as men, do they need to? Women's races typically evolve in a way unlike men's. First of all, women's road races aren't as long — sometimes no more than half the men's distance. I have no hard evidence to back this up, but it seems that women's races are, therefore, more likely to end in a pack sprint. But then a rider, or better, a couple of riders, who are strong enough to break from the women's field early in the race, are more likely to stay off the front and finish ahead of the field than in a men's race.

What all of this means is that women road racers should concentrate more on the high quality of their training than on high mileage. Not that building an aerobic base with long, steady rides is unimportant — it certainly is. A woman, however, must place more emphasis on developing her muscular-endurance, power and speed-endurance for the unique demands of her shorter and relatively faster race. Somewhat shifting the emphasis of training from volume to these abilities is likely to produce better results in women's road races.

Team Women on Wheels climbing Lookout Mountain near Denver. Increased quality of training may help women racers more than increased quantity.

STRENGTH

The average woman's total body strength is about a third less than the average man's, but that difference isn't distributed equally. Women are relatively stronger in their legs and weaker in the abdominal region and arms. While women don't race with men, this comparison makes it apparent where a woman's greatest opportunity for improvement lies. By increasing the strength of her arms and abdominal region, a woman can improve her climbing and sprinting relative to her competition. Powerful riding out of the saddle requires strength to stabilize the upper body against the torque applied by the legs. Spaghetti arms and an accordion abdominal dissipate the force produced by the legs.

Due to the size and shape of a woman's pelvis, it is important to especially emphasize abdominal strength.

Dede Demet leads a climb in the Garden of the Gods stage of the 1995 Colorado Cyclist race. By increasing the strength of the upper body, women can improve their climbing and sprinting.

MENTAL

Society expects less of women in sports and offers less — less media coverage, less prize money, less crowd support and less time to train due to greater family responsibilities. That women make it in sport is a testament to their perseverance and dedication.

Despite the socio-cultural obstacles, I have found that women have a somewhat healthier view of winning and losing than do men. Since women tend to strive to attain personal standards and are less preoccupied with defeating other riders, they are less devastated by losing and recover faster emotionally. Men take losing, when they feel they should have won, as a mark against their "manhood."

Women, however, carry even heavier and deeper psychological baggage than men in another area. Women are more likely to associate poor performance with lack of ability. After all, as youngsters society taught most women that sport was for boys, and girls were not particularly good at it. When men have a bad race, they view the problem as a lack of effort — ability is not the issue.

Developing confidence in ability is critical to success. Positive self-talk, self-affirmations and supportive people are perhaps more critical to a woman's progress as an athlete than to a man's.

DIET

Due to a greater propensity to store body fat, women athletes tend to restrict their caloric intake, especially from foods high in fat and protein. And yet high protein intake has been shown as more necessary for endurance athletes than for the population at large, or even for body builders, who often consume protein in excessive quantities. A low-protein diet can easily cause a decline in aerobic capacity, fatigue and anemia in women cyclists.

Many women cyclists consume fewer than 2,000 calories a day, but often require more than 3,000. With an average of 5 mg of iron per 1,000 calories in the typical American diet, a female athlete may only be getting 10 mg daily, but need 15 mg. Vegetarian diets, favored by many women, are even lower in iron and provide a less absorbable type of iron. Over the course of several weeks, borderline iron deficiency or even anemia can creep up on a woman athlete.

Eating more calories or including red meat are ways to solve this dilemma, although not popular ones for many women. There are other ways to improve iron intake and absorption including eating high-iron-content foods with orange juice or vitamin C and cooking in iron skillets with acidic tomato sauces. It may also be a good idea to talk with a health-care provider about supplementing with iron. Don't supplement iron without medical guidance. It is also wise to avoid food products that hinder iron absorption such as tea, wheat bran, antacids and calcium phosphate supplements.

Women, indeed all riders, should have their blood tested in the winter to establish an iron-level baseline.

CONTRACEPTIVES AND PERFORMANCE

A recent study at the University of Illinois showed that women who are on the pill may have an advantage in endurance sports such as cycling. During long endurance runs at a low intensity, women taking oral contraceptives showed an increase in growth hormone. They used significantly less carbohydrate and more fat for fuel than those women not taking the pill. This suggests that using oral contraceptives may improve a woman's capacity for burning fat, may allow her to get into shape faster and may extend her endurance range in races. I am not aware of any other studies that have tested this finding, so the results should be taken with some reservation.

If you are not currently using an oral contraceptive, but are considering it, talk with your health-care provider before starting. Don't take the pill only for race — performance reasons.

MASTERS

On April 4, 1994, I spoke at an American College of Sports Medicine workshop in New York City. The topic for the workshop was masters athletes — those over the age of 40. For two hours before my presentation I listened as one doctor after another talked about "normal" performance declines with aging.

When I finally got my turn to speak, I was beginning to think we were all supposed to give up sport as we got older. I told the audience not to believe half of what they had been hearing. The reason people slow down so much after age 40 is not as much physiology as it is psychology. We *think* we should be slower.

I reminded the audience of 41-year-old Eamann Coghlan, who just became the first person over 40 to run less than four-minutes for the mile. He didn't do this by reading statistics on what is *supposed* to happen with age. I pointed to 40-year-old Dave Scott, who was planning a comeback at that year's Ironman — not to just finish, but to win (he finished second). And how about Mark Spitz who took a serious shot at making the 1992 U.S. Olympic swimming team 20 years after his seven gold medals in Munich. Then there was Carlos Lopes who, at age 37, won the Olympic marathon. Most recently, 42-year-old Kent Bostick surprised everyone by qualifying for the 1996 Olympics by defeating 28-year-old Mike McCarthy by nearly one second in the 4000 meter pursuit.

These aging athletes are just the tip of the iceberg. There are hundreds of masters in the world of sport who are within seconds or inches of their best performances of all time. In cycling, athletes such as George Hansen, Vic Copeland and Irene Asher — all in their 50s — are still mixing it up with the under-30 youngsters.

In the last 10 years, there has been tremendous growth in the number of USCF members who are older than 40. Between 1984 and 1993 there was a 75-percent increase in the number of members in their 40s. In 1996, 20 percent of USCF racers were older than 40. What just 10 years ago was a young man's sport is becoming a sport for both sexes and all ages.

ABILITY AND AGE

There's no denying that there's a loss of ability for racing with advancing age. The best indicators of this in road cycling are age group records for the individual time trial. The 40k records reveal an average slowing of 20 seconds per year, about

0.6 percent, after the ages of 25 to 35. For the 20k, ITT times slow about 12 seconds per year from age 20 to 65 — a 0.7-percent decline.

These small drops in performance result from continuing losses of the three basic abilities — endurance, strength and speed. While longitudinal studies of highly-trained athletes are few and far between, it appears that the decline of each of these abilities is similar to what the ITT records show: about 6 percent per decade. That is well below the expected decline of 10 percent per decade that's found in the "normal" population after age 25.

A rider's body goes through several changes following its second decade. Typical of aging are drops in aerobic capacity, maximum heart rate, the amount of blood pumped per heart beat, the activity of muscle cell enzymes, breathing efficiency, blood vessel elasticity, nervous system speed of response and muscle mass. The only thing that has been shown to increase is body fat. Not a pretty picture.

But wait, there's more.

Flexibility is also lost with age. This is in part due to a drop in the amount of body fluids the body can store in later life. An aging immune system doesn't work as well as it once did, either — a good reason to take antioxidants. Then there's heat. Getting older means not sweating as much in hot, dry conditions, yet our urinary systems are more effective at flushing water, thus decreasing blood volume. To make matters worse, the thirst mechanism isn't as sensitive as it once was. All of this means a greater likelihood of overheating and dehydrating.

BEATING THE CURVE

So how is it some continue to perform at nearly the same high level for years? While slowing down with age to some extent may be inevitable beyond the age of 35, these riders have found that the rate of decline can be dramatically reduced by a willingness to train with the same high intensity and volume as they did when they were younger. In fact, some of the top masters riders are even doing more now than before. One scientific study has shown that it's possible to maintain aerobic capacity, a good indicator of fitness, for 10 years past your youth. Another has demonstrated that aerobic capacity drops of 2 percent or less can be accomplished well into an athlete's 50s.

TRAINING IMPLICATIONS

How willing and able are you to train as much as you did when younger — or even more? Here are some suggestions for improving your racing even as you get older.

Strength train year round. While younger and more muscularly-blessed athletes may stop strength training in the late winter, masters should continue throughout the year. The stronger you are, the more force you can apply to the pedal. Greater strength means lower perceived exertions at all levels of power output.

Train a minimum of 7 to 10 hours a week on average throughout the year. That means an annual volume of at least 350 to 500 hours.

Take a full 12 weeks in the Base period. Don't cut it short. You must maximize your endurance, strength and speed before upping the intensity. Be sure to stay proficient at spinning at high cadences.

Once you have established your base fitness, put less emphasis than younger riders do on endurance and more on power, speed-endurance and muscular-endurance. That means greater attention to jumps, sprints, intervals and time trialing than to long workouts. Your longest ride should be only as long as your longest race time.

After you have established your base, allow for more recovery time than you had in the past. Few masters can handle more than two or three high-quality workouts a week and get away with it for long. Many masters have found it is possible to race quite well on two break-through workouts a week. For example, in the Build period, at mid-week combine a muscular-endurance workout with speed-endurance or power, doing the faster portion first. Then recover for two or three days and complete a high-intensity group ride or tune-up race on the weekend. Take a day off every week. If you find recovery to be especially difficult, change the pattern of weekly training hours in Table 8.5, so that there are only two weeks between recovery weeks instead of three. Omit the first week in each case.

Train in the heat once or twice a week, including higher-intensity workouts on hot days, once you feel adapted. Be especially cautious with your levels of hydration. Drink a 16-ounce bottle of sports drink every hour during a ride whether you feel like it or not. Sip water throughout the day.

Stretch after every workout and again later in the day. Try to become more flexible now than you've been in years. You can do it if you are dedicated.

In road races, stay in the front third from the start. Due to the wide range in

The Training Bible

abilities and experience levels at masters races, the groups tend to break up sooner than senior races do.

JUNIORS

In 1982, my son Dirk competed in his first bicycle race at age 12. On that cold September day, he raced three laps around the block in baggy wind pants with a big smile on his face — and finished dead last. But he was hooked. From this inauspicious start, Dirk went on to win the junior Colorado Road Race Championship, make the U.S. National team, race as an amateur in Europe for five years and turn pro at age 22.

Dirk Friel in the 1996 Tour DuPont, 14 years after his first race as a junior.

COACHES

As a junior, Dirk was an exceptional athlete, one in whom I saw a great deal of promise. I wanted to coach him, but knew that would not work. A father is a young athlete's worst possible mentor, so I hired Pat Nash, a local coach who specialized in juniors, to work with my son. Dirk's early and continuing success was largely due to Pat's careful nurturing. My major concern, which I expressed to Pat, was that Dirk still be enthusiastically riding, racing and improving at age 25. A good coach helped to make that possible.

If you are a junior and new to racing, try to find a coach who has a local team and rides along on workouts. You and the coach will get to know each other better that way, and he or she will be better able to help you grow as a racer. Avoid coaches and teams more concerned about winning the next race than in developing the team tactics, skills and fitness that come from a long-term approach.

TRAINING

By age 17, you and your coach should develop an annual training plan like that described in Part IV. Prior to age 17, your training should be mostly centered on the basic abilities of strength, endurance and speed with occasional races. In your early years as a cyclist, it is best that you participate in at least one other sport. Even the top champions, such as Miguel Indurain, did this. Don't specialize in cycling before the age of 17 — your long-term development will be greater because of this.

In the first two years of riding, when you are participating in other sports, an annual training volume of 200 to 350 hours is best. By age 17, you should be able to increase the volume, if you have been handling that level without difficulty. But do so gradually. More is not always better, and often worse.

Each year the number of races you enter should increase a little until, by age 18, you are racing as often as seniors. When you begin to race, emphasize team tactics more than winning. Learn what it takes to break away, to block, to work with other riders in a break, to lead out a teammate and to sprint. Cycling is much like football or basketball in this respect — teamwork produces greater results than everyone riding only for themselves.

Regardless of your age when you begin to do weight-room strength workouts, the first year should only include the Anatomical Adaptation (AA) phase described in Table 12.1. Working both with machines and free weights, perfect your lifting form for each exercise in this first season. In the second year of strength training, follow the "novice" guidelines on Table 12.1. The first time you do the Maximum Strength (MS) phase use a weight no greater than 80 percent of your estimated one-repetition maximum. The most common injury that occurs in juniors starting to lift weights is to the low back. Be careful. By the third year you should be ready to move into more serious weight work, assuming you are at least 17 by then.

MISCELLANEOUS

Before the start of each season get a complete physical from your doctor. This is something even the pros do and will allow you and your coach to start the year with a "clean bill of health."

With the growth you may still be experiencing, one of your biggest challenges will be replacing equipment. You can go broke buying new equipment every year, and yet it's especially important that your bike fits. One way to get around the high cost of constant replacement is to buy the used bikes of other juniors who have outgrown theirs. That may provide a market for your old bike and a ready source of new ones.

When you purchase a handlebar computer, look for one that displays cadence. This is useful for helping you improve leg speed.

IMPROVING

Always try to remember that you are in bicycle racing for the long haul. That's easy to say, but there will be times when you want to accelerate the program and do more because one of your friends is. Before you change the plan, talk with your coach.

In his book, *Greg LeMond's Complete Book of Bicycling*, LeMond describes how when he was 15 he wanted to ride even more since one of his friend was putting in twice as much mileage. He was smart, however, and held back. The next year his friend was out of cycling, and LeMond went on to become America's greatest cyclist. Be patient.

Why do you want to race? It certainly isn't for money or to attract the opposite sex — most of the time they won't even understand what you're doing. I would be willing to bet that the reason you are racing is for fun and personal challenge. Keep that perspective: learn to laugh at yourself, to accept your successes, and to learn from mistakes. This really should be fun.

REFERENCES

Bemben, D.A., et al. Effects of oral contraceptives on hormonal and metabolic responses during exercise, *Medicine and Science in Sport and Exercise*, vol. 24(4), 1992.

Bompa, T. *From Childhood to Champion Athlete*, Veritas Publishing, 1995.

Brown, C. and J. Wilmore. The effects of maximal resistance training on the strength and body composition of women athletes, *Medicine and Science in Sports*, vol. 6, pp. 174-177, 1974.

Child, J.S., et al. Cardiac hypertrophy and function in masters endurance runners and sprinters, *Journal of Applied Physiology*, vol. 57, pp. 170-181, 1984.

Cohen, J. and C.V. Gisolfi. Effects of interval training in work-heat tolerance in young women, *Medicine and Science in Sport and Exercise*, vol. 14, pp. 46-52, 1982.

Cunningham, D. A., et al. Cardiovascular response to intervals and continuous training in women, *European Journal of Applied Physiology*, vol. 41, pp. 187-197, 1979.

Dill, D. et al. A longitudinal study of 16 champion runners, *Journal of Sports Medicine*, vol. 7, pp. 4-32, 1967.

Drinkwater, B.L. Women and exercise: Physiological aspects, *Exercise and Sports Sciences Reviews*, vol. 12, pp. 21-51, 1984.

Drinkwater, B.L. (ed.). *Female Endurance Athletes*, Human Kinetics, 1986.

Ekblom, B. Effect of physical training in adolescent boys, *Journal of Applied Physiology*, vol. 27, pp. 350-353, 1969.

Heath, G. A physiological comparison of young and older endurance athletes, *Journal of Applied Physiology*, vol. 51(3), pp. 634-640, 1981.

Legwold, G. Masters competitors age little in ten years, *The Physician and Sports Medicine*, vol. 10 (10), p. 27, 1982.

LeMond, G. and K. Gordis. *Greg LeMond's Complete Book of Bicycling*, Perigee Books, 1988.

Mayhew, J. and P. Gross. Body composition changes in young women and high resistance weight training, *Research Quarterly*, vol. 45, pp. 433-440, 1974.

Pate, R.R., et al. Cardiorespiratory and metabolic responses to submaximal and maximal exercise in elite women distance runners, *International Journal of Sports Medicine*, vol. 8 (sup. 2), pp. 91-95, 1987.

Parizkova, J. Body composition and exercise during growth and development, *Physical Activity: Human Growth and Development*, 1974.

Pollock, M., et al. Effect of age and training on aerobic capacity and body composition of master athletes, *Journal of Applied Physiology*, vol. 62(2), pp. 725-731, 1987.

Pollock, M., et al. Frequency of training as a determinant for improvement in cardiovascular function and body composition of middle-aged men, *Archives of Physical Medicine and Rehabilitation*, vol. 56, pp. 141-145, 1975.

Rogers, et al. Decline in VO_2max with aging in masters athletes and sedentary men, *Journal of Applied Physiology*, vol. 68(5), pp. 2195-2199, 1990.

Seals, D.R., et al. Endurance training in older men and women, *Journal of Applied Physiology*, vol. 57, pp. 1024-1029, 1984.

Shangold, M.M. and G. Mirkin (eds.). *Women and exercise: Physiology and sports medicine*, Davis Publishing, 1988.

Shasby, G.B. and F.C. Hagerman. The effects of conditioning on cardiorespiratory function in adolescent boys, *Journal of Sports Medicine*, vol. 3, pp. 97-107, 1975.

Wells, C.L. *Women, Sport, and Performance: A Physiological Perspective*, Human Kinetics, 1991.

Wilmore, J., et al. Is there energy conservation in amenorrheic compared with eumenorrheic distance runners? *Journal of Applied Physiology*, vol. 72, pp. 15-22, 1992.

Wilmore, J. and D. Costill. *Physiology of Sport and Exercise*, Human Kinetics, 1994.

Chapter 15

Using a Training Journal

I like life. It's something to do.

— RONNIE SHAKES

Each athlete responds to training in his or her very unique way. If two cyclists who test similarly do exactly the same workouts day after day, one will eventually become more fit than the other. One may even become *over*trained on a regimen the other thrives on. So it is critical that you follow a program designed just for you. To do otherwise is to place limits on your potential.

How can you determine what constitutes the optimum training method for your unique needs? While races and testing reveal how you're doing, learning the causes of your performance improvements or declines can be discovered in training records. Keeping a journal is your third most important task when not working out. It ranks right behind eating and resting.

In addition to offering the opportunity for keener analysis, a journal also helps you grow by increasing motivation. Motivation comes from recording successes such as training goals accomplished, higher levels of training, subjective feelings of achievement and personal race performance records.

But be forewarned: Training journals can have a darker downside. I've known athletes who realized on Sunday afternoon they were a few miles or minutes short of their weekly goal and so went out for a short ride to reach the magic number. This is how you go about building "junk" miles. Becoming overly invested in the numbers you record can be a problem. Instead of using your journal as a score card, think of it more as a diary — a place where important and personal information is recorded.

PLANNING WITH A TRAINING JOURNAL

The training journal is the best place to record your weekly training plan. Chapters 9 and 10 offered guidance in how to determine what workouts should be done each day. Figures 9.1 and 10.1 recommended specific daily training structure. The training journal suggested in Figure 15.1 brings the final pieces of the training plan together by providing a space to outline your planned workouts each day. It is a good idea to plan the next week's training regimen at the end of each week. After reviewing how the preceding week went, sit down with your annual training plan and jot down what you'll do and when you'll do it. Using the workout codes from Chapter 9 and the workout durations from Table 9.1 makes this quick and easy. Once you get on to it, planning an entire week in detail only takes about 10 minutes.

You don't have to use my training journal. Many athletes, indeed most elites, prefer to use a simple blank notebook in which they can record as much data as they want in any way they want. The only problem with such a system is that it makes recall and analysis laborious since you may have to search every page for the critical information. A standardized form makes these tasks much easier.

At the top of Figure 15.1, there are spaces to write in three weekly goals. These are quite specific actions you need to accomplish to stay on track to your training objectives, which are tied to season goals. Consistent success in achieving short-term, weekly goals brings long-term success.

Weekly goals should focus on what the BT workout and race objectives are for that week. If you properly selected weekly workouts based on your limiters and strengths, depending on what period of the season you're in, achieving their scheduled outcomes brings you one step closer to the season's goals. For example, if you've scheduled SE intervals (workout code A2) to include 5 x 4 minutes building to the 5b zone on each, a weekly goal may be "20 minutes of SE intervals."

WEEK OF

Fig. 15.1 Weekly Training Journal

WEEK'S GOALS (check off as achieved):

☐ 1. ....
☐ 2. ....
☐ 3. ....

MONDAY

Warnings: Rate first four below on scale of 1-7. 1=best, 7=worst. 5+ is a warning. 3 warnings=day off.

Sleep quality ☐ *Fatigue* ☐ *Stress* ☐ *Soreness* ☐ *HR above/below normal* ☐ *Weight* ☐

| **Wrkt 1** Plan: Duration: | Actual_____ Distance_____ Weather_____ Other_____ Comments: |
| **Wrkt 2** Plan: Duration: | Actual_____ Distance_____ Weather_____ Other_____ Comments: |

Time by Zone
Wrkt 1   Wrkt 2

	Wrkt 1	Wrkt 2
1		
2		
3		
4		
5		
Ttl		

TUESDAY

Warnings: Rate first four below on scale of 1-7. 1=best, 7=worst. 5+ is a warning. 3 warnings=day off.

Sleep quality ☐ *Fatigue* ☐ *Stress* ☐ *Soreness* ☐ *HR above/below normal* ☐ *Weight* ☐

| **Wrkt 1** Plan: Duration: | Actual_____ Distance_____ Weather_____ Other_____ Comments: |
| **Wrkt 2** Plan: Duration: | Actual_____ Distance_____ Weather_____ Other_____ Comments: |

Time by Zone
Wrkt 1   Wrkt 2

	Wrkt 1	Wrkt 2
1		
2		
3		
4		
5		
Ttl		

WEDNESDAY

Warnings: Rate first four below on scale of 1-7. 1=best, 7=worst. 5+ is a warning. 3 warnings=day off.

Sleep quality ☐ *Fatigue* ☐ *Stress* ☐ *Soreness* ☐ *HR above/below normal* ☐ *Weight* ☐

| **Wrkt 1** Plan: Duration: | Actual_____ Distance_____ Weather_____ Other_____ Comments: |
| **Wrkt 2** Plan: Duration: | Actual_____ Distance_____ Weather_____ Other_____ Comments: |

Time by Zone
Wrkt 1   Wrkt 2

	Wrkt 1	Wrkt 2
1		
2		
3		
4		
5		
Ttl		

THURSDAY

Warnings: Rate first four below on scale of 1-7. 1=best, 7=worst. 5+ is a warning. 3 warnings=day off.

Sleep quality ☐ *Fatigue* ☐ *Stress* ☐ *Soreness* ☐ *HR above/below normal* ☐ *Weight* ☐

| **Wrkt 1** Plan: Duration: | Actual_____ Distance_____ Weather_____ Other_____ Comments: |
| **Wrkt 2** Plan: Duration: | Actual_____ Distance_____ Weather_____ Other_____ Comments: |

Time by Zone
Wrkt 1   Wrkt 2

	Wrkt 1	Wrkt 2
1		
2		
3		
4		
5		
Ttl		

WEEK OF   Fig. 15.1 Weekly Training Journal

FRIDAY   Warnings: Rate first four below on scale of 1-7. 1=best, 7=worst. 5+ is a warning. 3 warnings=day off.

Sleep quality [ ]   Fatigue [ ]   Stress [ ]   Soreness [ ]   HR above/below normal [ ]   Weight [   ]

Wrkt 1 Plan: Duration:	Actual_____ Distance_____ Weather_____ Other_____ Comments:	Time by Zone Wrkt 1 Wrkt 2

| | | 1 [ ][ ] |
| | | 2 [ ][ ] |

Wrkt 2 Plan: Duration:	Actual_____ Distance_____ Weather_____ Other_____ Comments:	3 [ ][ ] 4 [ ][ ] 5 [ ][ ]

Ttl [ ][ ]

SATURDAY   Warnings: Rate first four below on scale of 1-7. 1=best, 7=worst. 5+ is a warning. 3 warnings=day off.

Sleep quality [ ]   Fatigue [ ]   Stress [ ]   Soreness [ ]   HR above/below normal [ ]   Weight [   ]

Wrkt 1 Plan: Duration:	Actual_____ Distance_____ Weather_____ Other_____ Comments:	Time by Zone Wrkt 1 Wrkt 2

| | | 1 [ ][ ] |
| | | 2 [ ][ ] |

Wrkt 2 Plan: Duration:	Actual_____ Distance_____ Weather_____ Other_____ Comments:	3 [ ][ ] 4 [ ][ ] 5 [ ][ ]

Ttl [ ][ ]

SUNDAY   Warnings: Rate first four below on scale of 1-7. 1=best, 7=worst. 5+ is a warning. 3 warnings=day off.

Sleep quality [ ]   Fatigue [ ]   Stress [ ]   Soreness [ ]   HR above/below normal [ ]   Weight [   ]

Wrkt 1 Plan: Duration:	Actual_____ Distance_____ Weather_____ Other_____ Comments:	Time by Zone Wrkt 1 Wrkt 2

| | | 1 [ ][ ] |
| | | 2 [ ][ ] |

Wrkt 2 Plan: Duration:	Actual_____ Distance_____ Weather_____ Other_____ Comments:	3 [ ][ ] 4 [ ][ ] 5 [ ][ ]

Ttl [ ][ ]

WEEK'S SUMMARY
1. **Total training time (including strength) this week was** [:] hrs : min
2. **I felt like I was...** [ ] **overtraining ....** [ ] **on the edge ....** [ ] **O.K.**
3. **I had soreness in my** _____ **caused by** _____ .
4. **Comments on this week:**

When you accomplish that goal check it off. By periodically scanning weekly goals, you have a quick check of how you're doing throughout the year. Figure 15.2 shows how this is done. (Please see page 188)

WHAT TO RECORD

If you've never kept a journal, you may find record keeping a bit scattered at first, until you figure out what to write down every day. I ask the athletes I coach to record data in their journals in five categories:

- Morning warnings
- Workout basics
- Time by zone
- Physical comments
- Mental comments

MORNING WARNINGS

Every morning on waking your body "whispers" what it can handle that day. The problem is, most of us refuse to listen. A journal helps the body be heard if certain indicators of readiness are checked. These are sleep quality, fatigue, stress level, muscle soreness and heart rate. The first four should be rated on a scale of 1 to 7, with 1 being the best situation (for example, an excellent night's sleep) and 7 the worst (for example, extremely high stress).

Take your pulse while still laying quietly in bed and record it in beats per minute above (positive number) or below (negative number) your average morning pulse rate. If you record a 5, 6, or 7 for any of the first four indicators or a positive or negative 5 or greater for heart rate, consider that a warning that something is wrong.

Another way of taking resting heart rate that has been shown as a more reliable indicator with some athletes, is to take lying down pulse as above and then to stand for 20 seconds and take the pulse again. A heart rate monitor is best in this case. The variance in difference between the two is the indicator. An example may better explain this method:

Lying-down heart rate	46
Standing heart rate	72
Difference	26

Record your variance from a normal difference in the "HR above/below nor-

WEEK OF APRIL 28   Fig. 15.2 Weekly Training Journal Example

WEEK'S GOALS (check off as achieved):

☑ 1. 24 MINUTES OF CRUISE INTERVALS.
☐ 2. 15 MINUTES OF SE INTERVALS.
☑ 3. GOOD EFFORT FOR CLUB RIDE.

MONDAY   *Warnings: Rate first four below on scale of 1-7. 1=best, 7=worst. 5+ is a warning. 3 warnings=day off.*

Sleep quality 1   *Fatigue* 2   *Stress* 2   *Soreness* 1   *HR above/below normal* +1   *Weight* 152

Wrkt 1
Plan: WEIGHTS 3 x ME
Duration:

Actual ME   Distance —   Weather —   Other —
Comments: 3 SETS OF ME, FELT STRONG!

Wrkt 2
Plan:
Duration:

Actual____ Distance____ Weather____ Other____
Comments:

Time by Zone	Wrkt 1	Wrkt 2
1		
2		
3		
4		
5		
Ttl	1:00	

TUESDAY   *Warnings: Rate first four below on scale of 1-7. 1=best, 7=worst. 5+ is a warning. 3 warnings=day off.*

Sleep quality 1   *Fatigue* 1   *Stress* 1   *Soreness* 2   *HR above/below normal* -1   *Weight* 152

Wrkt 1
Plan: M2
4 x 6' (2')
Duration: 1:30

Actual M2   Distance 29M   Weather 36°   Other TRAINER
Comments: ON TRAINER AT 7AM. A LITTLE HARD TO GET GOING. FELT STRONG ON #1-3. #4 WAS HARD. GOOD WORKOUT!

Wrkt 2
Plan: E1
Duration: :30

Actual E1   Distance 7M   Weather 52°   Other TRAINER
Comments: EASY SPIN. FELT GOOD TO WORK OUT KINKS. GOT HOME LATE.

Time by Zone	Wrkt 1	Wrkt 2
1	25:00	:30
2	42:00	
3	2:10	
4	18:20	
5	2:30	
Ttl	1:30	:30

WEDNESDAY   *Warnings: Rate first four below on scale of 1-7. 1=best, 7=worst. 5+ is a warning. 3 warnings=day off.*

Sleep quality 3   *Fatigue* 2   *Stress* 3   *Soreness* 1   *HR above/below normal* 4   *Weight* 151

Wrkt 1
Plan: E1
Duration: 3:00

Actual E1   Distance 46M   Weather 68°   Other FRONT.RD.
Comments: A LITTLE SLEEPY ALL DAY. STRESS-FUL DAY AT WORK. RODE WITH BILL. NEEDED EASY RIDE TO UNWIND.

Wrkt 2
Plan:
Duration:

Actual____ Distance____ Weather____ Other____
Comments:

Time by Zone	Wrkt 1	Wrkt 2
1	2:39	
2	:13	
3		
4		
5		
Ttl	2:52	

THURSDAY   *Warnings: Rate first four below on scale of 1-7. 1=best, 7=worst. 5+ is a warning. 3 warnings=day off.*

Sleep quality 3   *Fatigue* 5   *Stress* 4   *Soreness* 1   *HR above/below normal* 6   *Weight* 150

Wrkt 1
Plan: A2
5 x 3' (3')
Duration: 1:00

Actual A2   Distance 20M   Weather 62° WIND   Other HWY 1
Comments: ONLY DID 3 INTERVALS. HAVEN'T FULLY RECOVERED FROM TUESDAY AND WORK PROBLEMS. POWER PRETTY GOOD, THO.

Wrkt 2
Plan: E1
Duration: :30

Actual E1   Distance 6   Weather 56°   Other TRAINER
Comments: EASY SPIN. FELT GOOD. RAINING.

Time by Zone	Wrkt 1	Wrkt 2
1	18:00	:20
2	30:00	
3	10:00	
4	3:10	
5	7:50	
Ttl	1:09	:20

WEEK OF APRIL 28

FRIDAY
Warnings: Rate first four below on scale of 1-7. 1=best, 7=worst. 5+ is a warning. 3 warnings=day off.

Sleep quality [2] Fatigue [5] Stress [5] Soreness [2] HR above/below normal [+5] Weight [151]

Wrkt 1 Plan: OFF Duration:	Actual____ Distance____ Weather____ Other____ Comments: NEEDED THIS DAY OFF! CAME AT THE RIGHT TIME.
Wrkt 2 Plan: Duration:	Actual____ Distance____ Weather____ Other____ Comments:

Time by Zone

	Wrkt 1	Wrkt 2
1		
2		
3		
4		
5		
Ttl		

SATURDAY
Warnings: Rate first four below on scale of 1-7. 1=best, 7=worst. 5+ is a warning. 3 warnings=day off.

Sleep quality [1] Fatigue [3] Stress [2] Soreness [1] HR above/below normal [+1] Weight [152]

Wrkt 1 Plan: A1 Duration: 2:30	Actual A1 Distance 58 M Weather 75° Other BIG LOOP Comments: CLUB RIDE — BIG CROWD. EVERY — ONE RIDING HARD TODAY. I FELT GOOD AT START AND MADE FIRST BREAK. AFTER
Wrkt 2 Plan: Duration:	Actual____ Distance____ Weather____ Other____ Comments: THAT I JUST HUNG ON. FIRST HOT RIDE OF YEAR.

Time by Zone

	Wrkt 1	Wrkt 2
1	22:00	
2	36:00	
3	35:00	
4	42:40	
5	24:20	
Ttl	2:40	

SUNDAY
Warnings: Rate first four below on scale of 1-7. 1=best, 7=worst. 5+ is a warning. 3 warnings=day off.

Sleep quality [2] Fatigue [3] Stress [1] Soreness [3] HR above/below normal [4] Weight [151]

Wrkt 1 Plan: E2 Duration: 3:30	Actual E2 Distance 63 M Weather 77° Other TO LYONS Comments: NICE DAY FOR A LONG RIDE. WITH TOM L. CAN FEEL YESTERDAY'S WORKOUT IN MY QUADS — A LITTLE SORE.
Wrkt 2 Plan: Duration:	Actual____ Distance____ Weather____ Other____ Comments: WILL GET MASSAGE TOMORROW.

Time by Zone

	Wrkt 1	Wrkt 2
1	1:44	
2	1:48	
3		
4		
5		
Ttl	3:32	

WEEK'S SUMMARY
1. **Total training time (including strength) this week was** [13 : 33] hrs : min
2. **I felt like I was...** ☐ overtraining .... ☑ on the edge .... ☐ O.K.
3. **I had soreness in my** QUADS **caused by** SATURDAY'S RIDE.
4. **Comments on this week:**

CLUB RIDE, MY FIRST RACE EFFORT OR THE YEAR, WAS AN EYE OPENER! I HAVE A LONG WAY TO GO YET. OF COURSE, ALL THE STRESS AT WORK DIDN'T HELP. FEEL REAL GOOD ABOUT TUESDAY'S CRUISE INTERVALS.

mal" box. For example, if your average difference over several days is found to be 26, but one day the difference is 32, record a variance of +6 — a warning sign for that day. This may be a better warning method for you than just the lying-down type. You may be able to determine which method is better for you by doing both for three to four weeks during a period of hard training.

Two morning warning scores of 5 or higher mean reduce training intensity today. Three or more morning warnings is your body telling you to take the day off — you need more recovery. Failure to heed the morning warnings your body is whispering to you, forces it to eventually "shout" by giving you a cold or by leaving you too exhausted to workout for several days.

Ratings of 4 or less are generally good signs that your body is ready for serious training. The lower the scores, the harder the workout can be any given day.

A recent study at the University of Queensland in Australia showed these indicators to be relatively reliable measures of overtraining and burnout. But they are not necessarily the best for everyone. You may find others that work better for you. If so, record them in the same manner.

Checking and recording body weight every morning after visiting the bathroom and before eating can also reveal the state of your body. Short-term weight loss is a measure of fluid levels, so if your weight is down a pound from the previous day, the first thing you should do is drink water. A pint of water weighs about one pound. A study done in Oregon a few years ago found that afternoon weight loss is also a good indicator of overtraining, and may be the easiest-to-measure initial indicator. (Chapter 17 discusses overtraining in greater detail.)

WORKOUT BASICS

This is the detail stuff that will help you remember the workout months later. Include the "Actual" workout by code (in the "Comments" section briefly describe the reason for change from the plan, if any), the "Distance," "Weather" and "Other" variables such as course or equipment used (for example, mountain bike or fixed gear bike).

TIME BY ZONE

On the right side of the training journal are two columns titled "Wrkt 1" and "Wrkt 2." The "Wrkt 1" column provides spaces to write in the time spent in each training zone for the first workout of the day. This could be heart rate or power data and serves as a good check of how the workout profile went in relation to the plan. A few weeks or even a year later you can compare this information following a repeat of the same workout.

The "Ttl" box at the bottom of the first column is a space to write in the total duration of the workout. This should be about the same as the planned duration.

The "Wrkt 2" column is completed in the same way for the second daily workout. If you worked out just once, leave it blank.

PHYSICAL COMMENTS

Observing how you are performing in workouts and races is critical to measuring progress. After each workout, record such information as average heart rate, heart rate at the end of work intervals, highest heart rates observed and average speed. If you have sophisticated equipment, you may record average power, maximum power and lactate levels. Later, you may use any or all of this data for comparisons under similar conditions. Also record aches or pains no matter how trivial they may seem at the time. Season-wrecking injuries often start as insignificant discomforts. Later, it may be helpful to trace when, why and how.

Women should record their menstrual periods to help them get a clearer picture of how it effects training and racing.

For races, you may want to record warm-up, key moves, limiters, strengths, gearing, results and notes for the future. Race information may also be recorded using Figure 15.3, Season Results. (Please see page 192) This will come in handy when you need to seek sponsors or change teams. Putting together a race resumé is much easier when all of the information is in one location.

MENTAL COMMENTS

Here is where most journal keepers fail. Training and racing are usually thought of as strictly physical and what's happening inside the head is unimportant. Sometimes emotions are the most telling aspect of physical performance.

Always include your perception of how hard or easy the workout or race was. It's not necessary to be overly scientific about this. Just say something such as "A tough workout," or "Felt easy." These tell a lot about your experience. Commenting on how enjoyable the workout was is also revealing. Repeated remarks about training being a "drag" is a good sign that burnout is imminent just as frequent "Fun

The Training Bible

Figure 15.3

Sample training diary

Figure 15.3 Season Results

Year _____

Date	Race	Distance	Time	Place (starters)	Comments

workout" speaks volumes about your mental state.

From the Mental Skills Profile completed in Chapter 5, you should have a good idea of what needs work. If, for example, confidence is lacking, look for and record the positive aspects of the workout or race. What did you achieve that was at the limits of your ability? What were your successes today? Remembering and reliving accomplishments is the first step in becoming more confident.

Mental comments should also include unusual stressers in your life off the bike. Visiting relatives, working overtime, illness, sleep deprivation and relationship problems all affect performance.

WEEK'S SUMMARY

At the end of the week, complete a short summary of how things went for you. Total your training time. This will come in handy later in the year when it's time to decide training volumes for the new season. Check how you felt physically this week. It's not a good idea to frequently feel "on the edge" of overtraining, though that feeling is inevitable whenever you're trying to become more fit. The third week of a four-week training block is when this typically happens. If you never feel on the edge, you are not working hard enough.

Indicate any soreness felt during the week no matter how trivial it may seem at the time. There may be a pattern developing that will be easier to find if you noted it here.

Summarize how the week went, noting the successes, the areas needing work, racing and training revelations and notes for the future, such as how to deal with a problem you experienced this week. For example, you may have had a head cold coming on and discovered something that helped you fight it off.

ANALYSIS

When training and racing aren't going so well, looking back in the journal to what was happening in more positive times can sometimes get you back on track. In addition, you'll find that by comparing recent workouts to what you were doing a year or more ago provides a solid gauge of improvement. When trying to regain the top form from an earlier period, look for patterns such as types of workouts done then, morning warning levels, stress, recovery between BT workouts, equipment used, training volume, training partners and any thing else that may provide a clue. Become a detective.

Recently, an athlete asked me to review her training journal. She was training hard, putting in lots of quality miles, and was very focused on her goals. Yet she wasn't in top form at the A-priority races, and sometimes even had trouble finishing.

The first thing I noticed in her journal was that she ignored her warning signs. She faithfully took her resting heart rate every day and recorded hours of sleep and fatigue level. Yet she always did the planned workout regardless of what the morning warnings said. She was so driven to succeed that she let nothing get in her way — not even her own body. I told her about a 1968 study in which rats were forced to swim six hours a day, six days a week. After 161 hours of swimming, they showed great improvement in their aerobic capacities. But after 610 hours, their aerobic powers were no better than the untrained, control-group rats. She was an overtrained rat, I told her.

We also talked about how to peak and taper for a big race. It was obvious that she was not rested on race days. She trained through the A races as if they were the same as her C-priority races. We discussed how backing off in the days and even weeks before an important event allows the body to absorb all of the stress that has been placed on it and grow stronger.

The next time I talked with this rider was several weeks later, and she was riding well and pleased with her results. Had it not been for the detailed journal she kept, I would have never been able to so exactly determine the causes of her lackluster performance.

REFERENCES

Abraham, W.M. Factors in delayed muscle soreness, *Medicine and Science in Sports and Exercise*, vol. 9, pp. 11-20, 1977.

Berdanier, C.D. The many faces of stress, *Nutrition Today*, vol. 2(2), pp. 12-17, 1987.

Brown, R.L. Overtraining in athletes: A round table discussion, *The Physician and Sports Medicine*, vol. 11(6), p. 99, 1983.

Czajkowski, W. A simple method to control fatigue in endurance training, in *Exercise and Sport Biology*, International Series on Sport Sciences, P.V. Komi (ed.), Human Kinetics, vol. 10, pp. 207-212, 1982.

Dressendorfer, R., et al. Increased morning heart rate in runners: A valid sign of overtraining? *The Physician and Sports Medicine*, vol. 13(8), pp. 77-86, 1985.

Galbo, H. *Hormonal and Metabolic Adaptations to Exercise*, Stuttgart: Georg Thieme Verlag, 1983.

Chapter 16

FUEL

Never eat more than you can lift.

— MISS PIGGY

The human body has not changed significantly in more than a million years, but there has been an exponential increase in information about the human body over the last 30 years. Some of this knowledge has caused us to make dramatic and even complex adjustments in the ways we live and train, though not always. Take diet, for example.

Going back a million years to the Stone Age, we find that Paleolithic men and women had a simple diet. Despite the absence of food pyramids and RDA, they did not suffer from the diet- and lifestyle-induced diseases we now experience: heart disease, hypertension, diabetes and some types of cancers. Nor were they runts. Research has shown that Stone Age men and women were about the same size as we are today. The men averaged five-feet-eleven inches and the women were about five-feet-six inches. Indeed, it wasn't until the advent of agriculture about 10,000 years ago that humans lost stature they would not regain until the last 200 years.

With the advent of an agrarian lifestyle came also higher infant mortality, reduced life spans, iron deficiency, bone disorders such as osteoporosis and dental cavities. Modern man is still afflicted with many of these same disorders.

In only 10,000 years (less in most parts of the world), agriculture has completely reshaped our diets and our health. While a hundred centuries may seem like a long time, it's really not in the context of nearly 2 million years of man's time as a genus on earth. If man's existence were represented by 24 hours, farming would have been around for only the last eight minutes, far too little time for the body to have adapted to the diet currently popular. Modern men and women have bodies meant for a diet quite different from what most eat now.

It is reasonable to believe that the diet man ate for most of his existence, until the arrival of farming, is the diet for which we are best suited today. What was that diet? Paleolithic man primarily ate the meat and organs of wild game, uncultivated vegetables and fruit. They did not eat grass seed (grains), dairy products, animals fattened on corn in feedlots, or, with the rare exception of honey, calorie-dense, nutritionally-empty foods. Their diet was high in fiber, low in saturated fat and high in protein from the meat of extremely lean animals.

While it is not possible to fully adopt earliest man's menu, it is possible to eat in a manner which more closely resembles that optimal diet. Such a menu includes a macronutrient breakdown somewhat different from the high carbohydrate, low protein regimen commonly described as best for the athlete. A diet that more closely follows that of Paleolithic man would be composed of one-third or more protein, 20- to 25-percent fat and half or less from carbohydrate. Since meat was undoubtedly Stone Age man's dietary staple, some paleontologists believe he ate even more than one-third of his calories as protein. This issue has not been resolved, and certainly won't be here.

The focus of this book is training, not diet, but there is no denying the complex tie-ins between nutritional practices and exhaustive exercise. Eating foods optimally designed for the human body will reduce body fat, improve recovery, decrease down time due to illness and generally enhance athletic performance. The older you are, the more critical diet is for performance. At age 20, you can make a lot of mistakes and get away with it. At age 40 everything is critical, especially diet. For many female athletes who are chronically low in iron stores, such a diet is crucial to athletic success.

The next section briefly discusses details of a diet based on the Paleolithic model. For a more detailed discussion of structuring meals in this way, read *Protein Power* by Michael and Mary Dan Eades (Bantam Books, 1996) or *The Zone* by Barry Sears (Harper Collins, 1995). The second section of this chapter looks at supplements that have the potential to bolster your health and fitness. The last discusses leading-edge ergogenic aids.

DIET

Nearly every serious athlete I meet tells me that they load up on carbohydrate, carefully limit their fat intake and eat little or no meat. They have bought in to the carbohydrate craze. If this describes the way you eat, get ready for a dietary revolution and better performance. There is an accumulating body of evidence that high carbohydrate, low protein diets are not as beneficial to health and fitness as is slightly lowering the carbohydrate and eating more protein than most athletes commonly do.

Greg LeMond eating a pre-race breakfast before the 1990 Paris-Nice stage race with an obviously pleased sponsor looking on. Adequately fueling the body before a race is important to success.

PROTEIN

Protein is more important for endurance athletes than for those in power sports such as American football, baseball and basketball. An intense, one-hour criterium can cause the depletion of up to 30 grams of protein, about equal to the amount of protein in a three-ounce can of tuna. Replacing these losses are critical to recovery and improved fitness. Without such replenishment, the endurance athlete's body is forced to cannibalize protein from muscle.

The daily requirement of protein for the hard-training cyclist, based on recent research, appears to be about 0.9 grams per pound of lean body mass (about 2 grams per kilogram of body weight). For a lean 128-pound woman who carries 12-percent body fat, the need for protein is about 101 grams daily. A 154-pound rider with eight-percent body fat needs about 127 grams of protein in a day.

Protein is found in both vegetable and animal forms, and the quantity required, regardless of source, can be difficult to consume unless you closely watch your diet. To get 127 grams of protein from vegetable sources would mean eating 17 cups of spaghetti, 14 cups of yogurt, or 21 bagels. The same 127 grams could also come from 15 ounces of chicken or lean steak, or 17 ounces of tuna. This is a lot of food from either type, but there is an added benefit in getting protein from animal sources: All of the necessary amino acids in the right proportions, easily absorbable iron, zinc, calcium and vitamin B-12 are present and the protein is more absorbable due to less fiber in the meat.

So what happens if you fail to get your daily need for protein when training hard? Occasionally missing out probably has no measurable impact on performance, but regular avoidance of high quality protein accompanied by a volume of high-intensity exercise can have a significant impact on training and racing. Besides being a minor fuel source during strenuous exercise, protein is responsible for building muscle, making hormones that regulate basal metabolic rate and for fighting off disease.

There's no doubt that during prolonged, high intensity exercise, the body turns to stored protein, eventually resulting in the loss of muscle. A 1992 study of 16 hikers who spent 21 days in the Andes Mountains traveling five hours a day on foot with an average elevation gain of 2,500 feet per day, found significant loss of muscle mass. This may explain why some endurance athletes have a gaunt look during several weeks of rigorous training with low intake of protein.

Without meat in the diet, the risk of low iron levels is also high. One study linked low iron levels with injuries in runners. Those lowest in iron had twice as many injuries as those highest in iron. Besides providing protein, lean red meat is also a good source of easily absorbed iron.

CARBOHYDRATE

When you eat a high-carbohydrate meal or snack the pancreas releases insulin to regulate the level of blood sugar. That insulin stays in the blood for up to two hours, just in time for the next carbohydrate snack, during which time it has other effects, such as preventing the body from utilizing stored fat, converting carbohydrate and protein to body fat and moving fat in the blood to storage sites. This may explain why, despite serious training and eating a "healthy" diet, some athletes are unable to lose body fat.

Some carbohydrates enter the blood stream sooner than others, producing

Adriano Baffi in the feed zone in stage 10 of the 1996 Tour DuPont. On-bike fuel can determine the outcomes of a long race.

an exaggerated insulin increase and quickly bringing about all of the negative aspects of high insulin described above. These rapidly digested carbohydrates are high on the glycemic index — a relatively new food rating system developed for diabetics. Foods low on the glycemic index produce a less dramatic rise in insulin and help avoid the craving for more sugary food that comes with eating high glycemic carbohydrates.

Table 16.1 (see page 200) lists common high and low glycemic foods. To control the negative side of the insulin response, choose foods on the low end of the index. High index carbohydrates are best eaten during exercise and in the 30 minutes immediately afterward, otherwise they should be consumed in moderation in combination with fat and protein.

FAT

We have gone too far. In the past 10 years or so, we've created such a terrifying specter of dietary fat that many athletes now see all types of fat as the "enemy" and try to entirely eliminate it from their diet. Don't get me wrong, some types of fat need to be reduced — especially saturated fat and trans fatty acids, the man-made fats found in many highly processed foods and called "partially hydrogenated" on the label. Partially hydrogenated fats lead to artery clogging the same as the saturated variety common to feedlot cattle.

Table 16.1

Glycemic index of
common foods

Glycemic Index				
High glycemic (80% or higher)				
Apricots	Bananas	Carrots	Corn	Corn chips
Corn flakes	Crackers	French bread	Grapenuts	Honey
Mango	Molasses	Muesli	Oat bran	Pastries
Potatoes	Raisins	Rice	Rye crisps	
Shredded wheat	Soda pop	White bread	Whole wheat bread	
Moderate Glycemic Index (50-80%)				
All-bran cereal	Baked beans	Beets	Garbanzo beans	Navy beans
Oatmeal	Oranges	Orange juice	Pasta	Pinto beans
Potato chips	PowerBar	Spaghetti	Yams	
Low Glycemic Index (30-50%)				
Apple	Apple juice	Apple sauce	Barley	
Black-eyed peas	Dates	Figs	Grapes	Yogurt
Kidney beans	Lentils	Lima beans	Peaches	Pears
Peas	Milk	Rye bread	Sweet potatoes	Tomato soup
Very Low Glycemic Index (less than 30%)				
Cherries	Grapefruit	Peanuts	Plums	Soy beans

Don't confuse these "bad" fats with all types of fat. There are, in fact, "good" fats that not only prevent dry skin and dull hair, but more importantly help maintain a regular menstrual cycle in women and avoid colds and other infections common to serious athletes. You may find that eating these essential fats improves your long-term recovery and capacity to train at a high level, if you previously have been low in them.

A study at State University of New York illustrates this. Researchers had a group of runners eat a higher-than-usual fat diet consisting of 38-percent fat and 50-percent carbohydrate calories for one week. The second week they ate a more typical high-carbohydrate diet with 73 percent of calories coming from carbos and 15 percent from fat. At the end of each week the subjects were tested for maximum aerobic capacities and then ran themselves to exhaustion on a treadmill. On the higher-fat diet their max VO_2 was 11 percent greater than when they were on the high-carbohydrate diet. On the higher-fat diet they also lasted nine percent longer on the run to exhaustion. The study was not without fault, however, since test sujects were not provided with a carbohydrate drink during the runs.

The good fats are called "monounsaturated" and "omega-3" and were well balanced in our Paleolithic ancestors' diet. Monounsaturated fats include the oils and spreads of almonds, avocado, hazelnut, macadamia nut, olive and walnut. Omega-3 fats are found in fish oils and wild game. The red meat of wild game also provides significant amounts of both monounsaturated and omega-3 fats.

The bottom line on fat is to select the leanest cuts of meat (wild game, if possible), trim away all visible fat from meat, include fish and fowl, eat low- or non-fat dairy, avoid trans fatty acids and regularly include monounsaturated fat in your diet.

RECOVERY

While eating as Paleolithic man did will likely improve your health and even your performance, it is not without its limitations. By lowering carbohydrate intake to around 50 percent of total calories, for the first two or three weeks you are following this diet, recovery time is likely to increase. To speed recovery, continue to consume high glycemic index food and drink during and immediately after high intensity training and racing. I don't recommend making this dietary shift within two weeks of an A race. Recovery is discussed in greater detail in Chapter 18.

WATER

Many athletes don't drink enough fluids, perpetually leaving them on the edge of dehydration. In this state, recovery is compromised and the risk of illness rises. Drinking throughout the day is one of the simplest and yet most effective means of boosting performance for these athletes. Since sports drinks and most fruit juices are high glycemic index, the best fluid replacement is water.

Get in eight to 12 glasses a day, based on your body size and training load. Use your rate of urination and urine color as a guide. You should need to visit the toilet at least once every two hours during the day and your urine should be clear. If you are not achieving these standards, drink more.

ANTIOXIDANT SUPPLEMENTS

For many years, registered dietitians and others who study nutrition have recommended that athletes meet all of their vitamin needs with food rather than pills. Some are now changing their opinions when it comes to serious athletes.

The Training Bible

Here is why.

The process of metabolizing food and oxygen for exercise, releases free radicals that cause damage to healthy cells. This is much like the rusting of metal — a breakdown caused by oxidation. Intensive and extensive exercise produces large numbers of free radicals that threaten your health and ability to recover following workouts. Hard training is likely to aggravate the condition.

For example, one study measured by-products of free radical damage in highly-trained athletes, moderately-trained athletes and a sedentary group. The researchers found that the highly-trained athletes had the highest levels of damage, while the moderately trained subjects had the least. The sedentary group was in the middle.

In recent years, studies have shown that vitamins C and E reduce damage and prevent colds associated with extreme physical exertion by combining with the free radicals to stop the oxidative process. The research typically uses large doses of each of these micronutrients — usually hundreds of times the RDA. Because the calculation involves variables such as age, sex, diet, body fat, size and training load, it is difficult to determine the necessary amounts for each individual. Recommended daily intakes based on these studies generally fall into these ranges:

Vitamin E	400-800 IU
Vitamin C	300 mg-1000 mg.

The problem is that in order to get even the lowest of these dosages you would have to eat *all* of the following foods *every* day!

Asparagus	15 spears
Avocado	31
Broccoli	4 cups
Peaches	33
Prunes	30
Tomato juice	12 ounces
Spinach	17 cups
Wheat germ	¼ cup

While some cyclists I know put away 3000 to 4000 calories a day, none eat such foods in these volumes. Do you?

While eating a wholesome diet from a wide-ranging menu is absolutely necessary for optimal health and fitness, few people, including athletes, achieve the recommended standards. For example, it has been estimated that the minimum goal of eating five fruit and vegetable servings per day is accomplished by less than 10 percent of the American population.

While it is true that serious athletes tend to eat more than average citizens, they seldom eat enough of the right foods. A 1989 study of triathletes who competed in the national championship; the Hawaii Ironman or the Huntsville, Alabama, Double Ironman, found that as a group they had inadequate caloric intakes due to unusual eating habits. They also demonstrated poor food selection resulting from rigorous training schedules and limited time for eating.

Athletes often rely on daily multiple vitamins, but these seldom provide vitamins C and E in large enough volumes. Highly-trained athletes may need to supplement their diets with individual dosages, especially vitamin E. It appears that these supplements should be taken with meals twice a day for best results.

Vitamin C has a low level of risk associated with usage at the above level, but high dosages of vitamin E can cause problems for those who are deficient in vitamin K. Check with your health-care provider before starting supplementation.

ERGOGENIC AIDS

Several years ago university researchers asked a group of elite athletes to answer a question: "If you could take a pill that would ensure a gold medal in the next Olympics, but you would die within five years, would you take it?" The overwhelming answer was "Yes!"

Such attitudes have led elite athletes to experiment with anabolic steroids, erythropoietin (EPO), amphetamines and other banned ergogenic aids. Some have consequently died in their quest for athletic excellence. Others have simply wasted their money on products that have no benefit beyond a placebo effect and have not withstood scientific investigation.

There is no magic pill that will guarantee an Olympic medal — or even a better-than-average performance. Training is still the single most important component of athletic excellence. There are, however, a few products that go beyond a normal diet and which science has generally found effective. I say "generally," because as with the scientific study of almost anything, there are often contradictory results. Also, not all ergogenic aids have the same benefits for everyone. Individualization applies here just as it does in training.

Here is a summary of some found to be best for endurance athletes. Before trying these or any other dietary supplement, it is a good idea to talk with your health-care provider. Diabetes, hypertension, or other serious medical problems may be reasons you should not use one or more of these supplements.

BRANCHED-CHAIN AMINO ACIDS

During workouts lasting longer than about three hours, the body turns to protein to provide fuel — perhaps as much as 10 percent of the energy requirement. Three essential amino acids — ones that must be present in the diet since the body can't synthesize them — make up about a third of muscle. These are leucine, isoleucine and valine. Collectively they are called branched chain amino acids (BCAA).

Several studies have shown that supplementing the diet with BCAA enhances endurance in several ways:

• BCAA help to maintain the immune system following exhaustive workouts and races reducing the likelihood of overtraining. Thus they have the potential to speed recovery.

• BCAA have been shown to maintain muscle mass, power and endurance during exhaustive, multi-day endurance events such as stage races or crash training.

• BCAA may help to reduce mental fatigue and increase speed late in a race.

• BCAA promote the use of fat for fuel while conserving glycogen.

BCAA may be purchased in health food stores and drug stores that sell food supplements. They should come in a brown bottle to protect the capsules from light, and the label should indicate that each of the individual amino acids is preceded by an "L" as in "L-valine." This ensures adequate absorption.

There are four times in your season to use BCAA — during the maximum strength (MS) phase, in the Build training period, for long and intense races or stage races and while training intensely at high altitude. Here are guidelines for supplementing with BCAA:

• Take about 35 mg of BCAA for each pound of body weight daily, but only at the times indicated above. A 150-pound cyclist would take 5,250 mg, or about five grams daily. A 120 pounder could consume 4,200 mg, or about four grams a day.

• One to two hours before an MS strength workout, a high-intensity workout in the Build period, or an A-priority race take one-half of your daily dose.

Then again one to two hours before bed time the same day take the other half.

• During a stage race, double your normal dosage taking one-third before the race, one-third an hour or two before your post-race nap and one-third before turning in for the day.

MEDIUM-CHAIN TRIGLYCERIDES

Medium chain triglycerides (MCT) are processed fats that are metabolically different from other fats in that they are quickly absorbed by the digestive system and aren't readily stored as body fat. Studies have shown that use of MCT can improve endurance and late-race speed in long races.

In a recent study at the University of Capetown in South Africa, six experienced cyclists rode for two hours at about 73 percent of maximum heart rate. Immediately after this steady, but low-intensity ride, they time trialed 40 kilometers at maximum effort. They did this three times on different days using a different drink for each attempt. One drink was a normal carbohydrate sports drink. Another was an MCT-only beverage. The third ride used a sports drink spiked with MCT.

With the MCT-only drink their average 40k time was 1:12:08. The carbohydrate sports drink produced a 1:06:45. With the mixed MCT-carbohydrate beverage their time was 1:05:00 — a significant improvement.

The scientists believe that the MCT spared glycogen during the two-hour warm-up. The riders were then able to better utilize carbohydrate during the more intense time trial.

An MCT-sports drink mix may benefit your performance late in races that last three hours or longer. You can create such a long-race drink for yourself by mixing 16 ounces of your favorite sports drink with four tablespoons of MCT. You can purchase liquid MCT at a local health food store.

CREATINE MONOHYDRATE

How would you like to sprint farther and faster, recover more rapidly, power up small hills quicker and reduce soreness after races? A relatively recent discovery, creatine monohydrate, may be the ticket. Many cyclists have tried it and report good results.

Creatine is a substance created in the liver, kidneys and pancreas and found in muscle tissue. The muscles use it to form creatine phosphate, a fuel used mostly during maximum efforts of up to about 15 seconds and, to a lesser extent, in intense efforts lasting a few minutes.

The amount of creatine formed by the human body is not enough to boost performance, but scientists have found that by supplementing the diet for a few days preceding the event, performance *can* be enhanced. In order to get an adequate amount of creatine from the diet, an athlete would have to eat up to five pounds of rare meat or fish daily. Supplementing appears to be quite effective in increasing stored creatine.

A few years ago, scientists from Sweden, Britain and Estonia tried creatine supplements on a group of runners. Following a creatine-loading period the runners ran a 4 x 1000-meter interval workout at maximum effort. Compared with the pre-test results, the creatine-supplemented subjects improved their total 4000-meter times by an average of 17 seconds while the placebo-control group slowed by one second. The relative advantage the creatine users experienced increased as the workout progressed. In other words, they experienced less fatigue and were faster at the end.

There is still not a lot known about creatine supplementation, but the benefits are probably greatest for maximizing the gains from interval and hill repeat workouts, in races on the track and in short races on the road such as criteriums. Vegetarians may stand to realize greater gain from using creatine since they typically have low levels.

According to scientists who have been working with creatine, there appears to be little health risk since it is passively filtered from the blood and puts no extra workload on kidneys.

Most studies have used huge dosages such as 20-30 grams a day, but there is reason to believe that as little as 8-10 grams daily for seven days prior to an important, A-priority event will "load" the athlete. As with most supplements, larger cyclists should use the greater amount. Divide your daily creatine supplement into three dosages taken with meals. Just as with carbohydrate loading, creatine monohydrate loading should only be done three or four times a year.

Creatine can be purchased at health food stores and will probably cost $2-$3 a day during the loading phase. It is wise to talk with your health-care provider before supplementing with creatine monohydrate.

SODIUM PHOSPHATE

The German Army used sodium phosphate in World War I, and even in the 1930s, German athletes knew of it's worth. It has not received a great deal of publicity in recent years, though some athletes have known about it for years, but kept the secret.

Sodium phosphate has the potential to improve a 40k time trial significantly, allow you to hang on when the pace would normally have you off the back and make high intensity efforts feel much easier.

In 1983, researchers working with elite runners found that sodium phosphate increased aerobic capacity by nine percent and improved ventilatory threshold (like lactate threshold) by 12 percent. A more recent study of cyclists in Florida showed that using phosphate improved low-level endurance time significantly, lowered 40k time trial times by eight percent and raised lactate threshold by 10 percent, while lowering perceived effort. Pretty heady stuff.

It appears to bring these changes by causing the hemoglobin in the red blood cells to unload their stores of oxygen more completely. A greater supply of oxygen allows the muscles to operate aerobically at higher speeds and power outputs that would normally be anaerobic.

Follow this routine to load with sodium phosphates:

Days before "A" race	Daily dosage
16-19	1-1.5g
14-15	none
9-13	1-1.5g
7-8	none
6-race day	1-1.5g

It's best not to continue using it more than three or four times each season as continued supplementation reduces the benefits. In studies, the greatest gains from sodium phosphate were apparent one week after the loading stopped, meaning that races over two weeks can reap the benefits. I'd suggest saving its use for A races only.

Twin Labs, Inc. makes a product called Phos Fuel that works well. Take one with a meal on each dosage day.

If you have a low dietary intake of calcium, sodium phosphate can cause a calcium deficiency. In this case, you'd be advised not to use it. Better yet, increase your intake of dietary calcium. Do not use calcium phosphate as no performance benefits have been linked with it.

GLYCEROL

Are you an athlete who withers in the heat? In long, hot races do you cramp up in the last few miles? Do you dread riding on days when the temperature reaches the 90s? If so, glycerol may be just what you need to beat the heat.

As your body loses fluid there is a corresponding drop in performance. Even a one-percent drop in body weight due to dehydration reduces maximum work output by about two percent. This drop is a result of decreased blood volume since the plasma in blood supplies sweat. A five-percent loss of body weight is common in hot, long races. Losing seven percent of body weight due to fluid depletion is dangerous to health and may even require hospitalization. Some athletes suffer the effects of heat more than others.

Other than just the heat, other factors may cause you to dehydrate. All it takes is a missed hand-up at a feed zone, being given someone else's bottle with a drink that upsets your stomach, or a dropped bottle in a solo break. Beyond these problems, there are also physiological limits on how much fluid the human digestive tract can absorb during high-intensity racing. All of this can lead to disaster in what might have otherwise been an exceptional race.

Glycerol, a syrupy, sweet-tasting liquid, turns your body into a water-hoarding sponge. Used prior to a race, it causes the body to hold onto 50 percent more fluid than when using water only. Because of this, fluid losses through urination are decreased and there is more water available for sweat.

In one study using cyclists, body temperatures increased 40 percent less when using glycerol as compared with water only. Also, heart rate increased five percent less with glycerol and there was a 32-percent improvement in endurance. These are tremendous advantages that could take you from the DNF listing to the top 10. Who wouldn't want these benefits?

Two companies presently have glycerol products on the market — "Glycerate" by Advanced Kinetics (1-800-295-4335) and "Hydro Fuel" by One+ (1-800-438-9435). Follow the instructions on the package. Using more glycerol than recommended will not help you, and may even cause problems.

As with anything new, you should experiment with glycerol before a workout — not a race. There are anecdotal reports of headaches and nausea in some athletes. Better to find that out in training, rather than in the most important race of the season.

There have been no long-term studies on the effect of large doses of glycerol, but it generally considered to be as safe as water.

REFERENCES

Administration of branched chain amino acids during sustained exercise — Effects on performance and on plasma concentrations of some amino acids. *European Journal of Applied Physiology,* vol. 62, pp. 83-88, 1991.

Anderson, O. Carbs, creatine & phosphate: If the King had used these uppers, he'd still be around today, *Running Research News,* vol. 12(3), pp. 1-4, 1996.

An evaluation of dietary intakes of triathletes: Are RDAs being met? *Brief Communications,* pp. 1653-1654, Nov. 1989.

Antioxidants and the elite athlete. *Proceedings of Panel Discussion,* Dallas, Texas, May 27, 1992.

Antioxidants: Clearing the confusion. *IDEA Today,* pp. 67-73, Sept. 1994.

Branched-chain amino acid supplementation during trekking at high altitude. *European Journal of Applied Physiology,* vol. 65, pp. 394-398, 1992.

Branched chain metabolic support: A prospective, randomized double-blind trial in surgical stress. *Annals of Surgery,* vol. 199, pp. 286-291, 1984.

Cade, R., et al. Effects of phosphate loading on 2,3-diphosphoglycerate and maximal oxygen uptake, *Medicine and Science in Sports and Exercise,* vol. 16(3), pp. 263-268, 1984.

Eades, M.R. and M.D. Eades. *Protein Power,* Bantam Books, 1996.

Eaton, S.B. Humans, lipids and evolution, *Lipids,* vol. 27(1), pp. 814-820, 1992.

Eaton, S.B. and M. Konner. Paleolithic nutrition: A consideration of its nature and current implications, *The New England Journal of Medicine,* vol. 312(5), pp. 283-289.

Eaton, S.B. and D.A. Nelson. Calcium in evolutionary perspective, *American Journal of Clinical Nutrition,* vol. 54, pp. 281S-287S, 1991.

Effects of glycerol-induced hyperhydration prior to exercise on sweating and core temperature. *Medicine and Science in Sport and Exercise,* vol. 22 (4), pp. 477-483, 1990.

Elevation of creatine in resting and exercised muscle of normal subjects by creatine supplementation. *Clinical Science,* vol. 83, pp. 367-374, 1992.

Endurance training amplifies the pulsatile release of growth hormone: Effects of training intensity. *Journal of Applied Physiology,* vol. 72 (6), pp. 2188-2196, 1992.

Evans, W., et al. Protein metabolism and endurance exercise, *The Physician and Sports Medicine*, vol. 11(7), pp. 63-72, 1983.

Glycerol hyperhydration and endurance exercise. *Medicine and Science in Sports and Exercise*, vol. 24 (5), supplement, p. S157, 1992.

Guilland, J.C., et al. Vitamin status of young athletes including the effects of supplementation, *Medicine and Science in Sport and Exercise*, vol. 21, pp. 441-449, 1989.

Personal communication with Dr. L. Cordain, Department of Exercise and Sport Science, Colorado State University, Fort Collins, Colorado 80523.

Physiological responses to glycerol ingestion during exercise. *Journal of Applied Physiology*, vol. 71, pp. 144-149, 1991.

Sears, B. *The Zone*, Harper Collins, 1995.

Somer, E. *The Essential Guide to Vitamins and Minerals*, Health Media of America, 1992.

Stahl, A.B. Hominid dietary selection before fire, *Current Anthropology*, vol. 25(2), pp. 151-168, 1984.

Chapter 17

PROBLEMS

Start every day off with a smile and get it over with.

— W.C. FIELDS

There is no doubt about it: Cycling is an addiction. The addictive nature of racing on two wheels is usually a positive, but from time-to-time problems do appear.

We so desperately want to excel in racing, and yet things get in the way. Sometimes it seems that life just isn't fair. Or is it? Where do our problems come from? In our greed to become more fit in less time, we may overtrain. We workout despite the scratchy throat and lose 10 days to illness rather than five. Or our bodies seem invincible, so we push big gears in the hills repeatedly and wind up nursing a sore knee while watching the next race from the curb.

With rare exception, the problems we face in training and racing are of our own making. Our motivation to excel is exceeded only by our inability to listen to our bodies. The result is often overtraining, burnout, illness, or injury. This chapter describes how to avoid these problems, or , if necessary, how to deal with them.

OVERTRAINING

Overtraining is best described as a decreased work capacity resulting from an imbalance between training and rest. In the real world of cycling, that means decreasing performance is the best indicator of training gone awry. But when we have a bad race what do most of us do? You guessed it — we train *harder*. We put in more miles, or do more intervals, or both. It is a rare athlete who rests more when things aren't going well.

Of course, poor races don't always result from too much training. You could be "overliving." A 40-hour-per-week job, two kids, a spouse, a mortgage and other responsibilities all take their toll on energy. Training just happens to be the thing most easily controlled. You sure aren't going to call the boss to ask for the day off since you're on the edge of overtraining. (Try to imagine how *that* conversation would go.) Nor will you tell the kids to get themselves to the scout meeting. Life goes on. Your smartest option is to train less and rest more.

Figure 17.1 shows what happens when we refuse to give in and insist on more, more, more. Notice that as the training load increases, fitness also increases, up to our personal limit. At that point, fitness declines despite an increasing load. Training beyond our limit causes a loss of fitness.

Figure 17.1

The Overtraining Curve

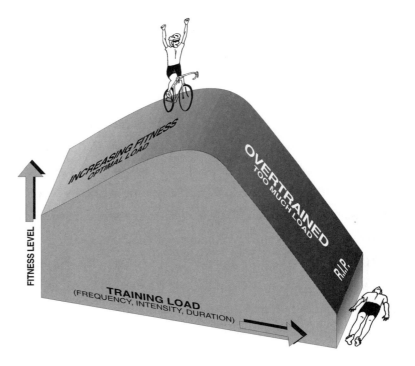

Increased training loads that eventually lead to overtraining come from one or more of three common training excesses:

1) workouts too long (excess duration)

2) exertion too high too often (excess intensity)

3) too many workouts in too little time (excess frequency)

The most common cause I see in competitive cyclists is excess intensity. Road racing is somewhere in the neighborhood of 90-percent aerobic and 10-percent anaerobic. Training should reflect that relationship. Placing too much emphasis on anaerobic training for a few weeks is a sure way to overtrain. That's why the Build period of training is limited to six weeks of high intensity plus two recovery weeks.

OVERTRAINING INDICATORS

The body responds to the overtrained state by issuing warnings in many forms (see table 17.1 Overtraining Indicators in Cyclists). These reactions are the body's way of preventing death by making further increases in stress volume all but impossible.

Table 17.1
Overtraining indicators

Overtraining Indicators in Cyclists

Behavioral	Physical
Apathy	Reduced performance
Lethargy	Weight change
Depression	Morning heart rate change
Poor concentration	Muscle soreness
Sleep pattern changes	Swollen lymph glands
Irritability	Diarrhea
Decreased libido	Injury
Clumsiness	Infection
Increased thirst	Amenorrhea
Sluggishness	Decreased exercise heart rate
Craving for sugar	Slow-healing cuts

If you've had blood testing during the Preparation or Base periods of training, you have a healthy baseline for later comparison. When you suspect overtraining during other periods of the season, it's a good idea to have your blood tested again. Table 17.2 lists the blood indicators of overtraining reported in a 1992 study of experienced middle- and long-distance runners. Realize that you are comparing your recent test results with the baseline established when you were

The Training Bible

Table 17.2

More indicators of overtraining

known to be healthy, not with standards for the general population.

Blood Marker Indicators of Overtraining	
Significant decreases of any of the following from individual baseline markers may indicate overtraining:	
Albumin	Iron
Ammonium	LDL cholesterol
Ferritin	Leukocytes
Free fatty acids	Magnesium
Glycerin	Triglycerides
Hemoglobin	VLDL cholesterol

None of the items listed in Tables 17.1 and 17.2 are "sure" indicators. Many of these situations may even exist in perfectly healthy athletes who are in top shape. In dealing with overtraining, there are no absolutes. You're looking for a preponderance of evidence to confirm what you already suspect.

STAGES OF OVERTRAINING

There are three stages on the road to becoming overtrained. The first stage is "overload." This is a part of the normal process of increasing the training load beyond what you are used to in order to cause the body to adapt. If great enough, but controlled, it results in supercompensation as described in chapter 10. During this stage it's typical to experience short-term fatigue, but generally you will feel great and may have outstanding race results. But also during this stage it's common to feel as if your body is invincible. You can do anything, if you want to. That belief brings on the next stage.

In the second stage, "overreaching," you continue to train at the same abnormally high load levels, or even increase them for a period of two weeks or so. Extending the Build period of training with it's higher intensity is a common cause of overreaching. Now, for the first time, your performance noticeably decreases. Usually this happens in workouts before it shows up in races, where high motivation often pulls you through. Fatigue becomes longer lasting than in the overload stage, but with a few days of rest it is still reversible. The problem is that you decide what's needed is harder training, which brings on the third stage.

The third and final stage is a full-blown overtraining syndrome. Fatigue is now chronic — it stays with you like a shadow. You are tired on awaking and throughout the day, on the job or in class, and yet have trouble sleeping normally at night. Your adrenal glands are exhausted.

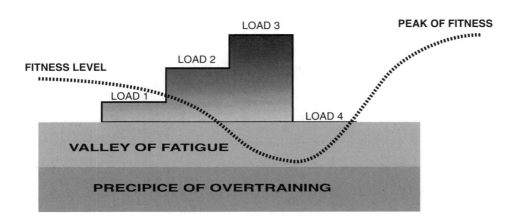

Figure 17.2
Valley of Fatigue.

THE GEOGRAPHY OF OVERTRAINING

I tell the athletes I train that in order to get to the "Peak of Fitness" they must travel through the "Valley of Fatigue" dangerously close to the "Precipice of Overtraining." Figure 17.2 shows how increasing the training load causes a decline in fitness and brings you closer to the edge of the Precipice. The idea is to go the edge infrequently, and then back off. By "infrequently" I mean once every four weeks or so. After three weeks of load increases, you need to allow for recovery and adaptation. Some athletes, especially masters and novices, may need to recover more frequently, perhaps after only two weeks. To do more is to fall over the edge.

As the body enters the Valley of Fatigue, overtraining indicators rear their ugly heads. You may experience poor sleep quality, excessive fatigue, or continued muscle soreness on a continuing basis. Once in the Valley, indicators may be minor in number and severity, but with too great an increase or too prolonged a period of stress, you're on the edge of overtraining. At this point, you wisely reduce training (Load 4 in figure 17.2) and rest more. Rest brings adaptation marked by fitness increasing to a level exceeding the starting level four weeks before. By repeating this process several times, you are eventually ready to peak.

If you fall over the edge into overtraining, the only option is rest. At the first signs of overtraining, take 48 hours of complete rest, and then try a brief recovery workout. If you are still not feeling peppy, take another 48 hours off and repeat the test ride. It could take five to eight weeks of this to fully beat back overtraining, at a great loss of fitness.

THE ART OF TRAINING

The art of training is knowing where the Precipice of Overtraining is for you. Highly motivated, young, or novice cyclists are less likely to recognize having crossed the line than are seasoned riders. That is why many cyclists are better off training under a coach.

Smart training requires constantly assessing your readiness to train. Chapter 15 provided a training journal format with suggested daily indicators to rate. Judiciously tracking these indicators will help you pay closer attention to the body's daily messages.

Unfortunately, there is no sure-fire formula for knowing when you have done too much and are starting to overreach. The best prevention is the judicious use of rest and recovery. Just as workouts must vary between hard and easy, so must weeks and months vary. It's far better to be undertrained, but eager, than to be overtrained. When in doubt—-leave it out.

BURNOUT

By August every year, many riders begin to experience burnout. It is not overtraining, there are no physical symptoms, but more a state of mind marked by decreased interest in training and racing, sometimes even frustration and a feeling of overwhelming drudgery when it comes time to get on the bike.

A mentally-fried athlete may have been experiencing a slump for a couple of weeks. Negative reactions to the slump lower self-esteem and motivation making focused concentration a thing of the past. This downward spiral leads to burnout.

A medical condition such as mononucleosis or anemia may be masquerading as burnout, but this is rare. For most of us, it is just a matter of timing. This is still a good time to get a blood test, just in case.

BURNOUT TIMING

That some cyclists become mental toast by August is not just bad luck or mere coincidence. About 220 to 250 days into heavy training without a break, athletes begin to experience burnout. If your serious workouts started in December or January, and there have been no breaks, August burnout fits right into that timeline.

Many riders race twice every weekend and do a hard club ride and BT workout at mid-week. That is a lot of intensity and emotional investment week after week. For this reason, Build periods should last no longer than eight weeks including R & R weeks. Serious racing without time off the bike for more than six weeks, less for some, may also lead to August burnout.

Those who experience burnout are usually zealous athletes who set high racing goals. By August, they have either attained the goals or have decided they are unattainable. Either situation may contribute to racing and training apathy.

Circumstances other than the two-wheeled variety may also contribute to your becoming mental toast. Emotional stresses such as job change, divorce and moving definitely lead to burnout. Environmental factors including heat, humidity, high altitude and pollution take a toll on enthusiasm. All of this may be compounded by a diet deficient in nutrients and water.

BURNOUT POTION

If there is no doubt that you are burned out and yet still have an important race at the end of the season, there are only three things to do

1) rest

2) rest

3) rest

Time off the bike is probably the hardest medicine to take for a usually-enthusiastic rider. But a week to 10 days of no training should have you ready to go again soon.

I can hear you now: "I'll lose all my fitness." No you won't, but even if you did, which would be better — fit but apathetic, or unfit and ready to go? It takes months to develop endurance, strength and speed. They won't slip away in a few days. After a short break, you'll be ready to race again with two weeks of Build 1 training, three weeks tops.

More important, you need to learn something from the experience: Don't let it happen again next year. The way to avoid burnout in August is to plan on a two-peak season by bringing yourself into race form in the spring for up to six weeks and then taking a short break of one week off the bike. After that, rebuild your base fitness and be ready to go with another late season peak.

The key to racing well when you want to is foresight. Good races in August don't just happen — they are planned.

ILLNESS

You would think that a lot of training would be healthy and help you avoid illness. That is not the case. Those who work out frequently are *more* likely to catch a bug than those who work out occasionally.

A study of runners in the Los Angeles Marathon found that those running more than 60 miles per week were twice as susceptible to respiratory illness as those who ran less than 20 miles each week. Runners who completed the marathon were six times as likely to be ill in the week following the race as those who trained hard for the race but for some reason did not run it.

ILLNESS AND TIMING

The six hours following a hard workout (3 zone or higher) or race has been shown as the most critical phase for remaining healthy as the immune system is depressed and less capable of fighting off disease. This six-hour period is a good time to avoid public places. Washing your hands frequently if you have contact with others during this time is also a good idea for staying healthy.

NECK CHECK

But what should you do when a cold or flu bug gets you down? Should you continue to train as normal, cut back, or stop altogether? Doing a "neck check" will help you decide. If your symptoms are a runny nose, sneezing, or a scratchy throat (all symptoms above the neck), start your workout but reduce the intensity to the 1 or 2 zones and keep the duration short. If you feel worse after the first few minutes, stop and head home. If the symptoms are below the neck, such as chest cold, chills, vomiting, achy muscles, or a fever, don't even start. You've probably got an acute viral infection. Exercising intensely in this condition will increase the severity of the illness and can even cause extreme complications, including death.

These below-the-neck symptoms are likely to be accompanied by the Coxsackie virus which can invade the heart muscle causing arrhythmia and other complications. I can speak from experience on this one. In November, 1994 I caught a bad cold with several below-the-neck symptoms including fever, achy muscles and coughing up mucous. Five months later, I had a full-blown Coxsackie virus in my heart. After a year of inactivity, I was finally able to start training again. No race or any amount of fitness is worth paying such a price. Don't take these symptoms lightly. Suspect Coxsackie virus is present whenever you have a respiratory infection with indicators below the neck.

RECUPERATING

After the illness has abated, you are likely to be run down for some time. There is a 15-percent reduction in muscle strength for up to a month following a bout of the flu. Aerobic capacity is also reduced for up to three months and muscles become acidic at lower levels of intensity during this time. This means you will feel weak when working out even though the acute stage is past. Following a below-the-neck illness, return to the Base period of training for two days for every day you had symptoms.

Trying to "push" past the flu will likely make your condition worse and cause it to last longer. It is best to get rid of the illness as soon as possible by allowing your limited energy reserves to go into fighting the disease rather than training.

INJURIES

There is nothing worse than an injury. It is not bad enough that fitness is slipping away, but so much of an athlete's life is tied to being physical that depression often sets in. No one wants to be around a lame athlete.

Some people seem prone to injuries. They get them doing what others do routinely. It is more than a nuisance. Here are some prevention tips that help keep injury-prone people healthy — most of the time.

EQUIPMENT

Get equipment that fits correctly. Riding a bike that is too big or too small sets you up for an injury. This is especially a problem for women cyclists who all too often ride bikes designed for men and for juniors riding bikes they'll "grow in to.".

BIKE SETUP

Having poor biomechanics can easily injure a joint, especially the knee, as it repeats the same movement pattern hundreds or thousands of times under a load. Once you have the right equipment, ask an experienced cyclist, bike shop, or coach to take a look at your position and offer suggestions for improvement. Be especially concerned with saddle fore-aft position and height.

Miguel Indurain carefully measures saddle height. Incorrect saddle position can easily cause injury.

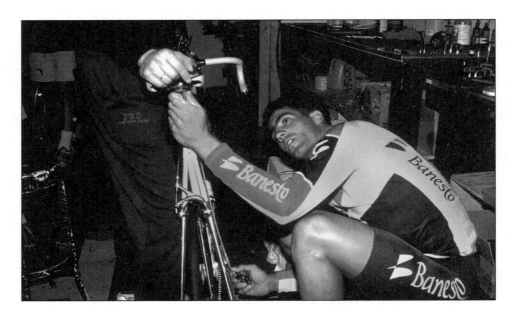

TRAINING

The most likely times to get injured are the two days after very long or very hard workouts and races. These days should be short and easy, reserved for cross-training, or days off altogether. In the same manner, two or three hard weeks of training should be followed by a week of reduced volume and intensity. This may be difficult to do when you know your cardiovascular and energy production systems are willing and able to handle it, but such restraint will keep you injury free.

STRENGTH AND STRETCHING

For most of us, our weakest link is the muscle-tendon junction. This is where tears and strains are likely to occur. Many muscle-tendon problems can be prevented early in the season by gradually improving the muscle's strength and range of motion. These are probably the most neglected areas for endurance athletes. Going for a ride is fun, but grunting through a combined strength and stretching session in the gym seems like drudgery. Hang in there, and you'll reap the benefits.

LISTEN

Learn to tell the difference between sore muscles that come from a high quality effort and sore joints or tendons. Pinpoint any discomfort and try to put the sensation into words. Don't just say "my knee hurts." Is it above or below the kneecap? Front or back of the knee? Is it a sharp pain or a dull ache? Does it hurt only while riding or all of the time? Is the pain worse going up stairs or down? These are the sorts of questions you will be asked when you finally seek professional help. Be ready for them.

If the pain is not gone with five days of reduced activity, it is time to see a health-care provider. Don't put it off. Injuries are easier to turn around in the early stages than later on.

Andy Pruitt examining Laura Peyke. If an injury is caught early it can be quickly turned around.

REFERENCES

Brenner, I.K.M. Infection in athletes, *Sports Medicine*, vol. 17(2), pp. 86-107, 1994.

David, A.S., et al. Post-viral fatigue syndrome: Time for a new approach, *British Medical Journal*, vol. 296, pp. 696-699, 1988.

Fitzgerald, L. Exercise and the immune system, *Immunology Today*, vol. 9(11), pp. 337-339, 1988.

Fry, R.W., et al. Overtraining in athletes: An update, *Sports Medicine*, vol. 12(1), pp. 32-65, 1991.

Fry, R.W. and D. Keast. Overtraining in athletes. *Sports Medicine*, vol. 12(1), pp. 32-65, 1991.

Heath, G.W., et al. Exercise and upper respiratory tract infections: Is there a relationship? *Sports Medicine*, vol. 14(6), pp. 353-365, 1992.

Hoffman-Goetz, L. and B.K. Peterson. Exercise and the immune system: A model of the stress response? *Immunology Today*, vol. 15(8), pp. 382-387, 1994.

Hooper, S.L. and L.T. MacKinnon. Monitoring overtraining in athletes: Recommendations, *Sports Medicine*, vol. 20(5), pp. 321-327, 1995.

Hooper, S.L., et al. Markers for monitoring overtraining and recovery, *Medicine and Science in Sports and Exercise*, vol. 27(1), pp. 106-112, 1995.

Keast, D., et al. Exercise and the immune response, *Sports Medicine*, vol. 5, pp. 248-267, 1988.

Kuipers, H. and H.A. Keizer. Overtraining in elite athletes: Review and directions for the future, *Sports Medicine*, vol. 6, pp. 79-92, 1988.

Lehmann, M., et al. Overtraining in endurance athletes: A brief review, *Medicine and Science in Sports and Exercise*, vol. 25(7), pp. 854-862, 1993.

Milne, C. The tired athlete, *New Zealand Journal of Sports Medicine*, vol. 19(3), pp. 42-44, 1991.

Nieman, D.C., et al. Infectious episodes in runners before and after the Los Angeles Marathon, *Journal of Sports Medicine and Physical Fitness*, vol. 30, pp. 316-328, 1990.

Sharp, N.C.C. and Y. Koutedakis. Sport and the overtraining syndrome, *British Medical Journal*, vol. 48(3), pp. 518-533, 1992.

Stone, M., et al. Overtraining: A review of the signs, symptoms and possible causes, *Journal of Applied Sport Sciences*, vol. 5(1), pp. 35-50, 1991.

Chapter 18

RECOVERY

Laugh and the world laughs with you,
snore and you sleep alone.

— ANTHONY BURGESS

Throughout this book, I have often referred to recovery and have occasionally offered how-to guidelines. This chapter will emphasize and more fully explain this important, and often underrated, aspect of training. Due to the nature of the sport, with its stage races and double-race weekends, cycling requires the athlete to be ready to go again within a few hours. In addition, the sooner a cyclist can do another BT workout, the sooner his or her fitness will improve. Recovery holds the key to both of these situations.

THE NEED FOR RECOVERY

It is reasonably easy to get athletes to train hard. Give serious riders tough workouts and they are not only challenged, but most are even happy. Competitive cyclists are successful, in part, because they have a great capacity and affinity for hard work. Without such drive, they would never make in the sport.

If daily, arduous training is all it took to bring victory, everyone would be atop the winner's platform. The greater challenge for the self-coached cyclist is not formidable training sessions, but rather knowing how, when and for how long to recover following tough workouts and races. Although that sounds like it should be easy, for most it is not. Recovery is the one area of training athletes have the most difficulty getting right.

Recovery determines when you can go hard again, and ultimately, your fitness level. Cut recovery short enough times, and the specter of overtraining lurks ever nearer. Go beyond the time needed to recover, and you end up wasting time and may even be losing the finer components of your fitness. Most serious athletes err on the side of not allowing enough recovery. They believe that "training" *only* takes place on the bike. It is how many miles they ride, how hard the workouts are and how often they ride that matters. To most, what they do off the bike has no relevance to fitness — it is viewed as "non-training" time and, therefore, of no consequence.

If you think that way, you are wrong. Off-the-bike-recovery time is critical to improving performance. The sooner you recover, the sooner you can do another quality workout. The sooner you can do another quality workout, the more fit you become. Another way of looking at it is as a formula:

Training = Workout + Recovery

In this formula, workout and recovery are of equal value — neither is greater than the other. So the higher the intensity of the workout, the greater the depth of recovery must be, not only in terms of time, but also of method. They must balance. If the balance is right, your fitness is bound to improve. Get the balance wrong often enough, and you are initially suffering, then off the back and finally overtrained.

You would think athletes would be more concerned about recovery. The first question to answer in writing a weekly training schedule should be, "How quickly can I recover?" With the answer to that question, the week can be scheduled.

Adequate rest and recovery is often the difference between leading the peloton and being off the back.

RECOVERY TIME

What happens inside the muscles during a hard workout is not a pretty sight. If you could look into your legs with a microscope after a hard race, what you would see looks like a battleground. The muscles appear as if a miniature bomb has exploded, with torn and jagged cell membranes evident. The damage can vary from slight to extreme, depending on how powerful the bomb/workout was. Under such conditions, it is unlikely the muscles and nervous system will be able to go hard again. Not until the cells are repaired, the energy stores rebuilt and cellular chemistry returns to normal will another all-out effort be possible. Your racing depends on how long that process takes.

Much of the time needed for recovery has to do with creating new muscle protein to repair the damage. Recent research conducted at McMaster University in Hamilton, Ontario and at the Washington University School of Medicine in St. Louis, found that this protein resynthesis process takes several hours. The study used young, experienced weight lifters and maximal efforts followed by observation of the muscles' repair process. Reconstruction work started almost immediately following the workout. Four hours after the weight session protein activity was increased about 50 percent. By 24 hours, post-workout it reached a peak of 109 percent of normal. Protein resynthesis was back to normal, indicating that repair was complete, 36 hours after the hard workout.

While this study used exhaustive strength training to measure recovery time, the results are probably similar to what could be expected following a hard race or cycling workout.

RECOVERY PHASES

The recovery process can be divided into three phases in relation to the workout — before and during, immediately following and long term. If each is carefully observed, recovery will be quicker and the next quality session made more productive.

RECOVERY BEFORE AND DURING THE WORKOUT

Recovery actually starts with a warm-up before the workout or race that will cause the damage, not after. A good warm-up before starting to ride hard helps limit damage by:

• Thinning body fluids to allow easier muscle contractions,

• Opening capillaries to bring more oxygen to muscles,

• Raising muscle temperature so that contractions take less effort,

• Conserving carbohydrate and releasing fat for fuel.

The recovery process should continue during the workout with the on-going replacement of carbohydrate-based energy stores. By drinking 18 to 24 ounces of a sports drink every hour, the training session is less stressful on the body and the recovery of the energy production system later on is enhanced. There are individual differences in how well carbohydrate drinks are tolerated and emptied from the stomach. Find a sports drink that tastes good and doesn't upset your stomach when riding hard. Before a race, make sure you have plenty of whatever works on your bike and prepared for hand-ups at feed zones. Making the drink more concentrated than is recommended on the label may cause you to dehydrate during a fast race, especially on a hot and humid day. Races and workouts longer than one hour are most likely to benefit from a sports drink. In races lasting longer than about five hours, solid food is also necessary.

Federico Echave hydrating during the 1996 Tour DuPont, A sports drink will benefit performance and recovery for races lasting longer than about one hour.

Recovery continues with a cool-down. If you complete the interval-portion of a workout and hammer all the way back to the front door and then collapse in a heap, recovery will be prolonged. Instead, always use the last 10 to 20 minutes of a hard ride to bring the body back to normal. The cool-down should be a mirror image of the warm-up, ending with easy pedaling in the 1 zone for several minutes.

RECOVERY IMMEDIATELY FOLLOWING THE WORKOUT

As soon as you are off the bike, the most important thing you can do to speed recovery is to replace the carbohydrate and protein just used for fuel. A long and hard workout or race can deplete nearly all of your stored glycogen, a carbohydrate-based energy source, and consume several grams of muscle-bound protein. In the first 30 minutes after riding, your body is several times more capable of absorbing and replenishing those fuels than at any other time.

At this time, you don't want to use the same sports drink you used on the bike. It's not potent enough. You need something designed for recovery. There are several such products now on the market. As long as you like the taste and can get 15-20 grams of protein and about 80 grams of simple carbohydrate from one of them, it will meet your recovery needs. You can easily make a recovery "homebrew" by adding five tablespoons of table sugar to 16 ounces of skim milk. Whatever you use, drink all of it within the first 30 minutes after finishing.

Dirk Copeland eating immediately following a stage of the 1996 Tour DuPont. Start the recovery process as soon as the race ends by taking in carbohydrate and protein,

LONG-TERM RECOVERY

For six to nine hours after a BT workout, you must actively seek recovery by using one or more specific techniques. This is critical when stage racing meaning the difference between finishing well in subsequent stages and failing to finish at all.

The most basic method is sleep. Nothing beats a nap for rejuvenation. In addition to a 30- to 60-minute, post-workout nap, seven to nine hours of sleep are

The Training Bible

needed each night. Other recovery methods are unique to each individual, so you will need to experiment with several of these to find the ones that work best for you.

Most of these methods speed recovery by slightly increasing the heart rate, increasing blood flow to the muscles, accelerating the inflow of nutrients, reducing soreness, lowering blood pressure and relaxing the nervous system.

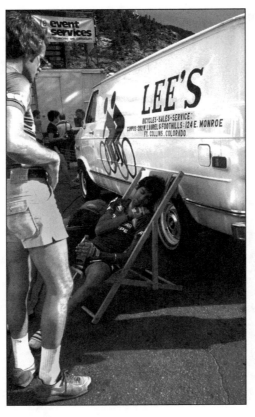

Alexi Grewal napping following a stage of the Coors Classic. Nothing beats a nap for rejuvenation.

Hot Shower or Bath

Immediately following the cooldown and recovery drink, take a hot shower or bath for 10 to 15 minutes. Do not linger, especially in the bathtub, as you will dehydrate even more.

Active Recovery

For the experienced rider, one of the best recovery methods is to pedal easily for 15 to 30 minutes several hours after the workout and before going to bed. Pressure on the pedals should be extremely light and cadence comfortably high with power and heart rate below the 1 zone.

Another effective active recovery technique is better for the novice, but also works well for seasoned riders. This technique is swimming, especially with a pull buoy between the legs, or simply moving in the water while floating.

Massage

Other than sleep, most riders find a massage by a professional massage therapist is the most effective recovery technique. A post-race massage should employ long, flushing strokes to speed the removal of the waste products of exercise. Deep massage at this time may actually increase muscle trauma. After 36 hours, the therapist can apply greater point pressure, working more deeply.

Due to the expense of massage, some athletes prefer self-massage. Following a hot bath or shower, stroke the leg muscles for 20 to 30 minutes working away from the feet and toward the heart.

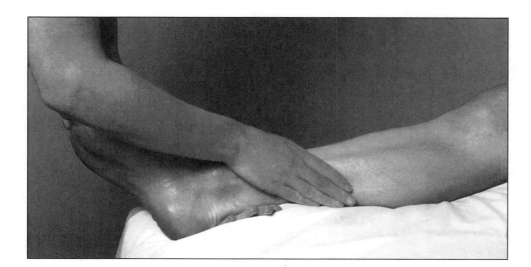

Other than sleep, most riders find massage by a professional therapist the most effective recovery technique.

Sauna

Several hours following a workout or race you may find that a dry sauna speeds recovery. Do not use a steam room for recovery as it will have the opposite effect. Stay in the sauna for no more than 10 minutes and begin drinking fluids as soon as you are done.

Relax and Stretch

Be lazy for several hours. Your legs want quality rest. Give it to them by staying off your feet whenever possible. Never stand when you can lean against something. Sit down whenever possible. Better yet, lay on the floor with your feet elevated against a wall or furniture. Sit on the floor and stretch gently. Overused muscles tighten and can't seem to relax on their own. This is best right after a hot bath or sauna and just before going to bed.

Walk in a Park or Forest

A few hours after finishing the workout or race, a short, slow walk in a heavily vegetated area such as a park or forest seems to speed recovery for some. Abundant oxygen and the aroma of grass, trees and other plants is soothing.

Other Methods

The sports program of the former Soviet Union made a science of recovery and employed several techniques with their athletes that may or may not be available to you. They included electro muscle stimulation, ultrasound, barometric chambers, sport psychology and pharmacological supplements such as vitamins, minerals and adaptogens. These require expert guidance.

By employing some of the specific methods described here, you can accelerate the recovery process and return to action sooner. Figure 18.1 illustrates how this happens.

Figure 18.1

Recovery time with and without specific techniques.

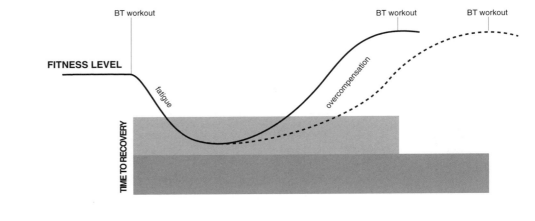

—— using specific techniques

- - - - - not using specific techniques

INDIVIDUALIZATION

While I have listed several possible methods to speed recovery, you will find that some work better for you than others. You may also discover that a teammate doing the same workouts as you and following the same recovery protocol springs back at a different rate — either slower or faster. This goes back to the principle of individualization discussed in Chapter 3. While there are many physiological similarities between athletes, we are each unique and respond in our own way to any given set of circumstances. You must experiment if you want to discover how best for you to recover. As always, do this in training rather than in the first important stage race of the season.

There are several individual factors affecting recovery. Younger athletes, especially 18 to 22 years old, recover faster than older athletes. The more race-experienced an athlete is, the quicker he or she recovers. If fitness is high, recovery is speeded up. Females were shown in one study to recover faster than males. Other factors influencing the rate of recovery are climate, diet and psychological stress.

How do you know if you are recovering? The best indicator is performance in races and hard workouts, but these are the worst times to find out that you're not ready. Typical signs that recovery is complete include a positive attitude, feelings of health, a desire to train hard again, high quality sleep, normal resting and exercise heart rates and balanced emotions. If any of these are lacking, continue the recovery process. By closely monitoring such signs, you should be able to determine not only the best procedure, but also the typical time needed to bounce back.

RECOVERY IN THE REAL WORLD

If you're following the periodization program suggested in this book, there will occasionally be periods of time when you experience an increasing load of fatigue. Despite your best recovery efforts, you will not unload all of the fatigue between planned workouts and will go into some BT workouts a bit heavy legged and lacking snap. Don't expect to be fully recovered for every workout, all the time. In fact, a little workout fatigue sometimes can bring benefits in the form of supercompensation which was discussed in earlier chapters. This can better prepare you for stage races and peak performances. You just don't want this to happen too often. Every three or four weeks, depending on your ability to avoid overtraining, a recovery week should be included to allow for the unloading of fatigue before starting a new three- or four-week block of training.

REFERENCES

Bompa, T. *Theory and Methodology of Training*, Kendall/Hunt Publishing, 1994.

Brunner, R. and B. Tabachnik. *Soviet Training and Recovery Methods*, Sport Focus Publishing, 1990.

Cade, J.R., et al. Dietary intervention and training in swimmers, *European Journal of Applied Physiology*, vol. 63, pp. 210-215, 1991.

Dragan, I. and I. Stonescu. *Organism recovery following training*, Bucharest: Sport-Turism, 1978.

Newham, D.J., et al. Muscle pain and tenderness after exercise, *Australian Journal of Sports Medicine and Exercise Science*, vol. 14, pp. 129-131, 1982.

Part VI

The

FINISH LINE

Jack Heid's Training Hints
BY JACK HEID
As it appeared in Cycling Almanac, 1952

---

1. *Plenty of hours on the bike at a moderate speed (approximately 15 m.p.h.)*

2. *Enjoy your training — don't punish yourself especially you juniors.*

3. *Save all your "cork" pulling for the race.*

4. *Slow training will make you strong and a few sprints will make you fast.*

5. *If you don't have a race every week, allot one day for a hard training ride.*

6. *In the winter I enjoy 25 miles every day and in the summer 40 miles—for track racing. For long road races you must put in more mileage.*

7. *Suggested gear for road training for track racing is 70, or lower.*

"Hand brakes and free wheels compulsory, speed gears optional."

Chapter 19

FREQUENTLY ASKED QUESTIONS

*Some people never learn anything because
they understand everything too soon.*

— ALEXANDER POPE

Every day athletes from around the world send me questions via e-mail and
fax. The following are frequently asked questions and my answers. They
touch on subjects mentioned in the book, but from a slightly different perspective.

SCHEDULING

*Q. I live in Florida and our race season starts in mid-February and ends in early June.
Then there are a few fall races. The problem is, I'm having a hard time deciding how
to organize the training periods. How should I do it?*

A. The determination of when to schedule each period of training depends on
when your first "A"-priority race is. Work backwards from that date allowing two

weeks for peaking, eight weeks for the Build period and eight to 12 weeks for the Base period. After the spring races, go back to the Base or Build period depending on your needs — base fitness (endurance, strength and speed) or intensity building (muscular-endurance, speed-endurance and power). I'd recommend a four-week period of Base before going back to Build.

Q. I do two hard rides a week (intervals and hills) and a fast group ride on the weekend. Is that too much?

A. It depends. If you have done a good job of building endurance, strength and speed, shifting to higher intensity for six to 10 weeks before important races is necessary to build race fitness. Continuing such training for longer than about 10 weeks could be too much. The bottom line is how it effects you. If you experience signs of overtraining such as poor performance, head colds, poor sleep, or irritability (there are many other indicators), you need to cut back or even take time off.

Q. In February, my club starts doing rides on Saturdays and Sundays. These usually become hammer sessions. Since our first race is in late April, is this too soon to be going hard?

A. One hard ride on the weekend is probably OK in February, but two is too much. I'd suggest an easy endurance ride on Sunday following a hard Saturday ride. With six weeks to go until the first "A"-priority race, you may want to occasionally do two back-to-back workouts.

Q. What workouts should I do during the weeks of my most important races?

A. The most important race-week workout is typically done at mid-week. This workout should emphasize your greatest ability and be only hard enough to slightly stress you. In other words, finish it feeling like you could have done more. Most cyclists also find that doing a few jumps the day before the race "reminds" their legs of what is required. All other workouts should be for recovery or endurance maintenance.

Q. During the Peak period, you said that the quantity of the workouts should decrease while the quality increases. I can see the quantity decrease, but I don't see how the quality increases.

A. If you have been doing 45 minutes of cruise intervals in the Build period, increase to 60 minutes in the Peak period. If 20 minutes of speed-endurance intervals were done in Build, go to 25 or 30 minutes in Peak. If you managed sprints at 600 watts in Build, aim for 630 in Peak.

Q. How many miles do I need in the Base period before starting speed work and more intense training?
A. Most riders need eight to 12 weeks of Base training with an emphasis on endurance building. There is no magic number of miles. Be sure to include leg-speed workouts such as form sprints and spin-ups to maximum cadence during Base. In the last four to eight weeks, begin riding hilly courses.

STRENGTH TRAINING

Q. Is it better to cool down after weights on rollers or a Lifecycle? Is the cool down important?
A. Spinning at high cadence for 10-20 minutes following weights helps to maintain "muscle memory". Pushing heavy weights slowly conditions the nervous system to operate that way. Your own bike on rollers is preferable, but if you can't get to your bike and rollers immediately after weights, then use the Lifecycle.

Q. Should I work legs separately or together on strength exercises such as leg press, leg curls and knee extensions?
A. I don't think it makes a lot of difference unless you have a strength discrepancy of 10 percent or more between your legs.

Q. I'm reluctant to cut back on the number of strength exercises as the season progresses. Why should I do that?
A. The reason for the reduced number of exercises is to allow you to conserve your energy for the increased training on the bike. Training should become more specific to racing as the season progresses. If racing required lifting weights at the same time, then there would be more emphasis placed on it during the season.

Q. Is it OK to ride on the same day I lift?
A. If you ride before weights, maintenance rides or form sprints can be done.

Form sprints may even improve the quality of your weight workout by stimulating the fast twitch muscles. After lifting, it is best to do a recovery ride.

Q. Weight training doesn't teach your muscles to fire in a sequence that's similar to cycling. Not even close. Why should I do it?

A. The only thing that is 100 percent like road racing is road racing. But that doesn't mean you should simply race all the time and never ride or workout otherwise. General training during the winter months begins to build greater fitness, which is refined as training becomes more specific by the spring. Weight training creates a reserve of strength that will greatly improve the force you can apply to pedals.

Q. I raced last weekend and my legs felt like they were full of lead. I'm riding four days a week, running two times and lifting weights twice. Am I doing enough to get in shape?

A. I suspect you're doing too much and not allowing your body to "catch up" with all of the training. Once the race season starts, general training such as weights and running need to be reduced in order for your fitness to be realized. The week before important races, training intensity and especially volume must also be cut back to allow your body to rest and get stronger.

INTENSITY

Q. What's the difference between lactate threshold heart rate and anaerobic threshold heart rate?

A. They refer to the same thing, but the term lactate threshold is becoming more popular since it better describes what is happening — the accumulation of lactate in the blood.

Q. I've tested myself and estimate my lactate threshold heart rate as 175. Based on what I've seen in races, my max heart rate is 181. Does this sound right?

A. Generally there are about 15-18 beats between lactate threshold heart rate (LTHR) and maximum heart rate. Try repeating the LTHR test when you are fresh with an assistant who pays close attention to your breathing and ratings of perceived exertion. Another method is to do a 10-mile time trial on a flat course. Divide your average heart rate for the ride by 1.01 to estimate LTHR.

Q. I've always read that you should do endurance rides slowly, but can you tell me why it's better to ride 100 km in four hours than in three?

A. There is no scientific evidence to support going slowly in the early stages of training. But a high level of aerobic fitness seems to make anaerobic training more effective. Creating race fitness requires making certain cellular changes. The first few weeks of endurance training should be low intensity in order to fully develop slow twitch muscles and aerobic enzymes before gradually stepping up the intensity later on to reap other training benefits. Hurrying the process results in missing or weak elements of basic fitness. There is plenty of time to ride fast later in the season.

Q. Before a hard, short hill (about 2-4 minutes long), should I sit in and be as recovered as possible, or should I prepare by bringing my heart rate up gradually?

A. Heart rate is not the determining factor in climbing. It's only an indicator of cardiovascular workload. The limiting factors for such a climb are power-to-weight ratio and speed-endurance. If both P-W ratio and speed-endurance are good, then you will be one of the riders determining the pace over the hill. If one is weak, you must sit in near the front as you approach the hill and conserve energy.

Q. How long should recovery rides be?

A. Duration of recovery rides depends on the individual. Generally, they are 25 to 50 percent of the longest ride. The idea is to keep them short enough so that additional stress is avoided. If a recovery ride increases your level of fatigue, it was too long.

Q. Which formula should I use to calculate my maximum heart rate and training zones?

A. I don't believe in using a formula. They're as often wrong as right. You need to be tested to find your lactate threshold heart rate. This can be done in a university lab or medical clinic. Or you can test yourself using the methods described in chapter 5.

Q. How can my club incorporate intense workouts into a group format? I'm referring to cruise intervals, speed-endurance intervals, sprints and lactate tolerance workouts.

A. Some workouts are difficult to do as a group, such as speed-endurance intervals. But such workouts can be done by dividing into pairs of similar ability and taking turns pulling while the other rider recovers in the draft. My club gets together on Saturday mornings for cruise intervals done like a time trial with 30-second starts. Sprints and lactate tolerance workouts are easily done in a group with a criterium format.

MISCELLANEOUS

Q. Will three weeks of training at 7500 feet in Colorado help me race better?

A. The major advantage from being at that altitude comes from living there, more than training there. Your blood will change in ways that positively effect your endurance. The disadvantage is a drop in average workout intensity since you'll be forced to ride at a slower speed due to a reduction in oxygen. This means your muscular system won't be stressed as much as it would have been at sea level. Training for power and speed-endurance become more important when living at altitude.

Q. Does cross training in the winter when you can't ride outside help, or is it a waste of time?

A. One of the most important aspects of fitness to be improved during the Preparation and early Base periods is cardiorespiratory function. This means the lungs, heart and blood. This system doesn't know the difference between cross country skiing, running, swimming, or cycling. By all means, include cross training at this time of year.

Q. I don't have much time to train, but I've been told that running is a more efficient use of time than is cycling. In the race season, should I run more and ride less?

A. At this time of year, running will not do you much good if you want to race a bike. In winter, it helps develop general fitness, but now more race-specific fitness is needed. That can only be had on the bike. Try including more high intensity training such as cruise intervals, tempo, threshold, speed-endurance intervals and sprints to make better use of your limited time.

Q. When I'm overtraining, my heart rate is very low compared with when I'm fresh.

This seems to contradict conventional wisdom.

A. This is a common situation for endurance athletes (but not power athletes). Endurance athletes may be depressing the activity of their adrenal systems when they overtrain causing a lowering of the heart rate.

Q. *How should I warm-up before a race?*

A. The duration and intensity of the race dictate how long and hard the warm-up should be. A criterium needs a longer and more intense warm-up than does a long road race. The warm-up should end by simulating the anticipated race-start effort with as little delay as possible before the gun.

Q. *I have about five to seven pounds of unwanted flab around the middle which will not come off. What should I do?*

A. What you describe is a common problem for many athletes. What I've found that helps is to make two changes in your diet. One is to avoid high glycemic index (HGI) carbohydrate foods except during and immediately after workouts and races. Typical HGI foods are bagels, bananas, bread, cereals, potatoes, raisins, pop, fruit juice, sports drinks and energy bars. Replace them in your diet with low glycemic index (LGI) foods such as apples, beans, cherries, peas, dates, figs, lentils, milk, peaches, pears, plums, tomato soup and yogurt. The second change is to include a handful of protein with every meal. This is best in the form of meat and non-fat dairy. Only slightly more than half of the food on your plate at each meal should be carbohydrate, especially HGI. Snacks should be the same ratio of carbohydrate to protein. I think you'll find that eating this way reduces your craving for sweets and leaves you satisfied longer following meals.

Q. *I only have time to train about 90 minutes four times a week. Is that enough time?*

A. It is if you only race in criteriums and short road races of up to about two hours duration. The key to training with a limited amount of time is intensity. High quality workouts for power, speed-endurance and muscular-endurance will help you get into excellent condition.

Q. *I'm 48 years old and in the Build period do hard workouts on Tuesdays, Thursdays and Saturdays. Lately I've been noticing that I still feel the effects of the Tuesday work-*

out on Thursday, and by Saturday I'm wasted. What should I do?

A. Either you need more than 48 hours to recover between hard workouts or you are not taking a recovery week often enough. Try this three-week pattern. In the first week do only two hard workouts spaced 72 or more hours apart. This could be on Wednesday and Saturday. Then train a week as you described. The third week reduce your volume by about 50 percent and do only one hard workout at week's end. Then start the pattern again.

Q. I like to ride a mountain bike, too. What type of workout would be best done off road and yet still help my road racing?

A. Riding a mountain bike on a hilly course is a great way to develop strength and provides a mental break from the roads.

EPİL⊙GUE

Writing this book was a bigger challenge than any race I've ever done. I never imagined it would take nine months to explain on paper what I do every day — design training programs for athletes. Now that it's done, I feel as if I've only scratched the surface. Deciding what to leave out was as difficult as determining what to include. There are other topics I wanted to cover, such as the future of training, mental skills training and more depth on training for the aging athlete. I want to touch on these topics briefly in closing.

There currently are two trends that will effect the direction of training for cycling in the next 10 years. The first is the development of cheaper, yet more sophisticated equipment for measuring the work output and physiological consequences of a ride or race. Within 10 years, nearly everyone will have a handlebar computer that displays more than just speed, distance, time and heart rate. Following races, we will discuss torque, watts and lactate levels as often as speed and distance. We will be able to determine our blood hormone levels and more accurately predict overtraining.

The other trend with portent for the future is the growth of coaching services that offer an increasing range of benefits to the athlete intent on improving. Not only will the average athlete of the future have access to a knowledgeable coach through such businesses, but also to a sports psychologist, exercise physiologist, registered dietitian, massage therapist and medical practitioner. This team approach to complete development of the cyclist will make the sport more competitive than it has ever been. The problem will be that such services will only be there for the athlete with money making sport less egalitarian.

I considered including a chapter on the psychology of training and racing, but this would require an author with a greater depth of clinical knowledge in this rapidly growing area. The refinement of mental skills is the next great frontier of bicycle racing.

The average cyclist is aging and this trend will continue into the near future. Many baby boomers who were the runners of the 1970s will become the cyclists of the late 1990s as they discover a need to reduce or eliminate running due to recurrent injuries. Many will want to remain active and competitive. Because of this trend, I thought about expanding the section in Chapter 14 on masters racing, but decided what is really needed is an entire book on the subject.

My intent in writing *The Cyclist's Training Bible* was to provide serious cyclists with a scientifically based method of training that would remove much of the guesswork so common in amateur sport. I hope I've helped you achieve that. Happy training!

RECOMMENDED READING

Baker, A. *Smart Cycling*, San Diego: Argo Publishing, 1995.

Bompa, T. *Periodization of Strength*, Toronto: Veritas Publishing Inc., 1993.

Bompa, T. *Theory and Methodolgy of Training*, Dubuque, IA: Kendall Hunt Publishing, 1994.

Borysewicz, E. *Bicycle Road Racing*, Brattleboro, VT: Velo-News, 1985.

Brunner, R. and B. Tabachnik. *Soviet Training and Recovery Methods*, Pleasant Hill, CA: Sport Focus Publishing, 1990.

Burke, E. *Serious Cycling*, Champaign, IL: Human Kinetics, 1995.

Eades, M.R. and M.D. Eades. *Protein Power*, New York: Bantam Books, 1996.

Freeman, W. *Peak When It Counts*, Mountain View, CA: TAFNEWS, 1991.

Janssen, P.G.J.M. *Training, Lactate, Pulse Rate*, Oulu, Finland: Polar Electro Oy, 1987.

LeMond, G. and K. Gordis. *Greg LeMond's Complete Book of Bicycling*, New York: Perigee Books, 1988.

Maglischo, E. *Swimming Faster*, Mountain View, CA: Mayfield Publishing Company, 1982.

Martin, D.E. and P.N. Coe. *Training Distance Runners*, Champaign, IL: Leisure Press, 1991.

Noakes, T. *Lore of Running*, Champaign, IL: Leisure Press, 1991.

Sears, B. *The Zone*, New York: HarperCollins Publishers, 1995.

Sleamaker, R. *Serious Training for Serious Athletes*, Champaign, IL: Leisure Press, 1989.

Wilmore, J.H. and D.L. Costill. *Physiology of Sport and Exercise*, Champaign, IL: Human Kinetics, 1994.

APPENDIX A

Annual Training Plan Worksheets, 1997-2002

Annual Training Plan: 1997

Athlete:

Annual Hours:

Season Goals:

1

2

3

Training Objectives:

1

2

3

4

5

WORKOUTS

Wk#	Monday	Races	Pri	Period	Hours	Details	Strength Phase	Endurance	Speed Skill	Muscular Endur	Speed Power	Power	Testing
01	Jan 6												
02	Jan 13												
03	Jan 20												
04	Jan 27												
05	Feb 3												
06	Feb 10												
07	Feb 17												
08	Feb 24												
09	Mar 3												
10	Mar 10												
11	Mar 17												
12	Mar 24												
13	Mar 31												
14	Apr 7												
15	Apr 14												
16	Apr 21												
17	Apr 28												
18	May 5												
19	May 12												
20	May 19												
21	May 26												
22	Jun 2												
23	Jun 9												
24	Jun 16												
25	Jun 23												
26	Jun 30												
27	Jul 7												
28	Jul 14												
29	Jul 21												
30	Jul 28												
31	Aug 4												
32	Aug 11												
33	Aug 18												
34	Aug 25												
35	Sep 1												
36	Sep 8												
37	Sep 15												
38	Sep 22												
39	Sep 29												
40	Oct 6												
41	Oct 13												
42	Oct 20												
43	Oct 27												
44	Nov 3												
45	Nov 10												
46	Nov 17												
47	Nov 24												
48	Dec 1												
49	Dec 8												
50	Dec 15												
51	Dec 22												
52	Dec 29												

Annual Training Plan: 1998

Athlete:

Annual Hours:

Season Goals:

1

2

3

Training Objectives:

1

2

3

4

5

Wk#	Monday	Races	Pri	Period	Hours	Details	Strength	Endurance	Speed Skill	Muscular End	Speed Power	Power	Testing
01	Jan 5												
02	Jan 12												
03	Jan 19												
04	Jan 26												
05	Feb 2												
06	Feb 9												
07	Feb 16												
08	Feb 23												
09	Mar 2												
10	Mar 9												
11	Mar 16												
12	Mar 23												
13	Mar 30												
14	Apr 6												
15	Apr 13												
16	Apr 20												
17	Apr 27												
18	May 4												
19	May 11												
20	May 18												
21	May 25												
22	Jun 1												
23	Jun 8												
24	Jun 15												
25	Jun 22												
26	Jun 29												
27	Jul 6												
28	Jul 13												
29	Jul 20												
30	Jul 27												
31	Aug 3												
32	Aug 10												
33	Aug 17												
34	Aug 24												
35	Aug 31												
36	Sep 7												
37	Sep 14												
38	Sep 21												
39	Sep 28												
40	Oct 5												
41	Oct 12												
42	Oct 19												
43	Oct 26												
44	Nov 2												
45	Nov 9												
46	Nov 16												
47	Nov 23												
48	Nov 30												
49	Dec 7												
50	Dec 14												
51	Dec 21												
52	Dec 28												

Annual Training Plan: 1999

Athlete:

Annual Hours:

Season Goals:

1

2

3

Training Objectives:

1

2

3

4

5

WORKOUTS: Strength, Endurance, Speed Skill, Muscular Endurance, Speed Power, Power, Testing

Wk#	Monday	Races	Pri	Period	Hours	Details							
01	Jan 4												
02	Jan 11												
03	Jan 18												
04	Jan 25												
05	Feb 1												
06	Feb 8												
07	Feb 15												
08	Feb 22												
09	Feb 29												
10	Mar 1												
11	Mar 8												
12	Mar 15												
13	Mar 22												
14	Mar 29												
15	Apr 5												
16	Apr 12												
17	Apr 19												
18	Apr 26												
19	May 3												
20	May 10												
21	May 17												
22	May 24												
23	May 31												
24	Jun 7												
25	Jun 14												
26	Jun 21												
27	Jun 28												
28	Jul 5												
29	Jul 12												
30	Jul 19												
31	Jul 26												
32	Aug 2												
33	Aug 9												
34	Aug 16												
35	Aug 23												
36	Aug 30												
37	Sep 6												
38	Sep 13												
39	Sep 20												
40	Sep 27												
41	Oct 4												
42	Oct 11												
43	Oct 18												
44	Oct 25												
45	Nov 1												
46	Nov 8												
47	Nov 15												
48	Nov 22												
49	Nov 29												
50	Dec 6												
51	Dec 13												
52	Dec 20												
53	Dec 27												

Annual Training Plan: 2000

Athlete:
Annual Hours:
Season Goals:
1
2
3

Training Objectives:
1
2
3
4
5

WORKOUTS

Wk#	Monday	Races	Pri	Period	Hours	Details	Strength	Endurance	Speed	Muscular Endurance	Speed Power	Power	Testing
01	Jan 3												
02	Jan 10												
03	Jan 17												
04	Jan 24												
05	Jan 31												
06	Feb 7												
07	Feb 14												
08	Feb 21												
09	Feb 28												
10	Mar 6												
11	Mar 13												
12	Mar 20												
13	Mar 27												
14	Apr 3												
15	Apr 10												
16	Apr 17												
17	Apr 24												
18	May 1												
19	May 8												
20	May 15												
21	May 22												
22	May 29												
23	Jun 5												
24	Jun 12												
25	Jun 19												
26	Jun 26												
27	Jul 3												
28	Jul 10												
29	Jul 17												
30	Jul 24												
31	Jul 31												
32	Aug 7												
33	Aug 14												
34	Aug 21												
35	Aug 28												
36	Sep 4												
37	Sep 11												
38	Sep 18												
39	Sep 25												
40	Oct 2												
41	Oct 9												
42	Oct 16												
43	Oct 23												
44	Oct 30												
45	Nov 6												
46	Nov 13												
47	Nov 20												
48	Nov 27												
49	Dec 4												
50	Dec 11												
51	Dec 18												
52	Dec 25												

Annual Training Plan: 2001

Athlete:

Annual Hours:

Season Goals:

1

2

3

Training Objectives:

1

2

3

4

5

WORKOUTS

Wk#	Monday	Races	Pri	Period	Hours	Details							
01	Jan 1												
02	Jan 8												
03	Jan 15												
04	Jan 22												
05	Jan 29												
06	Feb 5												
07	Feb 12												
08	Feb 19												
09	Feb 26												
10	Mar 5												
11	Mar 12												
12	Mar 19												
13	Mar 26												
14	Apr 2												
15	Apr 9												
16	Apr 16												
17	Apr 23												
18	Apr 30												
19	May 7												
20	May 14												
21	May 21												
22	May 28												
23	Jun 4												
24	Jun 11												
25	Jun 18												
26	Jun 25												
27	Jul 2												
28	Jul 9												
29	Jul 16												
30	Jul 23												
31	Jul 30												
32	Aug 6												
33	Aug 13												
34	Aug 20												
35	Aug 27												
36	Sep 3												
37	Sep 10												
38	Sep 17												
39	Sep 24												
40	Oct 1												
41	Oct 8												
42	Oct 15												
43	Oct 22												
44	Oct 29												
45	Nov 5												
46	Nov 12												
47	Nov 19												
48	Nov 26												
49	Dec 3												
50	Dec 10												
51	Dec 17												
52	Dec 24												
53	Dec 31												

Annual Training Plan: 2002

Athlete:
Annual Hours:
Season Goals:

1
2
3

Training Objectives:

1
2
3
4
5

WORKOUTS

Wk#	Monday	Races	Pri	Period	Hours	Details	Strength	Endurance	Speed Skill	Muscular Force	Speed Endur	Power	Musc Endur	Testing
01	Jan 7													
02	Jan 14													
03	Jan 21													
04	Jan 28													
05	Feb 4													
06	Feb 11													
07	Feb 18													
08	Feb 25													
09	Mar 4													
10	Mar 11													
11	Mar 18													
12	Mar 25													
13	Apr 1													
14	Apr 8													
15	Apr 15													
16	Apr 22													
17	Apr 29													
18	May 6													
19	May 13													
20	May 20													
21	May 27													
22	Jun 3													
23	Jun 10													
24	Jun 17													
25	Jun 24													
26	Jul 1													
27	Jul 8													
28	Jul 15													
29	Jul 22													
30	Jul 29													
31	Aug 5													
32	Aug 12													
33	Aug 19													
34	Aug 26													
35	Sep 2													
36	Sep 9													
37	Sep 16													
38	Sep 23													
39	Sep 30													
40	Oct 7													
41	Oct 14													
42	Oct 21													
43	Oct 28													
44	Nov 4													
45	Nov 11													
46	Nov 18													
47	Nov 25													
48	Dec 2													
49	Dec 9													
50	Dec 16													
51	Dec 23													
52	Dec 30													

APPEΠDİX B

Maximum Weight Chart

The Training Bible

MAXIMUM WEIGHT CHART

To determine one repetition max (1RM) from a submaximal lift of 2 to 10 repetitions:

1. Select from the top row of the chart the number of reps completed (for example, 5).

2. In the reps completed column find the weight used for the exercise (for example, 100).

3. From the weight used, look to the far lefthand "Max" column to determine predicted 1RM (in example, 115 pounds).

Reprinted with permission of Strength Tech, Inc., P.O. Box 1381, Stillwater, OK 74076.

Max	10	9	8	7	6	5	4	3	2
45	35	35	35	35	40	40	40	40	45
50	40	40	40	40	45	45	45	45	50
55	40	45	45	45	45	50	50	50	50
60	45	45	50	50	50	55	55	55	55
65	50	50	50	55	55	55	60	60	60
70	55	55	55	60	60	60	65	65	65
75	55	60	60	60	65	65	70	70	70
80	60	60	65	65	70	70	70	75	75
85	65	65	70	70	70	75	75	80	80
90	70	70	70	75	75	80	80	85	85
95	70	75	75	80	80	85	85	90	90
100	75	80	80	85	85	90	90	95	95
105	80	80	85	85	90	90	95	95	100
110	85	85	90	90	95	95	100	100	105
115	85	90	90	95	100	100	105	105	110
120	90	95	95	100	100	105	110	110	115
125	95	95	100	105	105	110	115	115	120
130	100	100	105	105	110	115	115	120	125
135	100	105	110	110	115	120	120	125	130
140	105	110	110	115	120	125	125	130	135
145	110	110	115	120	125	125	130	135	140
150	115	115	120	125	130	130	135	140	145
155	115	120	125	130	130	135	140	145	145
160	120	125	130	130	135	140	145	150	150
165	125	130	130	135	140	145	150	155	155
170	130	130	135	140	145	150	155	155	160
175	130	135	140	145	150	155	160	160	165
180	135	140	145	150	155	160	160	165	170
185	140	145	150	155	155	160	165	170	175

Max	10	9	8	7	6	5	4	3	2
190	145	145	150	155	160	165	170	175	180
195	145	150	155	160	165	170	175	180	185
200	150	155	160	165	170	175	180	185	190
205	155	160	165	170	175	180	185	190	195
210	160	165	170	175	180	185	190	195	200
215	160	165	170	175	185	190	195	200	205
220	165	170	175	180	185	195	200	205	210
225	170	175	180	185	190	195	205	210	215
230	175	180	185	190	195	200	205	215	220
235	175	180	190	195	200	205	210	215	225
240	180	185	190	200	205	210	215	220	230
245	185	190	195	200	210	215	220	225	235
250	190	195	200	205	215	220	225	230	240
255	190	200	205	210	215	225	230	235	240
260	195	200	210	215	220	230	235	240	245
265	200	205	210	220	225	230	240	245	250
270	205	210	215	225	230	235	245	250	255
275	205	215	220	225	235	240	250	255	260
280	210	215	225	230	240	245	250	260	265
285	215	220	230	235	240	250	255	265	270
290	220	225	230	240	245	255	260	270	275
295	220	230	235	245	250	260	265	275	280
300	225	235	240	250	255	265	270	280	285
305	230	235	245	250	260	265	275	280	290
310	235	240	250	255	265	270	280	285	295
315	235	245	250	260	270	275	285	290	300
320	240	250	255	265	270	280	290	295	305
325	245	250	260	270	275	285	295	300	310
330	250	255	265	270	280	290	295	305	315
335	250	260	270	275	285	295	300	310	320
340	255	265	270	280	290	300	305	315	325
345	260	265	275	285	295	300	310	320	330
350	265	270	280	290	300	305	315	325	335
355	265	275	285	295	300	310	320	330	335
360	270	280	290	295	305	315	325	335	340
365	275	285	290	300	310	320	330	340	345
370	280	285	295	305	315	325	335	340	350
375	280	290	300	310	320	330	340	345	355
380	285	295	305	315	325	335	340	350	360
385	290	300	310	320	325	335	345	355	365
390	295	300	310	320	330	340	350	360	370
395	295	305	315	325	335	345	355	365	375

The Training Bible

Max	10	9	8	7	6	5	4	3	2
400	300	310	320	330	340	350	360	370	380
405	305	315	325	335	345	355	365	375	385
410	310	320	330	340	350	360	370	380	390
415	310	320	330	340	355	365	375	385	395
420	315	325	335	345	355	370	380	390	400
425	320	330	340	350	360	370	385	395	405
430	325	335	345	355	365	375	385	400	410
435	325	335	350	360	370	380	390	400	415
440	330	340	350	365	375	385	395	405	420
445	335	345	355	365	380	390	400	410	425
450	340	350	360	370	385	395	405	415	430
455	340	355	365	375	385	400	410	420	430
460	345	355	370	380	390	405	415	425	435
465	350	360	370	385	395	405	420	430	440
470	355	365	375	390	400	410	425	435	445
475	355	370	380	390	405	415	430	440	450
480	360	370	385	395	410	420	430	445	455
485	365	375	390	400	410	425	435	450	460
490	370	380	390	405	415	430	440	455	465
495	370	385	395	410	420	435	445	460	470
500	375	390	400	415	425	440	450	465	475
510	385	395	410	420	435	445	460	470	485
520	390	405	415	430	440	455	470	480	495
530	400	410	425	435	450	465	475	490	505
540	405	420	430	445	460	475	485	500	515
550	415	425	440	455	470	480	495	510	525
560	420	435	450	460	475	490	505	520	530
570	430	440	455	470	485	500	515	525	540
580	435	450	465	480	495	510	520	535	550
590	445	455	470	485	500	515	530	545	560
600	450	465	480	495	510	525	540	555	570
610	460	475	490	505	520	535	550	565	580
620	465	480	495	510	525	545	560	575	590
630	475	490	505	520	535	550	565	585	600
640	480	495	510	530	545	560	575	590	610
650	490	505	520	535	555	570	585	600	620
660	495	510	530	545	560	580	595	610	625
670	505	520	535	555	570	585	605	620	635
680	510	525	545	560	580	595	610	630	645
690	520	535	550	570	585	605	620	640	655
700	525	545	560	580	595	615	630	650	665

APPENDIX C

Weekly Training Journal Format

WEEK OF
WEEK'S GOALS (check off as achieved):

- [ ] 1. ....
- [ ] 2. ....
- [ ] 3. ....

MONDAY
Warnings: Rate first four below on scale of 1-7. 1=best, 7=worst. 5+ is a warning. 3 warnings=day off.

Sleep quality [ ]   *Fatigue* [ ]   *Stress* [ ]   *Soreness* [ ]   *HR above/below normal* [ ]   *Weight* [_____]

| **Wrkt 1** Plan: | Actual_____ Distance_____ Weather_____ Other_____ | Time by Zone |
| Duration: | Comments: | Wrkt 1 / Wrkt 2 |

| **Wrkt 2** Plan: | Actual_____ Distance_____ Weather_____ Other_____ |
| Duration: | Comments: |

Time by Zone — Wrkt 1 / Wrkt 2: 1, 2, 3, 4, 5, Ttl

TUESDAY
Warnings: Rate first four below on scale of 1-7. 1=best, 7=worst. 5+ is a warning. 3 warnings=day off.

Sleep quality [ ]   *Fatigue* [ ]   *Stress* [ ]   *Soreness* [ ]   *HR above/below normal* [ ]   *Weight* [_____]

| **Wrkt 1** Plan: | Actual_____ Distance_____ Weather_____ Other_____ | Time by Zone |
| Duration: | Comments: | Wrkt 1 / Wrkt 2 |

| **Wrkt 2** Plan: | Actual_____ Distance_____ Weather_____ Other_____ |
| Duration: | Comments: |

Time by Zone — Wrkt 1 / Wrkt 2: 1, 2, 3, 4, 5, Ttl

WEDNESDAY
Warnings: Rate first four below on scale of 1-7. 1=best, 7=worst. 5+ is a warning. 3 warnings=day off.

Sleep quality [ ]   *Fatigue* [ ]   *Stress* [ ]   *Soreness* [ ]   *HR above/below normal* [ ]   *Weight* [_____]

| **Wrkt 1** Plan: | Actual_____ Distance_____ Weather_____ Other_____ | Time by Zone |
| Duration: | Comments: | Wrkt 1 / Wrkt 2 |

| **Wrkt 2** Plan: | Actual_____ Distance_____ Weather_____ Other_____ |
| Duration: | Comments: |

Time by Zone — Wrkt 1 / Wrkt 2: 1, 2, 3, 4, 5, Ttl

THURSDAY
Warnings: Rate first four below on scale of 1-7. 1=best, 7=worst. 5+ is a warning. 3 warnings=day off.

Sleep quality [ ]   *Fatigue* [ ]   *Stress* [ ]   *Soreness* [ ]   *HR above/below normal* [ ]   *Weight* [_____]

| **Wrkt 1** Plan: | Actual_____ Distance_____ Weather_____ Other_____ | Time by Zone |
| Duration: | Comments: | Wrkt 1 / Wrkt 2 |

| **Wrkt 2** Plan: | Actual_____ Distance_____ Weather_____ Other_____ |
| Duration: | Comments: |

Time by Zone — Wrkt 1 / Wrkt 2: 1, 2, 3, 4, 5, Ttl

WEEK OF

FRIDAY

Warnings: Rate first four below on scale of 1-7. 1=best, 7=worst. 5+ is a warning. 3 warnings=day off.

Sleep quality ☐ Fatigue ☐ Stress ☐ Soreness ☐ HR above/below normal ☐ Weight ☐

Wrkt 1
Plan:

Duration:

Actual_____ Distance_____ Weather_____ Other_____
Comments:

Wrkt 2
Plan:

Duration:

Actual_____ Distance_____ Weather_____ Other_____
Comments:

Time by Zone	Wrkt 1	Wrkt 2
1		
2		
3		
4		
5		
Ttl		

SATURDAY

Warnings: Rate first four below on scale of 1-7. 1=best, 7=worst. 5+ is a warning. 3 warnings=day off.

Sleep quality ☐ Fatigue ☐ Stress ☐ Soreness ☐ HR above/below normal ☐ Weight ☐

Wrkt 1
Plan:

Duration:

Actual_____ Distance_____ Weather_____ Other_____
Comments:

Wrkt 2
Plan:

Duration:

Actual_____ Distance_____ Weather_____ Other_____
Comments:

Time by Zone	Wrkt 1	Wrkt 2
1		
2		
3		
4		
5		
Ttl		

SUNDAY

Warnings: Rate first four below on scale of 1-7. 1=best, 7=worst. 3 warnings=day off.

Sleep quality ☐ Fatigue ☐ Stress ☐ Soreness ☐ HR above/below normal ☐ Weight ☐

Wrkt 1
Plan:

Duration:

Actual_____ Distance_____ Weather_____ Other_____
Comments:

Wrkt 2
Plan:

Duration:

Actual_____ Distance_____ Weather_____ Other_____
Comments:

Time by Zone	Wrkt 1	Wrkt 2
1		
2		
3		
4		
5		
Ttl		

WEEK'S SUMMARY

1. **Total training time (including strength) this week was** ☐ *hrs : min*

2. **I felt like I was...** ☐ **overtraining ....** ☐ **on the edge ....** ☐ **O.K.**

3. **I had soreness in my _____ caused by _____ .**

4. **Comments on this week:**

GLOSSARY

Aerobic In the presence of oxygen; aerobic metabolism utilizes oxygen.

Aerobic capacity The body's maximal capacity for using oxygen to produce energy during maximal exertion. Also known as VO2max.

Agonistic muscles Muscles directly engaged in a muscular contraction.

Anaerobic In the absence of oxygen; nonoxidation metabolism.

Anaerobic threshold (AT) When aerobic metabolism no longer supplies all the need for energy, energy is produced anaerobically; indicated by increase in lactic acid. Also known as lactate threshold.

Antagonistic muscles Muscles that have an opposite effect on movers, or against muscles, by opposing their contraction. For example, the triceps is an antagonistic muscle for the biceps.

Base period The period during which the basic abilities of endurance, speed and strength are emphasized.

Bonk A state of extreme exhaustion caused mainly by the depletion of glycogen in the muscles.

Breakaway A rider or group of riders that rides away from the main pack.

Build period The specific preparation mesocycle during which high intensity training in the form of muscular-endurance, speed-endurance and power are emphasized and endurance, strength and speed are maintained.

Capillary A fine network of small vessels located between arteries and veins where exchanges between tissue and blood occur.

Carbohydrate loading (glycogen loading) A dietary procedure that elevates muscle glycogen stores.

Cardiorespiratory system Cardiovascular system and lungs.

Cardiovascular system Heart, blood and blood vessels.

Chase The attempt to catch a breakaway.

Circuit training Selected exercises or activities performed rapidly in sequence; used in weight training.

Criterium A road race that is generally held on city streets or parks; a course usually one mile or less and marked by short straights and tight turns.

Cross training Training for more than one sport at the same time.

Duration The length of time of a given workout.

Endurance The ability to persist, to resist fatigue.

Ergogenic aid A substance or phenomenon that can improve athletic performance.

Fast-twitch fiber (FT) A muscle fiber characterized by fast contraction time, high anaerobic capacity and low aerobic capacity, all making the fiber suited for high power output activities.

Free weights Weights not part of an exercise machine (i.e., barbells and dumbbells).

Frequency The number of times per week that one trains.

Glucose Simple sugar.

Glycogen The form in which glucose (sugar) is stored in the muscles and the liver.

Growth hormone A hormone secreted by the anterior lobe of the pituitary gland that stimulates growth and development.

Hamstring Muscle on the back of the thigh that flexes the knee and extends the hip.

Individuality, principle of The theory that any training program must consider the specific needs and abilities of the individual for whom it is designed.

Intensity The qualitative element of training such as speed, maximum strength and power.

Interval training A system of high-intensity work marked by short but regularly repeated periods of work stress interspersed with periods of recovery.

Jump A sudden burst of speed which provides the initial acceleration for a sprint.

Lactate Formed when lactic acid from the muscles gives off a hydrogen atom on entering the blood stream.

Lactic acid A by-product of the lactic acid system resulting from the incomplete breakdown of glucose (sugar) in the production of energy.

Lactate threshold (LT) The point during exercise of increasing intensity at which blood lactate begins to accumulate above resting levels. Also known as anaerobic threshold.

Long, slow distance (LSD) training A form of continuous training in which the athlete performs at a relatively low intensity.

Macrocycle A period of training including several mesocycles; usually an entire season.

Mesocycle A period of training generally 2-6 weeks long.

Micro-cycle A period of training of approximately one week.

Motorpace Riding behind a motorcycle or other vehicle that breaks the wind.

Muscular-endurance The ability of a muscle or muscle group to perform repeated contractions for a long period of time while bearing a load.

Overload, principle of A training load that challenges the body's current level of fitness.

Overtraining Extreme fatigue, both physical and mental, caused by training at a volume/intensity higher than that to which the body can adapt.

Peak period The mesocycle during which volume of training is reduced and intensity is proportionally increased allowing the athlete to reach high levels of fitness.

Periodization Represents a process of structuring training into periods.

The Training Bible

Power The ability resulting from strength and speed.

Preparation period The mesocycle during which the athlete begins to train for the coming season; usually marked by the use of cross training.

Progression, principle of The theory that workload must be gradually increased accompanied by intermittent periods of recovery.

Quadriceps The large muscle in front of the thigh.

Race period The mesocycle during which workload is decreased allowing the athlete to compete in high-priority races.

Rating of perceived exertion (RPE) A subjective assessment of how hard one is working.

Recovery interval The relief period between work intervals within an interval workout.

Repetition The number of work intervals within one set.

Repetition maximum (RM) The maximum load that a muscle group can lift in one attempt. Also called "one-repetition maximum" (1RM).

Road race A mass-start race that goes from point to point, covers one large loop or is held on a circuit longer than those used for criteriums.

Set The total number of repetitions performed before an extensive recovery interval is taken.

Slow-twitch fiber (ST) A muscle fiber characterized by slow contraction time, low anaerobic capacity and high aerobic capacity, all making the fiber suited for low power, endurance activities.

Specificity, principle of The theory that training must stress the systems critical for optimal performance in order to achieve the desired training adaptations.

Speed In cycling, the ability to turn the cranks quickly.

Speed-endurance The ability resulting from the combination of speed and endurance allowing the athlete to maintain a high speed for an extended period of time.

Stage race A multiday event consisting of road races, time trials and possibly criteriums.

Strength The force that a muscle or muscle group can exert against a resistance.

Tapering A reduction in training intensity and volume prior to a major competition.

Time trial (TT) A race against the clock in which individual riders start at set intervals.

Transition period The mesocycle during which the workload and structure of training are greatly reduced allowing physical and psychological recovery from training and racing.

Ventilatory threshold (VT) The point during increasing exertion at which breathing first becomes labored. Corresponds with lactate threshold.

VO$_2$max The maximal capacity for oxygen consumption by the body during maximal exertion, also known as aerobic power and maximal oxygen consumption.

Volume A quantitative element of training, such as miles or hours of training within a given time.

Work interval High intensity efforts separated by recovery intervals.

Workload Measured stress applied in training through the combination of frequency, intensity and duration.

İNDEX

ABOUT THE AUTHOR

Joe Friel has coached adult endurance athletes — both amateurs and professionals — since 1980. From 1970 to 1980, he coached high school athletes. He has a masters degree in exercise science, and is an expert-level certified coach with USA Cycling. A nationally recognized authority on endurance training, he is a regular contributor to such publications as *VeloNews, Inside Triathlon, Performance Conditioning for Cycling, Masters Sports* and *Racing West,* and has written a training column for the *Fort Collins Coloradoan* newspaper since 1981. He lives and trains in Fort Collins, Colorado, with his wife, Joyce.

Joe Friel is available for workshops and personal coaching and can be reached by fax at 970/204-4221, or by e-mail at joefriel@aol.com.